With deep a[...]

for your g[...]

Lord's ministry

at

Biola College

and

Talbot Theological Seminary,

Carol Talbot

For This I Was Born

At age twenty in Australia: a bearing of distinction.

The Captivating Story of
Louis T. Talbot

For This I Was Born

By
CAROL TALBOT

MOODY PRESS
CHICAGO

ISBN: 0-8024-2822-3

Library of Congress Cataloging in Publication Data
Talbot, Carol.
  For this I was born.
  Bibliography & filmography: p. 282.
  1. Talbot, Louis Thompson, 1889-1976. 2. Clergy—
United States—Biography. I. Title.
BR1725.T23T34   269'.2'0924 [B]   77-10537
ISBN 0-8024-2822-3

CONTENTS

AS AN AMBASSADOR FOR CHRIST

GOD'S BENEDICTION ON HIS MAN

APPENDIX

FOREWORD

Dr. Louis Talbot was one of the spiritual giants of this generation. I first heard him preach during the 1930s. As pastor, Bible teacher, author and educator, he influenced not only me but thousands of theological students and pastors. His faithfulness to the infallibility of the Scriptures and the Gospel has been an inspiration to me for many years. Mrs. Talbot has captured in this book a spiritual and intellectual account of this remarkable, God-anointed man. I commend *For This I Was Born* to Christians everywhere; the biography of such a man will bless, inspire and instruct.

BILLY GRAHAM

PREFACE

You ARE INVITED to enjoy life with Louie Talbot—exciting, colorful, humorous, unique, warm-hearted, and dedicated unto God.

He will take you into ridiculous situations and you will come out laughing; he will take you into the presence of God and you will come out worshiping; he will take you into New Guinea, Borneo, and jungle warfare and you will come out praying; he will take you up some of life's unconquerable mountains and you will come out believing.

Where did he get that boundless capacity to enjoy life? What made him a leader so beloved that strong men wept when he left a pastorate? Why was he able to reach the depths of people's hearts?

What made him a power in the pulpit and a forceful leader in the world of Christendom? How was he able to raise tremendous funds when all else failed and everyone's purse was empty? What was the secret of his profound love and reverence for the Lord?

These questions surged through my mind as for three years I listened to his radio tapes; combed files, sermon notes, and letters; studied many years of minutes and church bulletins; viewed his films; corresponded or talked with people from every church he pastored and school he attended; and read the books he wrote. Members of his family in America and Australia shared their memories. As his wife in the evening years of his life, I talked with him heart to heart, searching out the ways of the Lord in molding a prankish youngster into a man of God.

As you walk through the pages of his life, picturing his arm thrown over your shoulders in typical Louie Talbot fashion, I pray you will find the answers to these questions in the blessing that may come to your heart.

SHOES TO MATCH THE ROAD

"Thy shoes shall be iron and brass; and as thy days, so shall thy strength be" (Deut 33:25).

OUR GRACIOUS FATHER, we thank Thee that we do not need to be great or mighty to come into Thy presence, and we come grateful for this promise that assures us of strength to meet responsibilities and carry trials no matter how great they may be.

As we find days that carry more tears, sorrows, and heartaches than a whole year beside, help us to remember that Thou hast given to us for that day grace and strength, the like of which we shall not know at any other time. How much like a range of mountains are our days. Some stand out like mountain peaks, others like low valleys.

We thank Thee for an all-inclusive assurance of strength. Help us to know the reality of Thy promise when pressures come from every side, pressure of home duties, of business relationships, of great decisions.

We are insufficient for these things, but no matter how difficult the path may be, Thou hast promised us shoes suited to the pathway our feet must trod, even though it requires shoes of iron and brass. Help us to live victoriously this day by the strength Thou dost provide.

In the Name of our wonderful Lord and Saviour Jesus Christ.

Amen.

Louis T. Talbot

1

ADVENTURE INHERITED

"I DON'T CARE how fast you can run around that track, Lou. Settle down to your studies, or when you get out of Newington College, you'll be *nothing!*"

With his British accent clothed in authority, John Talbot chided his son, a slender, brown-haired, blue-eyed, restless youth so filled with the electricity of life that he could hardly stand still long enough to listen to his father.

But the word *nothing* pierced Louie. That was one thing he did not want to be, and he determined he would bend all his efforts to become something. Years later when those efforts brought him from Australia to the Moody Bible Institute of Chicago, he was startled to hear the faculty and students singing "Oh to be nothing!"

God was putting His hand on Louie and molding him to accomplish great things for His glory as a leader of men, a power in the pulpit, an ambassador for Christ to twenty countries, and a cause for over a million hearts to smile and love.

He inherited his zest for life from his mother and father, John and Elizabeth, whose story always fascinated him:

John Talbot strode alone through the fog of London; he was struggling with the decision facing him. The year was 1877, and he was ready to leave for Australia, a land of new opportunities; but the thought of losing Bessie if he sailed so far away chilled him to his innermost being.

At twenty-four, John was slender and six feet tall, with reddish brown hair and eyes as blue as the seas he longed to sail. But it was the eyes of his cousin, Elizabeth Frayling (whom he had known most of his life as Bessie), that riveted his feet to England. Having lost everyone else that was dear to him, he determined to ask her parents again if he might take Bessie with him as his bride to Australia.

John's father had been killed in the Crimean War while he was serving in the Grenadier Guards, and his mother had been burned to death in an accident. John had grown up in England with his brother James, and the two orphans had been shuttled between friendly relatives. But James had left to seek his fortunes in America and was never heard from again. No trace was found of him.

Alone, John made his way to Bessie's home in the village of Calne, where he asked her parents again for their daughter's hand in marriage. They refused him because he was leaving England.

Beneath Bessie's cameo features and brown curls were a firm will and deep devotion, and she handled the situation with a wisdom that characterized her whole life. Because she was just twenty years old, she satisfied her parents by agreeing to wait, but she kept hope alive in John's heart by promising to follow him when he was established in Australia.

Letters took a long time to cross the seas, and they sometimes went through the hands of sympathetic cousins to insure delivery. Two years after John's departure, Bessie's mother and father stood forlornly on the dock and watched their gentle daughter leave alone on a rugged sailing ship bound for the other side of the world.

"How much longer do I have to stand here?"

After a long and rough voyage, the ship pulled into Melbourne Harbor. John was on the dock to welcome his bride, and they were married the same day. Traveling to Sydney, they established a home there under the Southern Cross, where Louis Thompson Talbot was born on October 19, 1889.

The sixth of eight children, Louie was named after John's friend in the liquor business. When John later became disappointed in this friend and wanted to change Louie's name, Bessie objected, "Every time you fall out with some of your friends, you're not going to change our children's names."

Among the five brothers and three sisters, Louie was one of the liveliest in imagination, mischief, and adventure; and he was always the one most in need of someone to pick up his belongings.

He made life exciting for himself and others because of his sheer enjoyment of living, but one day it nearly caused disaster. He had arranged a circus with his brothers and sisters, to take place in the loft over the washhouse, where they often played. Just before Sylvia was to jump through a ring of fire, Louie took the precaution of checking their mother's whereabouts. She was in the house, doing needlework; so Louie started closing the back door ever so softly.

Always on the alert, Bessie asked, "Why are you closing the door, Lou?"

"You're sitting in the sun, and I thought you might get too warm, Mum."

"Well, yes, I think I am. I'll just go up to the loft and cool off a little." Bessie's astuteness averted tragedy.

Although he enjoyed pranks that sometimes led him into mischief, Louie was sensitive and affectionate. His heart was tender toward any living creature that had been hurt. He brought home stray dogs and cats and any other animal he thought was hungry, wounded, or lost. It was only his mother's firmness that kept their large, three-story house from becoming a zoo; the extensive stables at the back became a menagerie.

In addition to raising bulldogs, Louie vied with his brothers in raising pigeons, kept a turtle hidden in his bed, and had a parrot in and out of his room according to his mother's vigilance. When the beleagured parrot died, Louie won, and his father had the parrot stuffed and put in a glass cage in his son's bedroom. But that did not end Bessie's feud with the parrot. Sometimes when the boys scuffled, they broke the glass cage, and there were feathers and glass to be cleaned up.

Tongues did click when the boys received pea rifles one Christmas and tried them out on the new glass windowpanes of a nearby boot factory.

Having observed their many escapades, a family friend commented, "I thought they'd all end up on the gallows."

In his early years, even church was not off limits for Louie's boyish mischief. Bessie and her eight children attended the Redfern
Congregational Church, which accommodated about six hundred
people. The Reverend Fred Binns looked down from the pulpit
each Sunday into nine pairs of blue eyes all in a row in the Talbot
pew. The five brothers often livened up the Sunday school, as well
as the morning and evening services.

Louie delighted in slipping live beetles into the coat pockets of
gentlemen entering the church; he even dropped one down the wing
collar of a deacon whose head was bowed in prayer. During a long
evening service, the gas lights dimmed and then went out. Having
become restless during the sermon, Louie had gone to the back,
turned off the gas, and then quietly returned to his seat to watch
what would happen as darkness closed in on the congregation. To
immortalize his name in that church, Louie carved his initials into
the family pew. All those pranks were just a lot of fun to him, until
his father heard about them.

Describing their family discipline, Louie said, "Dad was mayor,
and Mum was chief of police." Although their household reverber-
ated with fun and laughter, and John Talbot enjoyed hearing about
the shenanigans of his five sons, still he reprimanded them when
he felt that they had gone too far. Because Louie sometimes missed
the half-hidden twinkle in his father's eyes, he was more deeply
affected by such reprimands than his father intended. Louie later
explained.

"I became terrified of God. If I had been told of a desert place
where God was not, all my plans and purposes would have been
concentrated on the one effort of getting there, so distorted was my
view of God at that time."

Bessie kept a perceptive eye on the whole family. Early each
morning she locked herself alone in her room to pray for them.
When the youngest daughter, Gladys, asked her what she did in
there behind the closed door, the mother replied, "Someday I'll tell
you."

A great burden on Bessie's heart was the business of her husband,
who had become a wealthy business executive. In addition to es-
tablishing the Newtown Markets, he owned several places of business where liquor was sold. He was also the assistant manager and
head traveler for Tooth's Brewery, the largest in the southern hemi-

sphere at that time. He enjoyed his large family and provided well for them.

Bessie felt that it was an answer to prayer when her husband suggested they buy an organ to encourage the girls in their music. It became the center of their family life, and even the father, who seldom attended church, often joined in the singing of hymns around that organ. The children had profound respect for their father, while they loved their mother almost to the point of reverence. The organ drew them all even closer together, and it developed in Louie's heart a deep penchant for music.

His father spoke with authority.

In order to get the boys out from under their mother's feet on Saturdays, the father bought a sailboat for his five sons and named it *The Bessie.* He had Mr. Ball, one of his trusted servants, accompany them as they sailed on Botany Bay. The excursions in the sailboat provided the boys with some of the happiest moments of their childhood. Among the important aspects of these trips was always the big lunch sent along by their mother. The most often asked question of the day was "When do we eat?," a question Louie continued to ask almost every day of his life.

When he first went to school, sitting still and studying for long hours came hard to Louie, but when he tried to liven it up with practical jokes, he came face-to-face with old-fashioned English discipline. He recalled this story of his early days in what was known as the Common School:

One of his teachers was a stern-looking, middle-aged woman who wore a long, black skirt. "She walked from one side of the room to the other with a great big cane at her back, and you could see about a foot of it above her head. That teacher had an eternal feud with me. Although I tried to please her, I just couldn't, and many a time, unbeknown to my mother, I went to school with two pairs of pants on because I knew what was coming."

At the age of twelve, Louie entered Newington College, one of Australia's finest schools for boys. Sending his five sons there cost John Talbot a substantial sum, but it was the wisest investment he ever made. The college did much to shape Louie's life: it gave him a well-balanced education, the honor code, and a spirit of good sportsmanship. At the same time, it endeavored to change him from a prankster into an English gentleman of culture.

Louie enjoyed Newington; he thrived in its atmosphere and responded to its challenges. It was realized, as his studies progressed, that he had a retentive memory and a flair for the English language. The man who had the most influence on him was Dr. C. J. Prescott. A graduate of Oxford, he was a brilliant and humane man and had been a Methodist minister in England before becoming headmaster at Newington College.

But even at Newington there was one teacher Louie described as "very stern." In the school's publications, Ben Jarvie was described as a firm disciplinarian whose word is law and with whom no one trifles. This man had a strong impact on Louie. All his life, Louie reacted negatively to unnecessary sternness, but it developed in him the sternness of steel when required. He was a little afraid of Mr. Jarvie, and maybe that is why he excelled in what Mr. Jarvie taught— mathematics and cricket. Louie won a school prize in mathematics, became a significant player on the rugby and cricket teams, and was among the winners in the hundred-yard dash.

The boys came home for weekends and holidays. At four o'clock every morning, a school friend stood underneath Louie's bedroom window and called him until he woke up. Then the two of them took off on a long-distance run to keep in training for the sports program at Newington. Trouble developed because it woke up the whole household, and a big row erupted with Louie's brothers, who wanted to sleep late during the holidays.

Their mother settled it, "Lou, you'll have to find a quieter way to wake up."

His bedroom, which he shared with his brothers Will and Hubert, was on the second floor. To solve his problem, Louie tied the end of a long string around his big toe each night and weighted the other end with a rock, letting it out the window to the ground. When his friend came, he tugged at the string, which jerked Louie's toe and woke him. But one morning, this school chum realized he had a good thing going and kept pulling the string, tightening it on Louie's toe and drawing him hopping across the room on one foot. A skirmish between the two followed, and from then on the string was pulled with due respect for Louie's wrestling ability.

But his father took a dim view of all this time spent on running. It was then that his father said, "I don't care how fast you can run around that track, Lou. Settle down to your studies, or when you get out of Newington College, you'll be *nothing!*"

As his studies and experiences broadened, new concepts began surging in upon Louie. When Dr. R. A. Torrey came to Sydney in 1902, accompanied by the musicians Charles M. Alexander and Robert Harkness, Bessie took her family to the meetings. The crowds and singing were overwhelming. No one took any special notice of a youngster in the congregation. It was thirteen-year-old Louie Talbot, watching with wide eyes the stately personage of the scholarly Dr. Torrey, whose very pulpit in America Louie was later to occupy and of whose school he was to become president.

2

WHAT GREATER THING?

I<small>F</small> L<small>OUIE HAD AN IDOL</small> in his boyhood, it was his older brother Jim. He was gifted in song and dance and fluent in speech; and he acted in Shakespearean plays. His appearance and style bore strong resemblance to the actor Ray Bolger. He had chosen the stage for his career, and in Louie's eyes he was already a star. But up in her room alone, their mother spent many hours praying for Jim, with his brilliant mind and talent, and the Lord answered by bringing a lazy tramp steamer into Sydney Harbor.

There were only two passengers aboard that trading ship, which had been bartering its way through the South Sea Islands. One was the trader, and the other was Loyal L. Wirt. After Mr. Wirt had completed three years as a missionary to Alaska in the rough and tough days of the gold rush, his health broke. His physician recommended a leisurely cruise in the South Pacific to bake the arctic cold out of his bones. After sailing for many months to island ports, the ship had arrived at Sydney.

Mr. Wirt preached at a Congregational church in nearby Newcastle and was dumbfounded when the members asked him to become their regular minister.

"But that is impossible!" he exclaimed.

However, when the church handed him money for his family's passage, he cabled them to come and then moved into the manse for three years. Mr. Wirt commented, "Thus a kindly providence directs our feet over the rim of the horizon to destinies unsought and unexpected."[1] That destiny included Louie and Jim, and his own son, Sherwood E. Wirt, who was to become editor of Billy Graham's *Decision* magazine.

When a series of evangelistic meetings was planned for the Sydney area, Loyal Wirt was asked to take the campaign at Redfern, near the Talbot's home. The meetings were advertised each evening by groups of singers on street corners, and Pastor Binns recruited a reluctant Louie to carry a pole holding a kerosene lantern for these outdoor gatherings. It led to an experience Louie never forgot.

One evening, two young men who had served prison sentences for robbery wandered into the street meeting where Louie was holding the lantern. They were Charlie (Woodie) Woodward and Harry Dean, then members of a group of thieves, but later ministers of distinction. Woodie had hidden in a Methodist church, intent on stealing the organ, while the gang of thieves waited outside for his signal. But during the service, Woodie was converted and came out singing the praises of the Lord. The gang thought he had gone mad.

Right after their conversions, Woodie and his friend Harry tried to earn an honest living by selling rabbits, but they were not very successful. The Talbots bought the ones the men could not sell elsewhere, and rabbit became a regular dish on their table.

Always looking for opportunities to reach her family for the Lord, Bessie invited these men to stay for dinner each time they brought some rabbits. Louie sat spellbound as they told of their escapades in crime and the change Christ had wrought in their lives. In the meantime, he began holding the lantern more enthusiastically for the singing groups; he hoped some more criminals would wander into his street meetings as he continued to help advertise the Wirt campaign.

When Bessie urged her family to attend the meetings, Jim went to please his mother, but he found that Loyal Wirt was no ordinary preacher. A short man whose black hair was parted in the middle, he was a colorful and dramatic storyteller. Because of Jim's flair for the stage, the Lord had brought just the right man in answer to Bessie's prayers, even though He had to bring him clear from Alaska to Sydney. Jim was captivated by Mr. Wirt and his messages, and he went back night after night. When he came home from the meeting one evening, there was a new dimension in his personality. Jim was different.

He went to Louie's room and with great intensity and sincerity told him how he had experienced the transforming love and grace of the Lord Jesus Christ. Louie looked at Jim's face with wonderment. Although he could not comprehend all Jim was telling him, Louie knew in his heart that whatever Jim had, it was real and true and wonderful. If that something was Christ, Louie wanted Him.

A happy childhood and fine schooling. Seated, left to right: Will, Bessie Talbot, John Talbot, and Gladys. Standing, left to right: Hubert, Jim, daughter Bessie, John Jr., Sylvia, and Louie.

But Jim's conversion brought with it some problems. All the Talbot boys sooner or later had jobs selling liquor wholesale for their father's business. Jim felt that he could no longer sell the liquor. One day at the office he tried to persuade his father not to sell liquor at the Newtown Markets. He also told him that some of his business associates were dishonest and were deceiving him. With a rare flash of anger, the father said to Jim, "From now on, this business will no longer be 'Talbot and Sons.'"

"All right, Dad," Jim replied quietly. "That settles a question I've been pondering for some time. I'm going to enter the ministry and will be leaving home to attend school."

Still angry, the father replied, "Where will you get the money? You'll not get any from me."

"I don't know, Dad, but I'll get it somehow. Thank you for everything you've done for me." With a heavy burden on his heart for the father he loved, Jim turned and walked slowly out.

After leaving his Dad's office, Jim went to his pastor, the Reverend Fred Binns. He was a dedicated man of God, always on the committees that brought outstanding evangelists from America to his city, and he had become more than pastor to the Talbot family. His son married Bessie Talbot, the daughter named for her mother. Jim poured out his heart to this man who was pastor, friend, and relative; Jim told him how he had turned down offers for a career on the stage, how his experience with his father had gone, and how he felt called of the Lord to enter the ministry.

After prayer together, Mr. Binns told Jim of having heard Dwight L. Moody preach in England, of the love for God's Word it had created in his heart, and of the evangelistic zeal it had put into his whole life. He recommended to Jim that he attend the Moody Bible Institute of Chicago.

Jim wrote to the school for application papers and worked hard at any jobs he could find to earn money for passage and school expenses. The Reverend James Mathers, superintendent of the Sydney City Mission, invited Jim to preach there regularly. Jim's sincerity caused the men from skid row to listen, and although his preaching was amateur, he experienced the joy of seeing some of those men's lives changed by the power and grace of the Lord.

As Louie watched, he was astounded and thought, *I wonder if I could ever preach like Jim?*

When word came from Moody Bible Institute that Jim's application had been approved, there was great excitement in the Talbot household. But when Jim sailed for America, Louie felt as if part of his life were sailing away with Jim, and he became restless, as one who has lost his anchor and is in search of another.

Activities at Newington College helped Louie settle down after Jim left, and he became more interested in running, swimming, and tennis. As he grew into his late teens, he became a handsome young man with fine features and an active mind. Louie enjoyed life to the full, and a friend commented, "He is so brimming with personality that it fairly jumps out of his skin."

Although Newington was not able to eliminate his prankishness, it refined and cultured Louie. It also gave him a quality of distinction that was apparent all his life and can be seen in the picture taken when he was twenty years old.

One day his father's secretary came to Newington and took the Talbot boys home from school. They listened unbelievingly as they were told that, true to Jim's words, their father's business associates had deceived him. He was bankrupt.

Their father was in the depths of despair. Their property was taken by creditors, and it was traumatic for the family to leave the house they loved. In later years Louie described that moment.

"My mother was a very quiet soul, and she would get alone with God in regard to our family. We lived in a mansion, and my mother used to pray, 'Lord, if it's the only way Thou canst reach this family, including my husband, then sweep it all away.' And when it happened, the one in our home with the calm of heaven in her heart was my mother. She walked away from our wonderful home singing 'Beulah Land,' because she felt the Lord was going to use it to move the heart of our father."

Louie secured a job on the *Sydney Morning-Herald* as a copy-reader and collector of accounts. He did so well that he considered making newspaper work his career. However, he often pondered what he really wanted to do with his life. When he was twenty years old, he discovered the answer.

One day in 1909, Louie found himself caught up in a throng of thousands of people flocking to the Sydney Town Hall to hear Dr. J. Wilbur Chapman. With him were the same famous musicians who had accompanied Dr. Torrey—the singer Charles M. Alexander and pianist Robert Harkness. Before Louie reached the town hall, he could hear the singing soaring out into the night air. The building was filled, thousands were standing outside, and even Louie could not find a way to get through the door.

The next evening he arrived there early and obtained a seat in the highest row of the balcony. He was enthralled as that great crowd sang hymns he and Jim used to sing around the family organ.

The meetings grew in size and intensity until no building in Sydney could be found that was large enough to contain them. Night after night Louie was stirred by the singing, the forceful preaching, and the sight of lives being transformed. After the last meeting, he walked the streets in the darkness of the night, searching the depths of his soul and thinking, *What greater thing in life could there be than this?* Then he lifted his face toward the Southern Cross shining in the heavens and made the decision of his life—he would enter the ministry.

Among the first people Louie told was Mr. Mathers of the Sydney City Mission, who invited him to preach there as Jim had done. The faces of those down-and-out men stirred Louie's heart. He had great compassion for anything or anyone that had been hurt, and he talked to them out of his heart. His warm personality and unique sense of humor held their attention, and he had some of them laughing who had not smiled for a long, long time. He took a personal interest in the men, and he ended each meeting on his knees, with his arm around the shoulders of some destitute man as the two prayed.

When Louie saw how the lives of some of those derelicts were changed by Christ, he felt that it was the most wonderful thing he had ever seen. He decided then that all his life he would preach to broken hearts.

He wrote to Jim and asked what training he should take. Jim had graduated from Moody Bible Institute and was studying at Xenia Theological Seminary in Ohio when he wrote Louie: "You asked about the Institute. Would I go there if I had my time over again? Most assuredly, yes! . . . With regard to finances, I would say working your way sounds nice and romantic but I want to tell you from experience it is hard, real hard. To be honest with you, I can tell you it shook me to pieces for a while up there as it was an awful struggle to make ends meet. Yet I know it was the making of me. You have such a different attitude toward people and things when you have gone through the fire. . . .

"I must not tell you definitely to come to America or to stay at home. That is a matter between you and the Lord. Whatever steps you take, be sure you are in His will and then go ahead.

"I rejoice daily before the Lord that He has led you out in His service, but Lou, old man, be careful that day by day there may be the continual self-effacement, the self decreasing and the Lord increasing. I trust and pray that very clearly you may hear the voice behind you saying, 'This is the way, walk ye in it,' and that God's richest blessing may be yours."

Louie's application papers were approved by Moody, and he worked hard to obtain the necessary funds. He was ready to sail from Sydney at the age of twenty-one.

Just as he was leaving for the ship, his mother called him to her room and gave him a money belt into which she had sewn some gold sovereigns, money she had secretly saved for him. Louie put his long arms around his mother and held her for a few moments. He knew the loving sacrifice that must have gone into saving those pieces of gold.

Bessie felt that of all her children Louie was the most in need of someone to look after him. He had a lifetime habit of becoming utterly absorbed in whatever captured his interest, whether it was raising pigeons, racing, preaching, or talking to someone. At such times everything else would be excluded from his mind, especially mundane matters like schedules. His mother wondered how he would ever make it halfway around the world on his own.

3

LEARNING TO WALK WITH GOD

IT WAS ON A COLD, blustery evening in 1911 that Louie struggled through the door of Moody Bible Institute. It had been summertime when he left Australia, and he was wearing a summer suit, hanging on to his straw hat in the chilly winds of Chicago, and hauling his luggage. Startled students watched with amusement, wondering what the wind had blown into their school.

Louie later said of that arrival: "The first person I remember meeting was the student in charge of the dining room, and I immediately asked him, 'Where can I get something to eat?'

" 'Breakfast will be served in the dining room at seven o'clock in the morning,' was the sedate reply"; and Louie learned his first lesson in becomng a schedule-oriented student at Moody. He kept snacks under his bed!

Knowing how eager the family in Australia was for news, he kept up a running letter to them almost in diary form:

"I guess I am by this time what one would call a real, experienced traveller, having travelled some 18,000 miles without a mishap and very little expense. . . . I caught the famous *Mauretania*, 32,000 tons, which took me across the Atlantic. . . . We had a splendid time till after halfway, & then we struck a storm, which struck the ship, & then I was struck & had to excuse myself for a few days. . . .

"New York is a wonderful city and has buildings which astonish a new chum, so high that one almost has to lie on his back to see the top. The much spoken of Statue of Liberty is a massive construction & seems to be the pride of all true Americans.

"The train soon took me from city to city until after 28 hours journey I reached Chicago & spent no time in reaching the Institute. My word, I did sing the Doxology & clapped my hands when I dropped my portmanteau in my study. The morning I appeared for breakfast I received a grand reception from the students, perhaps because of the Kangaroo blood in me. . . .

"We took our first lecture today on the books of Daniel compared with Revelation. Dr. Gray treated the subject in a remarkable way and fairly opened my eyes. I once began to think that I knew a little about the Bible, but Dr. Gray has revealed to me my ignorance. I have been advised by all to take the straight-out Bible course first and then the music."

On May 5 he added more of his experiences: "We are digging into the book of Daniel compared with Revelation. My word, the first 7 chapters are no mystery to me now. . . . I have taken seven lectures this week and understand them very well. The study so far hasn't been as hard as I expected, but I believe I have a blessing of Jim's—a good memory. Don't judge by this that there is little to learn & memorize, because the study takes up one's time.

"I have a position in a boarding house as waiter for 1 hour's work a day. I receive my three meals—not bad pay you will say. . . . Next week will be a great week, as I am leaving here to go to St. Louis (to visit Jim) for a few days."

The students from Australia were assigned rooms on the fourth floor so they could be together. There was great rejoicing when another one joined them: Herbert G. Tovey also arrived freezing in a summer suit in winter time. Years later he was to become director of music for Louie at the Church of the Open Door and the Bible Institute of Los Angeles.

The students called the matron of the boys' dormitory "Mother Russell," and Louie's room was the bane of her existence. One day while she was taking visitors through the building, a strong odor came from beneath his bed. She soon disposed of the herring he had stored there for snacks.

Included in his circle of friends at Moody was a Hebrew Christian named Joseph Flacks, who occupied the room next to his. All Joe's loved ones—including his wife and all his children—had left him when he accepted the Lord Jesus as his Messiah and Saviour. They disowned him, and even held his burial service. One night Louie heard him sobbing in his room.

"I went in to see if there was anything I could do, and this is what he was saying, 'Press it harder, Lord; press it harder.'

"I asked what he meant by that, and he told me that he had just received a letter from his family, telling him never to write to them again. While he was wondering why he had to suffer so, he got on his knees to pray. Then it seemed that the Lord said to him, 'I am shaping your head for the crown, my child, I want you to rule with me.' "[1]

Louie's lifelong, loving concern for the Hebrew people started in that experience with Joseph Flacks.

While he was enjoyng his studies and fellowship at Moody, Louie's money was fast ebbing. At the restaurant where he worked for his meals as a waiter, he was so interested in the customers that during conversations with them he sometimes inadvertently tipped soup in their laps or down their necks. When he mixed up their orders, he convinced the patrons that what they received was better than their original orders. Because of his engaging personality, no one wanted him fired, but he needed more money.

He secured a job with Wells Fargo handling heavy shipments. Louie was slender, and this work developed his muscles. He became very strong. Thinking, however, that working on the elevated railway in Chicago's Loop would be more interesting, he applied for a job as a conductor.

When he had time to spare between station stops on the elevated railway, Louie memorized scripture verses that he had written on pieces of paper and kept in his pocket. His concentration on them, however, was so intense that he often forgot to call the stations. He was transferred to an express train.

When people on the express asked him whether his train stopped at certain places, agreeable Louie assured them all that it did. After the train had sped past their stops, he was confronted with irate passengers. Exuding good-natured charm, he assured them that there had been some mistake and that a returning train would stop at the desired stations. He would soon have most of the frustrated commuters smiling; but there were some who wrote down the number on his conductor's hat, and when word reached the railway officials, they did not smile.

Louie's practical Christian work assignment during his first year at Moody was at the Chinese Mission. It marked the beginning of his intense interest in foreign missions, and he began praying about going to China.

But as Louie attended meetings at Moody, he heard students tell

of their conversions, of being born again, of having a dramatic change come into their lives when they accepted the Lord Jesus Christ as their Saviour. Louie had seen that change in his brother Jim and in some of the men at the rescue mission in Sydney. He began wondering why he had not had a more startling change in his own life. While pondering this, he lost his assurance of salvation, but did not want anyone to know.

One day in early 1911, he saw that a certain pastor was to speak on assurance of salvation and eternal security. He attended the service, and the next day went to see the minister. As Louie recalled it later, the conversation went like this:

"My friend, I heard you preach last night, but I have a great problem. I believe on the Lord Jesus Christ and that He died for me, but I don't have any assurance of salvation."

"Who are you?" the minister asked with a searching look.

"I'm Louie Talbot."

"I've never heard of you. Who was your father?"

"John Talbot of Sydney."

"I've never heard of him either. Do you mean to tell me that the work the Lord Jesus Christ did on Calvary, a work that satisfies the heart of God, doesn't satisfy you? And are you going through life saying that you believe on the Lord Jesus Christ, but you are not sure that it satisfies *you* or meets *your* need or is sufficient to wash away all *your* sin? Who in the world do you think you are anyway?"

Although full assurance was not to come until later, Louie picked up his hat and walked down the street singing:

> Blessed assurance, Jesus is mine!
> O what a foretaste of glory divine!
> Heir of salvation, purchase of God,
> Born of His Spirit, washed in His blood.

Louie longed that his father might also know of this transforming love of Christ and wrote him this letter:

June 9, 1911

Dear Dad,

When the news of the death of Mr. Mathers came to me, this event laid it upon my heart to write a few lines to you. . . .

Father, Mr. Mathers was a Christian, & I do want you to become one. . . . You have realized the inconsistency of human friendship, but I point you to a friend who sticketh closer than a brother or son—a Friend who so loved that He left Glory & Majesty to die among shame & sin, & rise again that we might come to eternal joy; that He may be to you what He was to David who sang:

The Lord is my shepherd. I do not want for anything. He leads. He restores. He is with me. He prepares tables. He anoints with oil and commissions His angels to follow.

Father, accept Jesus fully into your life. Then accept everything that happens to you as being permitted by the will of Him who loves you. And there will roll in upon you, wave on wave, tide on tide, ocean on ocean an experience called the Blessed Life, because it is full of the happiness of the ever-blessed God Himself.

Jimmy & I pray that you will take this grand step.

Always claim from Him the virtue of which you feel the deficiency in yourself. In hours of unrest, Thy peace, Lord. In hours of irritation, Thy patience, Lord. In hours of weakness, Thy purity, Lord.

If you take this step, your life will become beautiful . . . & worth living, saying nothing for the blessed life to follow. . . .

"Let him that is athirst come. And whosoever will, let him take the water of life freely."

I had the pleasure of spending a few days with Jim. He has grown into a fine intellectual, Godly young man, of whom we all may well be proud. We both send our fondest love.

Your loving son,
Lou

As Louie's studies progressed at Moody, the books of Daniel and Revelation continued to fascinate him, and out of this fascination was to grow his widespread prophetic ministry. Studying under such teachers as William Evans and James M. Gray, Louie became firmly established in evangelical theology, and he never swerved from any of its tenets throughout his lifetime.

There was something in Dr. Gray's teaching and manner of life that caused Louie to revere him. One day in chapel Dr. Gray related the following incident, which meant so much to Louie that he often told it when giving messages on prayer. As he rememberd them, these were Dr. Gray's words:

"I spent part of my last vacation on a farm, and I learned something about prayer. The first morning my farmer friend said, 'Now Dr. Gray, you can stay here and make yourself at home. I've just purchased some new cows that don't know me, and I'm going down to feed them.'

"But I told my friend that I'd like to go with him and see how it was done.

"We went to the barn and the farmer took some alfalfa and threw it out to the cows, commenting to me, 'These cows need rock salt.'

"The farmer went into the barn and took out a big piece of rock salt, and then came to the fence and held it out. He stood there for almost half an hour, and those cows kept getting nearer and nearer, but then they stopped. After a while the farmer turned around, went back into the barn, and put the rock salt on a rack.

"The next morning we went out again, and after he had thrown the alfalfa to the cows, the farmer held out the rock salt again. This time they came a little nearer, but then they stopped and would not come any closer. The farmer then threw the rock salt back into the barn. He did that every morning, and each day the cows were getting a little nearer and a little nearer, and then one morning they were all around him licking the rock salt out of his hands.

"I said to him, 'Why did you go every day and stand there holding out the rock salt? Look at the time you lost—an hour every day for a whole week. Why didn't you just throw it over the fence and let them get the rock salt themselves?'

"And the farmer answered, 'Those cows needed something more than rock salt. They needed to know me; and therefore I made them come, and come, and come, until now they know me and I can do anything with them.'"

And Dr. Gray went on to say to the students: "My farmer friend taught me a lesson about prayer that day. Have you ever wondered why it is that God has held a thing out to you, and somehow you didn't want to come close to Him in order to get it? And as you have been spending time in prayer, He has been wooing you to His side. And then after He has granted your request, you realize that you have gained something of far more value than the thing you had originally wanted, something far more precious than rock salt. You have come to know Him."

Louie felt that he had learned a vital lesson about prayer.

Then one day Jim visited his brother and wrote about it to the family in Australia: "Louie . . . is going to make good. He is finding the work fairly easy and in the examination-tests he has gained full marks. The fact that he got 100 in both Daniel and Revelation speaks well, for many of the sudents go down on those. . . . I found he has the work very clear in his own mind. I told him to go for a record for the school, or to try and at least beat my record for two years of 98. This is not mere talk just to relieve your minds, but a firm conviction. *He is going to do well. You mark my word for it.*"

Louie recalled this incident of Jim's visit: "When my brother came to see me, he said, 'Lou, Chicago is a tremendous city in size, and I want you to learn this city. Otherwise you'll get lost.'

"Jim took me to the tallest building in Chicago and pointed out the north side, the south, the east, and the west, so I could get a vision of the city as a whole. Then I had to study maps to find the details of that great city with all of its streets. As I did this, I thought, 'That's a good way to study the Bible. First get a view of the Bible as a whole, then each book as a whole, and then the details of every chapter and verse.'"

When the new term opened in September, Louie became student pastor of a little church in Brainard, a few miles from Chicago, and he was elated. His responsibilities grew in teaching and shepherding his small flock, and he was fluent in the pulpit but still felt inadequate spiritually despite his experience earlier that year when he seemed to gain assurance of salvation. He longed and prayed for the deep walk with God that characterized the life of his brother Jim.

Then Louie went with other students from the Institute to hear the Reverend John Harper, pastor of the Walworth Road Baptist Church of London, who had been brought from England to fill the pulpit of the Moody Memorial Church for the month of November 1911. His preaching stirred the hearts of all who heard him. So great was God's blessing on his ministry that his stay was extended to three months, and soon meetings were being held each night, with prayer meetings in the daytime.

It was just what Louie wanted. His heart was hungry for more of the Lord Himself, and he attended as many services as possible. When Mr. Harper climaxed his meetings on the final night in January 1912, Louie's heart was overwhelmed, and he experienced one of the most sacred moments of his life. His doubts about his relationship to the Lord were cleared away forever that night. Louie reported, "I was an alien from God, even though I was studying for the ministry. While this man preached, I came to see how Christ took all my sins away. That night I walked down the aisle and knelt at the altar, where I found Christ. All hostilities ceased, and I had peace with God."[2]

Louie walked out of the Moody Church and down the street to the institute singing these lines by Isaac Watts:

> Were the whole realm of nature mine,
>   That were a present far too small;
> Love so amazing, so divine,
>   Demands my soul, my life, my all.

Not until early in the morning did Louie shut his eyes in sleep. He was rejoicing in his new-found peace with God. There was radiant joy and glory in his soul. He had experienced a confrontation with Christ and knew he had been born again. It plunged Louie's life and ministry from the shallows into the depths of walking with God. He had become nothing that Christ might become everything in his life, and it was then God put His hand on Louie to accomplish great things for His glory.

This encounter with his Lord was hallowed to his heart with deep solemnity by God's calling the speaker to heaven. The Reverend John Harper was returning to the Moody Memorial Church in April 1912 on board *The Titanic* when it sank after striking an iceberg.

During his second year at school, Louie developed more maturity as pastor of the Emmanuel Congregational Church in Chicago, and his interest grew in becoming a missionary to China. He was challenged by the life and death of Borden of Yale, and he later spoke of it on one of his radio broadcasts:

"I had the privilege of meeting one of the finest young men that I ever saw. His name was Borden, and his biography is entitled *Borden of Yale*. He inherited a vast sum of money; and after graduating from Yale University, life in the homeland looked very attractive to him. But he chose to go in a path leading in the opposite direction from the one many would have chosen in like circumstances. I was present at his ordination service held in Moody Church. Soon after that he set his face toward China, going out under the China Inland Mission. On the way to the field he stayed for a time in Egypt. There he contracted a disease, and after a few days of sickness, young Borden passed into the presence of the Lord.

"I shall never forget the morning when Dr. James M. Gray made the announcement to all of us students. The newspapers, including the *Chicago Tribune*, had the story on the front page, with a sketch of the life of William Borden. When many people read the news, they said, 'Oh, what a sacrifice!' But in my heart I said, 'Oh, what a privilege to lay down one's life in the Lord's service.'"

Louie was seeking the Lord's place of service; and although he had received no specific call to China, he felt a great burden for that land and a desire to preach the Gospel to those who had never heard. While still a student at Moody, he applied to the China Inland Mission to become a missionary in that country. Because he was a British subject, his application papers were sent to the Canadian office.

As a candidate, he spent several weeks in the mission's home in Canada and was interviewed by the board there. He was accepted as an "exceptional" candidate with a gift for evangelism. But before going to China, he wanted to finish at Moody and take further studies at a seminary, as Jim had done.

Louie graduated from Moody Bible Institute in April of 1913 with a grade average of ninety-six. The official "Remarks on Leaving" recorded in the school files by Howard W. Pope, a member of the faculty, are that Louie's personal character was "consecrated, sensible, aggressive," and that his practical Christian work was "excellent."

Louie had to have his photograph taken before the commencement exercises, but he had a boil on his face. The photographer assured him, much to his comfort, that he could touch up the proof so the boil would not show in the finished picture.

This set off a trend of thoughts in Louie's mind. "When we have our pictures made, we want all the blemishes and wrinkles taken out; we really do not want our true likenesses reproduced. But when God gives us a picture of ourselves, He leaves in all the blemishes, that we may see our need. . . .

"When I was a child, after I had played in the mud until I was covered with it, my mother had great difficulty in convincing me that I needed to wash. Finally, in order to prove that I needed a bath, she would hold the mirror up before me so that I could see for myself. The mirror could not wash me, however; it could only reveal the mud. That is what the law does. It reveals sin, but cannot wash it away."[3]

Louie rejoiced that as the photographer would give him a finished picture without a boil, so God offers a guilty person the free gift of His righteousness. The words of Robert Murray M'Cheyne came to his mind.

> When I stand before the throne,
> Dressed in beauty not my own;
> When I see Thee as Thou art,
> Love Thee with unsinning heart;
> Then, Lord, shall I fully know,
> Not till then how much I owe.

That beauty not his own, to which Robert Murray M'Cheyne referred, is the righteousness of God; this righteousness is provided in the redemption that is in Christ Jesus.

At graduation time, Moody Bible Institute received a letter asking the school for someone to become pastor of the First Congregational Church of Paris, Texas, a small church founded by Dr. C. I. Scofield.

Louie was selected. Still keeping seminary and China in mind for some future date, he accepted the pastorate.

The sleepy little town of Paris had no idea of the excitement that was riding toward it in the form of the new parson.

4

THROUGH DEEP WATERS

LOUIE COULD NOT AFFORD a car or care for a horse, so he bought a bicycle to call on each of the fifty-five members of his new church in Paris. He immediately plunged his little congregation into a study of Daniel and Revelation, and he had them all scrambling through their Bibles in search of passages many of them had not known existed.

He was going to preach one Sunday on the return of the Lord, and he wrote out the whole sermon by hand. "How I worked on that sermon," he commented. "I couldn't wait for Sunday to come. I went down to the church Saturday night to put the finishing touches on the sermon, and left the manuscript on the desk in my study. Then I went home just longing for Sunday to come.

"When I went down to the church early Sunday morning to go over that sermon, I found that it was gone. I wondered who in the world had been in my study. Then I heard the janitor down in the basement working with the furnace. I went downstairs and on seeing the janitor, I said, 'Mr. Williams, were you in my study this morning?'

" 'Yes, Mr. Talbot, don't worry. I've taken care of everything.'

" 'Did you see some papers on my desk?'

" 'Yes. There they are in the furnace. I believe in getting rid of all the rubbish.'

"I landed into that fellow, and said a lot of things that weren't so and told him to keep out of my study.

"But as I went upstairs, I would have given anything if I could have recalled those words. Then the church service began. As we were getting near the time when I was to preach on the Lord's coming, I was wishing that we could just dismiss them all. When I got up to preach, I took one look out of my eyes at Mr. Williams, who was sitting in the front row picking at his fingernails.

36

"I stood there in the pulpit and said to the congregation, 'My friends, before I can preach on the return of the Lord or preach on anything, I've got a little unfinished business to do.' And then I told them what had happened before the service began and how I had lit into Mr. Williams. I looked down at the brother and said, 'Mr. Williams, I'm sorry, and I want you to forgive me.' Then I walked down the steps and put my arm around him, and the old boy started to cry, and then I began to cry. Then the choir started crying, and then the whole congregation wept.

"God gave us a great day that Sunday. Some people got up and walked to the other side of the church and made things right with each other and with God. We were still feeling the influence of that day a year afterwards."

One Sunday Louie announced that the young people of the church were to meet him in the town plaza with the folding organ and hymn books for a Gospel service in the open air. What a reaction there was, for they thought it would make them conspicuous in the eyes of their schoolmates! But as the street meetings continued Sunday after Sunday, the young people began counting it a privilege to witness in this way under the leadership of their pastor.

First Congregational Church, Paris, Texas; now called the Paris Bible Church.

Then he took them for jail and poor farm services, cottage prayer meetings, and Bible study groups, all new experiences in the lives of those young people. They grew in the Lord and some of them went into full-time service for Him.

But just as the church was beginning to thrive under Louie's pastoring, a telegram that changed everything came. Louie's brother Jim was critically ill. Lou loved and admired him more than anyone he had ever known. He handed the telegram to Judge Scott, a leading member of the church and in whose home he was living. When the fatherly judge saw the anguish in Louie's face, he said, "You want to go to him, don't you, son? We'll look after the church. You just pack a bag and go."

Jim was pastor of the First Presbyterian Church in Ferguson, Missouri. He had just completed an intensive campaign of evangelistic meetings in a large tent when he was taken ill. Rheumatic fever had damaged his heart when he was a young lad and now was taking its toll. Although doctors had warned Jim that he must limit his preaching, his burden for lost souls was so great that he would not spare himself. Because of his deep prayer life and close walk with God, the students at Xenia Seminary had often referred to him as "a second Robert Murray M'Cheyne."

When Louie bent over the hospital bed, Jim spoke weakly, "It's all right, old boy. I'll get better. I have to. I must get to Australia—to speak to Dad—about his soul. Oh Lou, pray for Dad."

For a few days Jim seemed to improve, and Louie went out and made arrangements to take him to Australia. Jim lingered on for two weeks, during which time he talked to Louie about the intense burden on his heart for lost souls. It was for this magnificent obsession that Jim had burned out his young life.

Louie remembered vividly his brother's last night. "He rested his head in my arms and faintly sang with me some verses from one of his favorite hymns:

> Jesus, I am resting, resting
> In the joy of what Thou art;
>
> .   .   .   .
>
> Ever lift Thy face upon me,
> As I work and wait for Thee;
> Resting 'neath Thy smile, Lord Jesus,
> Earth's dark shadows flee.

Brightness of my Father's glory,
Sunshine of my Father's face,
Keep me ever trusting, resting,
Fill me with Thy grace.

[JEAN S. PIGOT]

"In between periods of quietness, Jim uttered words of prayer: 'Lord, we have trusted Thee. We do trust Thee, and we ever shall trust Thee for everything—in life, in death, and forever. Lord, I don't want to die, but I'll lay down my ministry and go Home—gladly—if that will show Dad his need of the Saviour.'

"He asked the Lord to sustain Mother, and as his strength failed told me always to preach the Word. And then the Lord took Jim away from me Home to glory. I bowed my head in acceptance of God's will, but I could no longer keep the tears back. I was twenty-three years old and had never been so torn apart. I stumbled away alone somewhere and wept for five hours."

The members of Jim's church turned to Louie for help in making the funeral service glorify the Lord. It was their need of him that strengthened Louie through the next few days.

Among the letters from Jim's friends to his mother and father was the following one from Mr. R. A. Pollock:

"Jim was more than brilliant; in many ways he was a genius; and had the body been able to stand the spirit, he could have been one of the best-known preachers in America and Australia. . . . I met your other son at Moody Bible Institute last March and hope he will be as great a man as his brother."

The Reverend Fred Binns, who had suggested to Jim that he attend Moody, was in England when he heard the news and wrote to the family: "It seems strange that Jim should have been called away when he was entering on his life work after he had given such splendid promise of great usefulness and when he had fitted himself by such a fine course of training. We cannot understand it. But the longer I live the more I feel that God has a two-fold work to do in regard to us—a work in us and a work by us. Jim has not ceased to serve—no; he serves now in the glorious presence of the King. He has received his promotion early."

Louie felt as if he had a deathbed commission from his brother to sail for Australia and endeavor to lead their father to the Lord. It was a saddened pastor who returned to Paris and asked for a leave of absence. It was granted on condition that he return to the church on his arrival back in America. He recommended that his friend from Moody days, Joseph Flacks, become interim pastor.

During the lonely voyage to Australia, Louie wrestled with his thoughts, his emotions, and his future. Did the Lord want him to minister His Word in China or America? Had God called him specifically to China or was it a burden for lost souls everywhere? He wished the Lord had taken him instead of Jim, and he immersed himself in God's Word. As he paced the deck, there were times when he felt as if the Lord drew near, walked by his side, and laid it upon his heart to take up the work of evangelism Jim had laid down.

By the time he reached Sydney, he had found peace of heart and was ready to comfort his family. One evening Louie went to his father's room. While sitting at his father's bedside, Louie told him of Jim's deep love for him and his dying words, "Lord, I don't want to die, but I'll lay down my ministry and go Home—gladly—if that will show Dad his need of the Saviour."

The father's eyes filled with tears of deep regret as he recalled the flash of anger when he had said to Jim, "From now on this business will no longer be 'Talbot and Sons.'" But his heart was full of bitterness toward the business friends who had deceived him and caused his bankruptcy, and he felt that that bitterness stood in the way of his becoming a true Christian.

As Louie told him that the Lord could take the bitterness out of his heart and then outlined the plan of salvation to him, the father prayed.

"Lord, I want to be a Christian. Make it possible for me to be a Christian."

The clear word was not to come, however, until four years later. When John Talbot then became ill and was on the way to the hospital, he said to his wife, Bessie, "The bitterness is gone. If the Lord should call me, I am ready, trusting in Him."

While he was in his homeland, Louie wrote to the Australian office of the China Inland Mission that he was returning to the United States for further studies and to continue his ministry there.

But as he sailed again for America, he felt very much alone. He did not know that the Lord had a girl who was just for him. She was in Paris, Texas, playing the church organ.

5

THE GIRL AT THE ORGAN

IT WAS IN THE SPRING OF 1914 that Louie arrived back in Paris, Texas. He went down to have a look around the church, stood at the pulpit for a few thoughtful moments, and then sat down at the organ. He had loved hearing his sisters play their favorite hymns when the family sang together. Placing his hands on the keys, he tried to play one of those old hymns.

When he looked up, he saw her standing quietly in the doorway, watching him. His playing tapered off as Audrey Hogue walked up the aisle, and when she spoke, her voice was like the music of the organ to him. While he had been in Australia, she had been engaged as the church organist by Joseph Flacks.

Audrey had never met Louie. She had expected a somber, older man, because the letters he had written the church from Sydney sounded to her like the writings of the apostle Paul. She could hardly believe that the hand that had written those serious letters so full of scriptural admonitions belonged to this attractive young man.

During the church services that followed, the music from Audrey's fingertips and heart flowed through that organ into the depths of Louie's soul. He inquired more about her. On learning that she gave piano lessons, he promptly enrolled as one of her pupils.

Her music and serene personality were like the balm of Gilead to Louie after the heartrending experience of Jim's death. As their relationship deepened, Louie was able to plunge into the work of the Paris church.

Joseph Flacks had been a good substitute pastor while Louie was gone, and Louie asked that Joe be kept on as his assistant. They would divide equally Louie's salary of $100.00 a month. The two men were both ordained as ministers of the Gospel on November 11, 1914, by an official council of Congregational churches and ministers.

The ordination sermon was delivered by the moderator, the Reverend Luther Rees.

Under the shepherding of its two pastors, the little church tripled in size and grew in the knowledge of the Word. In a later sermon, Louie recalled this incident of those days:

"One rainy night about eleven o'clock there was a knock on our door and there was a woman who was saturated with the rain.

" 'I want you to come with me,' she said. 'My son is dying. He's a saloonkeeper and is a very wicked man.'

" 'Well, give me the address and I'll go see him tomorrow.'

" 'No, I want you to come tonight.'

"As I reached for a Bible, she said, 'And don't bring a Bible or he won't listen to you.'

"I put on my overcoat and walked with her through the rain down the main street of that little Texas town, 'Tell me about your son.'

" 'He's not going to live very long, and I can't bear to think of his going out of this world into a Christless eternity.'

"And as she talked, I prayed, 'Lord, I can't take a Bible, so what in the world can I say to this man?'

"Then the Lord seemed to say to me, 'Don't you remember that your father supplied the whiskey, wine, and beer for fellows like that?' And I quickened my steps because I knew I had a contact with that man.

"We came to his house; and when he saw me, he said, 'What brings you here?'

" 'I'm interested in you, my friend, because your mother told me you are a saloonkeeper.'

" 'Well, what's wrong with that?'

" 'I thought you'd be interested in knowing my father was the head of the largest brewery in the southern hemisphere.'

"His interest perked up then, and I continued, 'But one day Somebody gave him a drink, and he's never thirsted again.'

"I'll never forget the look on his face as he said, 'Who brewed that?'

" 'Do you really want to know who brews the drink that once tasted of you'll never thirst again?'

" 'Yes,' he replied, 'I've never heard of one like that.'

" 'And you won't get mad?'

" 'No.'

"I told him that there was One who came down from heaven and said, 'Whosoever drinketh of the water that I shall give him shall never thirst.' I went to see him a number of times, and God touched that man and caused light to shine in his heart as he drank of the water of life.

"Just before he died, he said to me, 'I want to thank you for the interest that you took in me. I was on my way to hell, and I didn't know it. When you come to heaven, I'll be at the beautiful gate to welcome you into everlasting habitations.'

Pastor and bridegroom.

"When I left his home, I walked along kicking up the gold dust and singing 'Hallelujah.'"

Joseph Flacks and Louie used every form of evangelism they could think of in their service for the Lord. They seemed indefatigable, and the two men worked well together, except in the matter of Audrey. One evening Joe wanted Louie to go somewhere with him, so he phoned Audrey and canceled Louie's date with her. When Louie found out, his temper flared and he struck a match, touching it to Joe's hair. The fire was quickly snuffed out, but Joe never again canceled any of Louie's dates with Audrey.

A beautiful girl, with brown hair and grayish blue eyes, Audrey had a deep love for the Lord and an ability to lift people's hearts with her music. Louie asked her father for Audrey's hand in marriage. Although the whole family rejoiced, Louie was shy of announcing it to his church. He asked Audrey to wear the engagement ring out of sight on a long gold chain around her neck.

A year had passed since he returned from Australia. Joseph Flacks was doing well at the Paris church, and Louie felt that this was his opportunity to ask for a leave of absence to study at McCormick Theological Seminary in Chicago. He persuaded Audrey to study at the Bush Conservatory of Music near there and at Moody Bible Institute. Audrey asked that their engagement be announced before their departure, and the ring was transferred from the chain around her neck to the proper finger.

While studying at McCormick Seminary, Louie pastored a fledgling group called the Madison Street Church in Oak Park, Illinois, from March 1915, to June 1917. This church continued to grow, and later its new edifice was named the Calvary Memorial Church.

Audrey and Louie planned their wedding for Christmas vacation in 1916. A fire had damaged the piano in the Paris church, and Joseph Flacks asked Audrey to help him select a new piano in Dallas. While there, she purchased her wedding garments. Since Joe was to have part in the marriage ceremony, he said to the salesgirls in each store where she shopped, "I'm going to marry this girl, but she's not going to marry me." After arousing their curiosity, he went on to tell of Louie as the absent bridegroom and of Christ as the Bridegroom waiting for His bride, the Church.

The wedding was held on December 27, 1916. Dr. Robert Shuler, who was pastor of the First Methodist Church, of which Audrey had been a member, officiated, and Joseph Flacks assisted him. When it was time in the ceremony for the bridegroom to kiss the bride, Joseph Flacks, a Hebrew Christian, quoted the Scripture portion "to the Jew first" and kissed the bride before giving the bridegroom his opportunity.

Audrey's sister Ruth asked Louie, "What about China?"

"I feel the Lord wants me to take up the work Jim laid down," he answered. God had used Jim to bring his brother to this country and to hold him here for a great ministry, and it is possible that Jim has a part in eternity for all the Lord did through Louie.

His friendship with Bob Shuler continued throughout Louie's life. Dr. Shuler was often heard to say: "If you want to know what to do about the liquor-loving, double-dealing politicians, come to hear me; but if you want to understand prophecy, Daniel's image, the beasts of Revelation, and God's plan of the ages, go and hear young Talbot."

Dr. Shuler was later to write of Louie: "Few men in this generation have achieved success as has he. Some characteristics cling to him. He is persistent. He has tremendous faith. He is absolutely loyal to the Book from which he draws his message. He is a tireless worker. He has a more than natural ability to understand and interpret the Scriptures. He knows how to give all he has and hold

Audrey, his chosen bride.

back nothing. He knows and loves Jesus Christ. He has taken literally the Bible exhortation, 'Search the Scriptures.' "[1]

When the school term was over, Audrey and Louie gave full time to the work of their church in Paris. Their ministry continued to grow in that little Texas town, and both Louie and Audrey were happy in their home life and in the church. A blue-eyed baby girl named after her mother, but who was to grow up looking remarkably like her father, was born in 1918 on her mother's birthday, September 13.

Among those people deeply influenced by Louie's life and ministry in Paris was Wee Dickie Kerr, who became a hero in the baseball world. The Lord was preparing him in those days for the world series baseball games of 1919, when Dickie pitched for the Chicago White Sox against the Cincinnati Reds. Eight members of his team secretly sold out to throw the game, but Dickie Kerr pitched his heart out and his arm almost off to win. When the story came out, the White Sox were nicknamed the Black Sox. A reporter in Houston wrote that he could think of nothing that would stand as a greater reminder of baseball's integrity than a statue of Dickie Kerr.

Dickie and his wife, Cora, were grateful all their lives for Louie's ministry to them at the Paris church.

Then one day a call came for Louie to accept the pastorate of the Fourth Congregational Church of Oak Park, Illinois. This was near Chicago, where he hoped to continue his studies, and when he and Audrey sought the Lord's will, they both felt that it was His next step for them.

The people of the First Congregational Church of Paris did not want them to leave, but on January 8, 1919, Louie presided over his last business meeting at that church. Louie felt that his work there was finished, and his spirit quickened within him with every click of the wheels of the train taking them to Oak Park. He did not know that the move would have far-reaching effects on his life and ministry.

6

IN THE CRITICS' DEN

LOUIE DECIDED to rent a tent. On a humid summer day, he looked out over his congregation of about two hundred people crowded into the Fourth Congregational Church of Oak Park. The aisles were filled with chairs, and men and women were wiping perspiration from their necks and faces. He felt that people living in the Chicago area would enjoy open-air meetings during the warm summer months.

Consulting with his church board, Louie told them he wanted to invite surrounding churches to the outdoor services during the summer evenings, and one of the elders, a tall, slim businessman named William G. Nyman, gave him the encouragment he needed. The response of the invited churches was so encouraging that it was decided to hold the meetings every night during the summer.

Among the speakers of stature who addressed the tent congregation was the silver-tongued orator, William Jennings Bryan. He was nominated for the presidency of the United States three times and served as secretary of state under President Wilson. His voice filled the tent and all the outdoors like the resonant tones of an organ. The conflict between liberalism and fundamentalism was flaring in the churches at that time; and in a compelling address, Mr. Bryan spoke of his unshakable belief in the infallibility of the Bible. Among the most avid listeners was Louie himself.

The tent was always crowded out, and the meetings were held each summer for several years. Between eminent speakers, Louie filled the tent with his messages on prophecy. People became fascinated with his thirty-foot chart, entitled "From Creation to Re-Creation." Interest in his unique presentations intensified, and it brought his first experience with destructive critics. His teaching of Daniel and Revelation stirred keen interest in many churches and criticism in others.

He was carrying big advertisements in the paper, and he caused quite a stir as people gathered with their Bibles to hear the Word of God as revealed in the book of Daniel. But the pastor of a large church told his people, "I've studied Daniel and Revelation and have concluded that no one can understand these books," and he advised his people just to let them alone because they were the utterances of a "dreamer."

"That man might just as well have taken a penknife and cut Daniel and Revelation out of the Bible and cast them upon the hearth to be consumed by the flame," commented Louie on the radio. "But Daniel and Revelation are still in God's Book . . . , and when we have another edition of the Word of God, you'll find Daniel and Revelation still there. . . . I stand for the full inspiration of all the reputed Word of God."

"I would recommend . . . Sir Robert Anderson's work, *Daniel in the Critics' Den.* That is a good title, for Daniel is being assailed more in the 'critics' den' than he was in the lions' den! . . . Daniel could look down the centuries and see the things that were to come to pass because God, as it were, put a telescope to his eye and let him see His great plan and purpose through the years."[1]

But it was more than Louie's teachings on Daniel that brought out the crowds to hear him. Louie's love for the people themselves and his warm, personal interest in them emanated from his personality. One of the members of his church commented, "When talking with you, he made you feel that you were the most important person in the world to him at that moment." He had a way of getting through to people's hearts.

He stood firm in the critics' den.

Louie and William Nyman in Oak Park.

Anyone who had been hurt by life always brought out his tenderness of spirit. He walked from his home to the church every day, and he often noticed several sisters sitting on the veranda of a nearby home. It seemed to him that they had a great burden, and their eyes were often red. One day he stopped and talked to them, "I'm one of your neighbors and the pastor of this little church over here. There seems to be some sadness in your hearts and lives, and I was wondering whether I could do something for you."

One of the young women pointed upstairs, "Our brother was gassed in the war over in France; now he's come home, and he's struggling for breath."

They went upstairs, and there was a young man stretched on a bed straining to breathe. Louie talked to him for a while and then said, "My dear friend, are you a Christian young man?"

"Oh," he answered in a weak voice, "I've been trying."

"And how are you getting along?"

"What can I do lying here?"

"I've got wonderful news for you. You don't have to do anything. Someone came into the world and did it all for you." Louie told him of the death of the Lord Jesus Christ on the cross for him, and how the Lord Jesus said, "It is finished." Then Louie continued, "Everything that needs to be done has been done, and it will be finished for you the moment you accept that one sacrifice for sins forever."

Louie later commented, "That young man accepted the Lord Jesus Christ as his Saviour, and peace came into his heart."

Louie was deeply reverent in matters concerning the Lord, but there was another side to his personality, as told by Lillian Sutton:

"He could be fun and nonsense at the sleigh rides, hayrides, and parties of the young people, but a word for his Lord was paramount."

Everyone was invited to a wedding at the church, but invitations to the reception at the bride's home were limited. Thirteen of the uninvited teenagers piled into a Ford; some had to ride on the running boards, including a boy on crutches. They drove out to the house, hoping somehow to get in on the refreshments but remained outside empty-handed.

Louie was sitting at a window in the dining room, and he spotted them. As chatting guests carrying plates filled with wedding cake and other confections passed him, Louie casually picked up their candy and nut cups. Then he handed them to the young people through the window. Recalling that story, Ann Larsen commented, "Is it any wonder that all of us young people loved him?"

At this time a flu epidemic swept over the world, and when a letter came from Louie's homeland, the news it contained made it feel heavy in his hand. His mother, after caring for others who were ill, had died of the flu. Overwhelmed by memories of his mother, Louie went out and walked for several hours. He had loved her deeply and had planned on bringing her to America so he could provide her with every comfort in the closing years of her life. Although he felt a terrific loss, he knew she was with the Lord she loved. She had seen all her family accept Him as Saviour except for one son, and she had claimed him with a faith that God later honored.

When Louie wrote the family in Australia, his sympathy reached out to his sister Gladys, who faced a double loss: her mother had just died and her fiancé had been killed in the war. Louie offered to pay her way to America so that she might study at the Moody Bible Institute. Feeling lonely and with a heart she could not shake out of its sadness, Gladys accepted. She became beloved and respected at Moody not only in her student days, but also during the thirty-five years she served the Lord there in the registrar's office, on the faculty, and singing over the institute's radio station. Dedicated, beautiful, and dignified, Gladys became an inspiration to the students at Moody.

Louie was happy in his family and ministry. A baby girl named Betty was born to Audrey and Louie on June 17, 1921. Betty was a

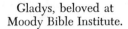

Gladys, beloved at
Moody Bible Institute.

roly-poly, hazel-eyed, good-natured, happy sister for their three-year-
old Audrey.

Louie was now becoming so well known that sometimes men of
note came to hear him preach. During one Sunday morning service,
he saw a distinguished gentleman come in late. Louie always felt
humble in the presence of those he considered great, and he recognized Dr. William R. Newell, a nationally known Bible teacher and
writer of the hymn "At Calvary" and books on Romans and Revelation.

Louie thought that the sermon he had intended to preach seemed,
in the presence of this man, inept and weak. With the pulpit presence that always characterized him, Louie rose to the occasion
with these words: "This morning we have in the congregation an
honored guest, Dr. William R. Newell, one of the most distinguished
teachers of the Word in this country. I am sure you would rather
hear him today than listen to me, so Dr. Newell, will you please
come to the platform?"

A twinkle came to the older man's eyes as he listened to the young preacher. Dr. Newell knew so well how Louie felt. Going to the platform, Dr. Newell shook Louie's hand and whispered to him, "Why should one piece of clay be afraid of another piece of clay?"

Dr. Newell said a few words of greeting and commendation to the congregation. Then, putting his hand on Louie's shoulder, he said in a kind voice, "Your people are waiting for your message, not one from an outsider." With these words, Dr. Newell returned to his seat in the front row.

By this time Louie could not even remember the sermon he had prepared. In desperation he took the best parts of his last three sermons and preached them over again.

Another Sunday morning there were several men in the congregation who concentrated their attention on everything Louie said and did. At the close of the service, as Louie stood at the door shaking hands with the people, one of these gentlemen said, "May we have a personal word with you?"

When Louie was free, he took them to his study. The request they made astounded him, and again the course of his life was changed.

7

BEAUTIFUL WESTMINSTER

"Now WHAT CAN I DO for you?" Louie asked the three gentlemen who had come to his study in Oak Park.

"We're from the First Westminster Presbyterian Church of Keokuk, Iowa, and have come to find out whether you would consider a call to become pastor of our church."

Louie found their words hard to believe. He knew the church, beautiful in its French Gothic architecture, with windows of imported stained glass depicting scenes from the Bible and lighting up the gray stones and steeple. It was more formal and aristocratic than the churches he had thus far served. He remembered preaching from its pulpit one time at the invitation of Jack Irwin, who was a member of the House of Representatives of the state of Iowa and was also Speaker of the House. The two men had met at Jim's church; and when Mr. Irwin's home church in Keokuk needed a pastor, he recommended Louie.

"What kind of a church has Mr. Talbot in Oak Park?" asked a member of the board when the pulpit committee returned to Keokuk after interviewing Louie.

"I don't care what kind of a church he has," responded one of those who had gone to hear him. "If he were preaching under a tree, it wouldn't matter. All that counts is that we secure him as our pastor!"

Louie began his ministry at the First Westminster Presbyterian Church in July 1922. Accustomed to traditional services, the congregation soon realized that they had an unusual preacher in their pulpit. While he could be reverent, dignified, and impressive in the worship services, Louie could also be unpredictable.

Just before his sermons on Sundays, Louie gave object lessons for children in the church services. One morning as the people gathered

to worship, they noticed that part of the ceiling had been removed
and that a long, wooden ladder extended from the pulpit right up
through the ceiling. They could hardly believe what they were seeing
in their stately church, but they never forgot that Jacob's ladder was
a type of the cross enabling man to go from earth to heaven.

Listening to those object lessons for children every Sunday was
Mr. Irwin's young son, John N. Irwin II, who became a brilliant
lawyer of Christian faith and integrity. He served in our government in various capacities during the administrations of Presidents
Truman, Eisenhower, Johnson, and Nixon. Included among his
presidential appointments were the positions of ambassador to France
and deputy secretary of state just before Dr. Henry Kissinger came
into the State Department.

After meeting doctors, lawyers, professors, government officials,

Beautiful Westminster.

and business executives among the members of the church, Louie studied harder on his sermons than ever before. He often paced up and down between the church and the manse, gesticulating and memorizing his sermons while his daughter Audrey followed him back and forth on her tricycle.

Noticing that large crowds milled around downtown on Saturday nights, with people socializing and farmers buying and selling, Louie mounted a soapbox and started preaching. He recalled that first meeting: "One man started heckling me, and a few days later he was suddenly stricken with a serious illness. I called at the hospital to see him. When I entered his room, his chin quivered as he told me, 'I didn't mean what I said the other night,' and he accepted Christ as his Saviour."

One of the Presbyterians watching his pastor preaching from a soapbox gave him a truck with a platform and organ. Soon the street meetings were causing traffic jams, and the police cooperated by roping off a section for them.

As news of Louie's preaching spread, attendance at the church increased until there were no empty seats. After coming to hear him several times, the minister of the Unitarian church told one of the elders, "I don't agree with your pastor's theology, but it does me good to see someone believe so thoroughly what he preaches."

Louie plunged with zest into the activities of the young people, and he reveled in their swims in the Mississippi River. He often swam across and back where the river was a mile wide.

Next to swimming, Louie enjoyed fishing. On one fishing excursion, Louie secretly took the fish his friend was catching, swam underwater, and attached them one by one to the fishhook of his little daughter Betty. She was delighted over all the fish she was catching, but Louie's friend could not understand why all his fish were disappearing.

One of Louie's favorite fishing companions was his dentist, who was also an elder in the church, Dr. R. G. Sinotte; their families vacationed together at the Fish Trays Lakes in Minnesota. Dr. Sinotte's son, Wells, shared this story of those days: "Louie had been fishing off of the boat dock, catching sunfish. When dinner was ready, he placed his fishing pole against a tree, with the worm still dangling on the hook. During the meal a chicken happened along and swallowed the worm along with the fishhook. The squawking and thrash-

ing around caused quite a commo-
tion. We stopped eating and investigated. My father removed the fishhook, but Louie felt so conscience
stricken over the chicken's suffering
that he undertook the responsibility
for its recuperation, whereupon the
chicken expired the next day."

Dr. Sinotte's daughter, Paralee,
recalls that "when he went calling
on his bicycle, he would have his
mind so on the Lord's work that he
would often start to his next appointment on foot, forgetting his
bicycle."

When entering home or office,
Louie immediately tossed his hat

Betty and Audrey.

and coat onto different chairs. One morning when he was ready to
leave for the church, there was not a single coat in his closet. Turning to his wife, he asked, "What in the world have you done with
my coats? Did you send them all to the cleaners?"

Audrey suggested he might find some in the church. There he
found four coats, each on its own chair.

One day a tramp, thinly clothed and cold, came into the church
for help. Anyone in need always stirred Louie's heart, and he gave
the tramp all the money he had in his wallet and a new, fur-lined
overcoat that had just been presented to him by a member of the
church. As the story circulated among the people of the congregation, they wondered who was the more astonished—the gentleman
who had given Louie the expensive overcoat or the tramp who received it.

Audrey's graciousness and Louie's wit made them popular dinner
guests. One evening at a dinner in his honor, Louie left his spinach
untouched: it was a vegetable he never liked. When asked by a
member of the church why he had not eaten his spinach, he turned
an embarrassing situation into laughter by replying, "If I had to
choose between spinach and sin, I'd choose sin!"

Because Louie was unique in his ways, problems in a church during his ministry were sometimes unique. There was, for instance, the problem of pigeons in the sanctuary of beautiful Westminster.

Most of the pigeons in Keokuk clustered in the cupola of the fire department, but some ventured into the tower of the church. Louie and James Fulton, one of the church elders, began feeding them. More and more of the fire-department pigeons began joining the Presbyterian pigeons. Periodically, Mr. Fulton took some to his wife, Florence, who made delicious pigeon pie and invited Louie over to enjoy it with them. Difficulty arose when some of the pigeons found their way into the church sanctuary. On Sunday mornings ushers would have to chase them out before the worshipers arrived.

At a meeting of the board, the problem was discussed; Louie and Mr. Fulton listened attentively but quietly, all the time trying to look serious. It was decided that chicken wire be stretched over the openings in the tower.

Not to be deterred, Mr. Fulton and Louie would roll up the wire until enough pigeons for a pie flew in, and then they would fasten the wire down again. Sometimes a stray pigeon would find its way into the sanctuary. Members of the board would examine the tower, only to find the wire securely in place. The mystery remained unsolved, and Louie and the Fultons continued to enjoy pigeon pie.

Several years later, when Louie was pastor of a church in another city, he was invited back to Keokuk for special meetings. He told them the secret of how the pigeons got into the church, describing the expressions and comments of the different board members as they had tried to figure it out. The congregation responded in like good humor. One of the members commented, "He told the story with much *inner* hilarity. He was always so full of the joy of living. He could also open the gates of heaven for me."

During the long, warm evenings of summer, the people of Keokuk enjoyed being outdoors. In his mind, Louie could see them gathered together on the cool lawn that spread from the church to the manse. He presented the idea of outdoor meetings to the leaders of the church. Some murmured that many feet would trample and ruin their well-manicured lawn, while others felt that the meetings would not have the dignity of a church service. But they found their pastor's enthusiastic personality irresistible, and his persuasion swept away their objections. All was made ready with lights, seats, a platform, and an organ. The crowds grew and meetings were held every night, with police to guide the traffic.

The members of Louie's congregation caught his enthusiasm themselves; and when the nearby Baptist church closed its Sunday evening services for the summer to attend the meetings, the Presbyterians gave them a sincere welcome to the refreshing, green lawns. It became the place to go on a summer evening, and Louie preached his heart out. One member commented, "Louie had an active and brilliant mind, and nobody else before or since let them have it like he did."

Then one day two strangers came to the Sunday morning worship service and sat in the second row. Louie described what happened, "Watching them out of the corner of my eye, I decided they were probably two traveling salesmen from out of town, and I let them have both barrels." He preached the Gospel that morning with all the might he could muster. And those two "salesmen" brought a whole new world into Louie's life.

8

OUR UNPREDICTABLE PASTOR

THE TWO GENTLEMEN Louie thought were salesmen turned out to be elders from the Oliver Presbyterian Church of Minneapolis; they were looking for a new pastor. "We went to the church and sat in the second row to get a good look at the Reverend Louis Talbot," Orrin Jacobs explained. "He seemed to preach directly at us. We were impressed with his ability and personality, so we invited him to Oliver Church for the midweek prayer meeting and two services on Sunday."

Louie was met at the station in Minneapolis by Dr. Rudolph Logefeil, who summed up the reaction of the congregation, "Mr. Talbot's warm friendliness and strong sense of humor, along with his love of the Word of God and his exceptional ability to present it in a practical way, made him very popular."

His first Sunday as pastor of Oliver Presbyterian Church was June 6, 1926. In the morning he preached on "The Old Paths," and in the evening his subject was "The Christ I Believe."

Because Louie was trying to get around Minneapolis on his bicycle, John Germann often drove him in his car. One day at the Germanns' home, Louie discovered he had worn a hole in his sock and asked John's wife, Eva, to darn it. As she was darning his sock, and Louie was resting his bare foot on a low table and wiggling his toes, in walked Louie's wife, Audrey. She stood there in shocked surprise. One year when asked what he wanted for his birthday, he replied, "Socks," and he received an avalanche of them.

Some people felt that it was time Louie gave up his bicycle and bought a car of his own.

"So I bought a new car without knowing much about driving one," Louie recalled, "and parked it in front of my house because I wanted all the neighbors to see my fine new automobile.

"But after a few hours a policeman knocked at my door and asked, 'Is this your car parked out here?'

" 'Yes, it is.'

" 'Well, come out here and have a look at it.'

"I went outside and the whole back end was bashed in.

" 'A streetcar conductor saw a truck strike your car and wrote down the license number. Here it is.'

" 'What can I do about it?'

" 'You'd better get a lawyer.'

"So I hired a lawyer, and he went to court, fought my case, and won it. When he sent me his bill, I told him, 'I have an Advocate who's been looking after my affairs for many years, and He's never sent me a bill yet.'

" 'Who's that?' the lawyer asked.

" ' "If any man sin," ' I replied, ' "we have an advocate with the Father, Jesus Christ the righteous." When you do something wrong, my friend, the devil accuses you in the presence of God; but you have an Advocate with the Father, and He will never send you a bill.' "

While driving to his appointments, Louie used the time to think through his sermons, and stories of his absentminded driving abound. On his way to a meeting at the Knox Presbyterian Church, where his friend the Reverend J. Renwick McCullough was pastor, Louie veered off the street to avoid an oncoming vehicle. Losing control, he ran his car through the backyard of a home and through several lines of wet clothes hanging up to dry; the wet clothes were draped all over Louie's car, which ended up in the basement of a new house under construction.

Scrambling out of the excavation, Louie said to the harried woman who was trying to retrieve her clothes from his car, "I'm the pastor of the Oliver Presbyterian Church, and I'll be back to see you. Right now I'm in a bit of a hurry."

Just then he saw a passing truck and hailed it, "Can you give me a lift? I've got a problem." The driver hitched a chain to Louie's car and pulled it out of the basement.

Louie did not know it, but the lady had called the police. As he was driving toward the Knox Presbyterian Church, he heard the police siren behind him. Louie had some explaining to do.

He enjoyed fun and action. At the annual church picnic there was a race in which all ages could participate. "You should have seen the pastor run like a deer," observed Orrin Jacobs. "He left all the rest behind and won the race."

Attendance at the church surged upward, especially at the evening meetings. "When Louie came to Oliver, he was liked right off the bat, and was unpredictable," commented V. A. Skiff. "We needed more room for Sunday school classes, and next to the church was a large house that Louie found we could obtain for a price." He started raising the money, and the house was purchased in 1929.

The people enjoyed the way he made himself at home everywhere he went. After an unsuccessful fishing expedition, he spent the

Oliver Presbyterian Church.

night at the home of Dr. and Mrs. Logefeil. Bernie Parsons brought over some fresh fish he had caught; but since they had just finished dinner, no one, not even Louie, felt like eating fish. They were put in the refrigerator. About 11:00 p.m. the Logefeils were awakened by a knock on their bedroom door. There stood Louie in his night-clothes. "I can't sleep for thinking of the fish in the refrigerator," he said. Everyone went to the kitchen and routed out the fish, which Mrs. Logefeil promptly fried, and they all enjoyed a midnight snack of sunfish and crappies.

One of the church's trustees, Selby Larson, owned a meat market, and he invited his pastor to make himself at home there any time. Louie often walked behind the counter, selected some choice cut of meat, and fried it in the back room; and he often asked the good-natured butcher to enjoy it with him.

Louie made his family's life at home equally interesting.

"We were always taking in stray animals," related his daughter Audrey, "and one of them was a jet black cat that sometimes made himself at home with us. Other times he would be gone for several months. One Sunday morning as we were leaving for church, this cat showed up on our doorstep as thin as a rail and expecting an immediate meal. Daddy picked him up, unlocked the front door, and carried him into the kitchen. There he opened the refrigerator and took out some liver. While the hungry, meowing cat joined us in watching him, Daddy stood by the stove, with his overcoat and hat still on, and cooked that liver to what he felt would be a cat's taste.

"My mother, feeling that the cat would enjoy the liver raw, and concerned because of the time, said, 'Louie, we'll be late for Sunday school, and those people are waiting for you.'

"To which Daddy replied, 'Those people aren't hungry,' and he continued cooking the liver for the cat.

"When Betty lost a tooth, I told her that a neighborhood friend had put her tooth under the pillow, and in the morning she found that the tooth fairy had put a dime there. Betty decided to try it. We did not know that Daddy had overheard our conversation. The next morning when we woke up, there were balloons and lollipops and other delightful trifles dangling on strings hanging from the ceiling. It looked like fairyland to Betty and me."

One evening when Louie and his wife were guests for dinner at the home of some members of his church, they were having a delightful time of chatting and laughing. Suddenly the hostess excused herself and went upstairs. After a while she came down carrying a small baby in her arms. As everyone admired the sleepy infant, Louie looked at the mother and asked, "Why in the world did you go and wake up that baby?"

"I didn't awaken her. Didn't you hear her cry?"

"You mean to tell me that in all the noise this bunch was making, you heard the cry of your baby upstairs?"

"Yes, I'm always listening for her cry."

Then Louie turned to the dinner guests, "Did any of you hear that baby cry?" When everyone answered in the negative, he continued, "God has given you mothers the wonderful gift of ears that are tuned to hear your own baby's cry. And that is the way the Lord is with us. In Psalm 40:1 David says, 'He inclined unto me, and heard my cry.' No matter how much noise is going on down here, no matter how faint our cries may be, the Lord has His ear inclined toward you and me, and His ear tuned to hear us when we cry unto Him."

These warm, human illustrations of biblical truths reached into people's hearts, making Louie an often requested speaker. His keen knowledge of prophecy brought him invitations to address conferences across the nation, and his inexhaustible energy enabled him to accept two additional ministries: radio and Christian education.

A pioneer in recognizing radio as a means of reaching countless people for Christ, he began verse-by-verse studies of the Bible over station WRHM on May 5, 1927; that ministry continued over various stations almost all of his life.

Then one of his friends, Dr. W. B. Riley, requested that Louie teach classes in personal evangelism at an institute that developed into Northwestern Schools. Teaching the budding young preachers exhilarated Louie, and this experience was to have a profound effect on his future ministry.

Anyone coming into Oliver Church during the week might hear that Australian drawl reverberating in some empty room at the back, where he often paced up and down, practicing aloud his sermons, radio messages, and lectures for the students.

The wife of one of his elders spent the last ten years of her life on a sickbed. She experienced considerable pain, but whenever Louie called on her, he found that sick woman giving thanks to God for the

testing through which she was passing. She died triumphantly in
Christ.

As Louie was walking into the pulpit of Oliver Church to conduct
her funeral service, the husband handed him a piece of paper. "We
found this poem in my wife's Bible," he said, "and I'd like you to
read it."

That poem became one of Louie's favorites. Here it is:

THE WEAVER

My life is but a weaving
  Between my Lord and me;
I cannot choose the colors
  He worketh steadily.

Ofttimes He weaveth sorrow
  And I in foolish pride,
Forget He sees the upper,
  And I, the underside.

Not till the loom is silent
  And the shuttles cease to fly,
Shall God unroll the canvas
  And explain the reason why.

The dark threads are as needful
  In the Weaver's skillful hand,
As the threads of gold and silver
  In the pattern He has planned.

When quoting that poem, Louie added these thoughts: "This
poem emphasizes the mystery of God's silence. I know other wonderful people of God who live constantly with pain, and some have
had tragedies come into their lives, and we wonder why God allows
it all. But when we get to heaven and look over the pathway along
which we have come, we'll see how one event links with another,
how the dark Fridays were just as necessary as the bright days of
the week, and we'll bless the hand that led and we'll bless the heart
that planned. All of God's ways with His people are going to be
vindicated at the judgment seat of Christ. For now, God wants us
to trust Him.

"During my boyhood days in Australia, I'd sit on the edge of a kitchen table and watch my mother make a cake. She'd break a bunch of raw eggs and empty the contents into a bowl, and then she'd put in some flour. Now who in the world would sit down and eat a bowl of flour? Then she put in some lard and other ingredients. Those things that she put in there I wouldn't eat separately; but after she mixed them all together and put them in the oven and baked them, all those things had worked together for good.

"The Spirit of God takes this thing and that thing and the other thing in our lives and makes them all work together for our good and for the glory of God. We're just in the mixing bowl now, and the finished product will not be seen until life's story is over."

One of the most poignant experiences during Louie's ministry in Minneapolis was that of Agnes, and he shared it with his radio audience. A young woman who was a hunchback belonged to his church, but she had the voice of a nightingale. Several nights a week she sang at the Minneapolis Rescue Mission, and the thing that gave her message in song such an impact was her deformity. Often Louie would say to her, "Agnes, I want you to sing this song just before I preach," and how she would lift that audience. Louie said that when she finished singing, "the congregation would be hushed, and I would be able to preach with power, vigor, and joy."

But one Sunday morning when he asked her to sing, she answered, "Mr. Talbot, I'm never going to sing again. I learned last night that I don't have the faith in God I thought I had."

Then Agnes told him that she had been to a healing meeting the night before; there she had been told that if she had enough faith in the Lord for the healing of her body, it would become normal. She went home that night, got down on her knees, and wept before the Lord. She was led to think that her lack of faith was why her body was still misshaped. When she prayed, she told the Lord she was going to trust Him for the healing of her body, just as she trusted Him for the healing of her soul.

As she told Louie this story, the tears ran down her face. "I woke up this morning and stood before the mirror expecting my body to be completely healed, but . . . I'm still a hunchback! So I've come to realize that I don't have any faith. I guess I didn't have any faith ten years ago when I trusted my soul to the Lord Jesus Christ, because if I really had faith, I'd be healed."

When her emotions subsided a bit, Louie explained: "Agnes, do you know that about nineteen hundred years ago there was a man who prayed the same prayer you prayed? It was over a physical infirmity. That man didn't have a hunchback, but he had a failing eyesight. . . . He naturally thought he could do a better work for God with a good pair of eyes, so he asked the Lord to remove the affliction. In fact, he prayed about it three times. Agnes, . . . do you know what God did for this apostle? He leaned over and put as it were His finger on the thorn. As he pressed it farther into his body, He said to Paul, 'My grace is sufficient for thee: for my strength is made perfect in weakness.' That satisfied the apostle Paul. . . . His attitude became, 'Therefore will I rather glory in my infirmities, that the power of Christ may rest upon me, . . . for when I am weak, then am I strong.'

"Agnes, one of the reasons you have such a wonderful testimony, and why men and women who have missed the way will listen to you, is because of the radiance of your life shining through a weak body."

And then Agnes looked up at him and said, "Mr. Talbot, what— do you want me to sing—this morning?"

"I gave her the hymn, and before I preached she sang. I'll never forget the radiant voice that came from that woman with the hunchback."

Louie continued in his radio message: "The Word of God does give us some partial answers to the question of why tears, sorrows, and heartaches come to the Lord's people. . . . Testings are a trust. If rightly used they enable us to honor God. We can understand about other things being trusts. Take money as an example. Some people have the gift of getting wealthy; and everything they touch seems to turn to gold. . . . There is also the gift of leadership, which is a trust. Scientific skill . . . is another. With these there comes the trust of sorrow and tears. . . . God gave Job the trust of severe testing, and this saint came out victoriously. The same can be true in our lives as we yield ourselves fully and completely to the Saviour."

Some of the tenderest moments of Louie's ministry were with the sick and the hurt. Mrs. Hildur Christensen was sitting outside the hospital operating room awaiting word from the doctor. Her sister had recently passed away and left five children. Her oldest son had just been injured in an accident and was having his arm amputated. He would either die or go through life without his arm.

"My heart was heavy," Mrs. Christensen said, "and then someone sat down beside me. Looking up, I saw Dr. Talbot. He stayed with me until the doctor told us that the boy came through all right, and then he offered a prayer of thanks and hope. Although we had often taken our children to hear his object lessons and wonderful sermons, we were not even members of his church. It is no wonder he was so deeply loved."

At an anniversary of the church, Harry Christensen commented "When Louie came to Oliver, the church's greatest preaching era began. He was the most forceful and dynamic preacher we ever had, but his secretary spent much of her time tracking him down so he would keep his appointments. One Saturday afternoon he was on the golf course playing with some Oliver friends when he suddenly dropped his club and streaked over the hill shouting, 'I've got a wedding in half an hour.' He had to reach the church and dress, but he made it."

One day some men came from Canada to hear Louie preach, and then they asked him whether he would consider becoming pastor of the Philpott Tabernacle in Hamilton, Ontario. He had been recommended to them by Dr. P. W. Philpott, after whom the tabernacle had been named, but who at that time was pastor of the Moody Church of Chicago. It was several months before Louie gave them his answer.

All his wonderful Presbyterian friends at Oliver Church were stunned when he announced his resignation, which became effective on April 29, 1929. They made him promise to return whenever possible for special meetings.

Orrin Jacobs had this parting word, "Louie was a gifted minister and leader, unique and colorful, with unusual enthusiasm and humor. Most certainly when he was born his mold was broken."

As Louie turned his face toward Canada, the English blood quickened in his veins. He did not know that this step would lead him on to the greatest work of his life.

9

"THE KING CAN WAIT"

As NEWS of the preaching and personality of the new pastor spread, the Canadian people crowded into every possible space at the Philpott Tabernacle in Hamilton.

Louie's ministry started there in June 1929, and the fifteen hundred seats were soon filled; the police even allowed people to sit on the steps of the balcony and stand during the services. One time so many stood in the baptistry that the floor of the tank gave way during the service. Men and women so packed the tabernacle to hear his prophetic messages that the doors often had to be closed an hour before the evening service began.

Bill Lawson worked at a nearby gas station, and on Saturdays he could hear Louie practicing his Sunday sermons out loud as he paced up and down the aisles of the empty church.

Even the children became fascinated with their new pastor. Dr. John R. Dunkin, who was between the ages of ten and fourteen during those years, recalled: "His vivid and energetic preaching was such that he became my hero. Our whole family watched in admiration from the south balcony of the tabernacle as he preached with periodic pugilistic gestures—his arm stabbing ahead while one of his legs kicked backward. He was an evangelistic preacher and prophetic Bible teacher, a loyal and winsome witness for our Lord Jesus Christ."

The depression that was hitting America during those years was also sweeping Canada, and Louie had a tender heart for the down-and-outs; he often gave them all the money he had on his person. He was among those most interested in the relief center set up in Hamilton for those in need. Every time he went there to minister spiritually to the people, he also sampled the mulligan stew served from its soup kitchen. Always a tease, Louie asked the cook one day what she put into the soup.

Philpott Tabernacle.

Tired, overworked, and busy, she replied, "Everything except the scrub brushes."

When she was looking the other way, Louie picked up one of the brushes with which she scoured the large utensils, and put it into a nearly empty kettle of soup. "What's that in this one?" he asked.

The poor woman looked with horror at the scrub brush in the soup and then at Louie; she was too embarrassed to speak. But the impish twinkle in his eyes changed that look of horror into a wholesome laugh for a weary cook, and gave her a story to tell for the rest of her days.

But sometimes his friends gave Louie his due by pulling some jokes on him. One of the members of the tabernacle secured some parking tickets from the friendly police, and whenever Louie found his car ticketed, he never knew whether it was the real thing or a prank.

The nondenominational atmosphere of the Philpott Tabernacle appealed to Louie because he was not limited by denominational lines. He enlarged the missionary vision of the church until new missionaries under various mission boards were supported. He taught the men's Bible class, and every department of the church seemed to come alive and grow under his leadership.

He had a large sign reading "Jesus Saves" erected on top of the church. One Sunday evening a man on his way to drown himself in the bay saw this sign and came into the church, where he found the Lord Jesus Christ as his Saviour and the help he needed.

Before Louie came to the church as pastor, there had been a split between former leaders, and a number of people had left and started a new church. Louie wanted to see this split healed. With understanding and prayer, he talked to both groups. The day came when he and some of the officials of Philpott Tabernacle went over and took communion with the dissenting group. Some of the members later came back to the tabernacle, and eventually the dissenting group dissolved.

Mr. and Mrs. J. E. Shaw were among the influential members of the tabernacle, and she described an accident that could have cost Louie his life. "Dr. Talbot's morning services were much enriched by his object talks to the children, but he met with near tragedy in trying out one of them in the vestry before the church service.

"As president of the Ladies' Meeting, I had to go into the vestry before church with an announcement for the pastor. What a shock I received! He had taken some gunpowder out of a bag and put it in a small dish. Then he had struck a match on the sole of his shoe. The lighted head of the match flew off and landed in the dish of gunpowder. Had it fallen into the open bag of gunpowder nearby, the whole place would have gone up in a fearful explosion. As it was, there was a blast, and the pastor's face and hands were badly burned. He was in serious condition, and my husband called a doctor at once. However, our pastor was more concerned about the services than himself. My husband promised to go for the assistant pastor, who was at another church that morning.

"Dr. Talbot was confined to his house for some time, and his face was swathed in gauze. One Saturday he phoned for my husband to come for him. Although his bandages were somewhat the worse for wear, he would not take time for his wife to change them. As he was leaving, his wife threw a shawl over his head and shoulders.

"On the way to our house, he insisted on stopping at a fish store on the main street to purchase some shrimp, of which he was very fond. With the shawl dragging along after him, he got out of the car and entered the store. A staring crowd collected outside the big plate glass window.

"A policeman who knew my husband came over to our car and asked, 'Do you know anything about this man with the bandages and shawl?' What a surprise that officer received when we told him that man was our pastor! We were all thankful that his life and eyesight had been spared and tragedy averted.

"He was very thoughtful of the feelings of people. If he had hurt anyone, he would lose no time going to that one and trying to make things right. He was outstanding in that respect and greatly loved because of it. He had the respect of the public, with even the police doing anything they could to help him."

Jack Penhall commented, "Busy as Mr. Talbot was, he always was the first one to go to anyone in trouble or sorrow, and he knew just how to deal with each problem."

In a radio message on prayer, Louie told of an experience that made a vivid impression on him during those days: He stood on a vantage ground watching Niagara Falls, and for some minutes he was just taken up with those millions of gallons of water going over the cliffs into that great abyss. And as he stood there, he noted that far down below, where the water hit the depths, there was a spray, and it was rising in the form of a mist. It came up and up until it reached the ledge over which that tremendous volume of water was falling, and he said to himself: *Why, that mist coming up is just a picture of worship.* Those millions of gallons of water pouring and pouring and pouring down upon that open abyss showed something of the river of God's grace—all His goodness and all of His mercy being poured down upon mankind.

And then as the mist kept rising up to the very ledge over which the water was pouring, his thoughts continued. *It seemed as though the water, after it hits the bottom of that pit, is coming up and saying to the river, "I thank you, I thank you, I thank you."* Thus it pictured for us worship ascending from the heart of man on earth up to the throne of God in appreciation for all His goodness, mercy, and love, which He is pouring down upon us.

And as Louie stood there watching, he thought of the second chapter of Daniel, where it is told how God answered Daniel's prayers and revealed to him the meaning of King Nebuchadnezzar's dreams. "Daniel was not in a hurry to get away from God. He had prayed for light. He had prayed to God to reveal this secret of the king, and when God gave it, he remained on his knees. He as much as said, 'the king can wait,' and he just dwelt in the presence of God and blessed Him. That's worship."

While he was pastoring the Philpott Tabernacle, Louie said to his wife, Audrey, "We're going to stay here for the rest of our lives."

Then a letter came from the Church of the Open Door in Los Angeles asking him if he would preach in the pulpit there from June 21 to August, 1931. Dr. Philpott, who was serving as pastor there, had requested that the letter be sent to Louie. The auditorium where the church worshiped had been built originally for Dr. Torrey and was part of the Bible Institute of Los Angeles.

Louie considered it a sacred privilege to stand in Dr. Torrey's pulpit, but was glad when it was time for him to return to the tabernacle in Canada, where he felt so much at home.

However, in October Dr. Philpott resigned, and Louie received a letter asking him whether he would become the pastor of the Church of the Open Door and be linked up with the Bible Institute of Los Angeles, which had a debt of over a million dollars.

"I was very much disturbed," he reported later. "At night I used to pray, telling the Lord how thankful I was that He had taken me to the Philpott Tabernacle, but I'd never mention this letter to the Lord. I was afraid that He would lead me . . . into all these debts.

"Then when I was praying, the Lord seemed to say to me, 'My son, what about that letter in your pocket? You haven't talked to Me about it.' It seemed as though the Lord was holding His yoke before me and saying, 'Take my yoke upon you, and learn of me, and ye shall find rest unto your soul.' "

On his knees before the Lord, Louie struggled against it, but could find no rest of heart.

"Then I said 'Yes' to the Lord and good-bye to that wonderful body of people in Canada, and immediately I found the rest that He gives by being yoked up with Him."

Members of the Philpott Tabernacle at first could not believe that he was leaving, and one of them wrote, "It was a sad day when he left. Some of the elders—big, strong men—actually wept." While another commented, "His secret was that he really loved people and they knew it."

But Louie turned his face toward Los Angeles, where the greatest ministry and the heaviest trials he had ever known awaited him.

10

THE PROPHET AND THE YOKE

IT WAS A HALLOWED MOMENT for Louie when he stepped into the pulpit of the Church of the Open Door in Los Angeles on January 10, 1932. As a thirteen-year-old boy in Sydney, he had sat wide-eyed in a crowd listening to the distinguished Dr. Torrey; at forty-two, Louie was becoming pastor of the church, with its vast auditorium containing two balconies and four thousand seats, that had been built for that great man of God. Louie stood there for a moment in awe and wonder at the way God had led in his life.

The congregation was accustomed to pastors more mature in years and experience, and to some members Louie appeared a bit youthful. Would he be equal to the tremendous responsibilities awaiting him? Could he draw young people and new life into a congregation that was mostly middle-aged and older, a congregation of about a thousand people surrounded by three thousand empty seats? What about the insurmountable debt of nearly 1.5 million dollars that encumbered the Bible Institute of Los Angeles in whose auditorium the church met? If the institute failed, the church would have no home. The whole nation was in the grip of a disastrous depression, and every possible source of money had already been drained.

It was a formidable task and a heavy yoke that fell on Louie's shoulders that day.

But he was like a breath of fresh air in that cavern of bleakness. His humor and ability to enjoy life and just be himself in all circumstances made people chuckle at themselves. One afternoon while Louie was preaching, an old gentleman in the front row fell asleep. Pausing in his sermon and smiling down kindly at the elderly man, he said, "Have a good sleep, brother, I appreciate your confidence. It shows you don't feel it necessary to stay awake and check up on my theology."

Pacing back and forth across the platform while he preached,

It was a sacred honor to occupy
the pulpit of Dr. R. A. Torrey.

Louie held the Bible in his left hand
and gestured with his right. On
Sunday mornings his sermons often
focused on the greatness of God
and balm for the heart, and on Sunday afternoons and evenings his exposition of the Scriptures and biblical prophecy stimulated people's
thinking. His energy seemed inexhaustible. He preached three times
on Sundays, gave object lessons for
the children in church, and taught
verse-by-verse Bible studies at the
men's Bible class and Wednesday
night prayer meetings. Within a
month of his arrival, he started
broadcasting the Sunday evening services over the radio, and through
it all the way of salvation was woven into every message. The empty
seats in the church began filling up.

On Sunday mornings, when the choir sang the anthem, he would
turn in his pulpit chair and watch them, absorbed in their singing.
Irene Howell described how his appreciation of music put new life
into the choir:

"He was oblivious to everything else when the message of God's
love and grace was presented in song. It seemed to inspire him as
he started his sermon.

"The choir rehearsed every Thursday evening. Many times, near
the end of the rehearsal, a shadow could be seen coming down the
stairs that led from the church offices to the first balcony. He would
walk silently to the platform, pull a chair over to the side, and sit
facing us, looking at each member in turn, his face becoming aglow
as he listened to us sing of God's glory. His very presence and enjoyment lit up the whole choir. Our weariness would fade away. As we
closed, he sent us on our way with a little humor and something to
inspire our hearts. At the end of many a long evening of rehearsal,
we left happy and refreshed.

"One night at choir rehearsal, someone asked when and where our
next social would be. He promptly replied, 'Let's make it next Friday
night at my house, and I'll buy the steaks.' This met with a tremen-

dous round of applause. When we arrived at his home Friday night, there he was decked out in a chef's hat and apron. When people looked for the host that night, they could find him cooking steaks at the grill and enjoying it all with good humor. People who tried to play jokes on Louie found that he was always a step ahead of them.

"Whenever he was at any of our gatherings, we could be assured of a lively evening, but we always left feeling that our love for the Lord and our walk with Him were just a little deeper."

When Louie suggested that dress in the choir should be more uniform, but the church could not afford robes, the members of the choir volunteered to make their own robes and did an impressive job.

As a pastor, Louie had a way of making everyone feel as if he were part of the team. He invited the officers of each society and organization connected with the church, including all Sunday school teachers, to meet with him and the social committee of the executive board every month for a time of fellowship and discussion.

Everyone wanted to get better acquainted with the new pastor. Among the dinner invitations that came to Louie and his wife, Audrey, was one from a very elegant home in Beverly Hills. Dr. Sutherland told the story as he had heard it:

"There was a trick shop down on Sixth Street, and one day Dr. Talbot went in there and saw a little mechanical cockroach. He didn't know what he would do with it, but thought it might come in handy sometime, so he bought it and put it in his pocket. On the way out to this home in Beverly Hills, he felt in his coat pocket and there was this mechanical cockroach. When dinner was ready to be served, the guests were invited from the drawing room into the dining room. The tomato soup had been poured and was on the table. As Dr. Talbot went past the chair of the hostess, he slipped this mechanical cockroach into her soup.

"The hostess asked him to return thanks, and after everyone was seated, she was keeping the conversation lively and putting her spoon into her tomato soup. All of a sudden she felt a foreign substance down there, and she pulled it up the side of her soup plate. Out came the cockroach in her spoon. Everybody saw it; everyone was quiet; there was nothing the hostess could do. She was embarrassed and flustered as she looked around the table, not knowing what to say, until she came to Louie. The impish twinkle in his eyes gave him away. At first there was a gasp of unbelief, and then everyone's embarrassment turned to hilarity. The hostess didn't have to worry about keeping the conversation lively after that, and it became her favorite icebreaking story at future dinner parties."

But as economic disaster continued to sweep across the country and millions of people could not get work, some members of the Church of the Open Door were without the bare necessities of life. Louie opened a church commissary to which all who could were urged to bring food to share with those who were hungry. So great was the need that the dispensing of food had to be limited to families with children.

When the church had to make cutbacks to balance its budget, Louie requested that his salary be cut $2,000 a year. The board of deacons did not want to grant this request, so Louie started a daily radio broadcast to minister the Word of God and raise funds for both the church and the Bible institute; he paid for the broadcasts himself. He had been deeply grieved on his arrival in Los Angeles to learn that the institute had sold its radio station. The school, to his thinking, had lost one of its greatest avenues for giving out the Gospel and raising funds for its needs. He found it frustrating that he had not been there to save it, and spent his summer vacation taking meetings for the insti-
tute to encourage prayer and gifts for the school.

People seemed paralyzed by the depression, businesses were failing everywhere, and the Bible Institute of Los Angeles, which was called Biola for short, was threatened by extinction because of its enormous debts. Louie dug into the school's history to find out how it had come to this point of financial disaster.

It was T. C. Horton who had infused his vision for a Bible institute into the heart of Lyman Stewart, one of the founders of the Union Oil Company. Biola's stately building was erected with funds given main-

Audrey and Louie at home in California.

ly by Lyman, and the erection of the school's branch in China was funded by his brother Milton. Lyman's wealth fluctuated with the fortunes of the Union Oil Company, and when costs for building the Los Angeles school zoomed unexpectedly, the cooperative Milton gave financial assistance.

In the early 1920s the school was free of debt, and under the leadership and teaching of Dr. R. A. Torrey, both the Church of the Open Door and Biola gained national stature. Although Lyman Stewart felt that future generations should support the school, he did provide some endowment, which included various stocks, four thousand shares of Union Oil stock, and the major interest in the Western Machinery Company.

Biola's historian, Dr. James O. Henry, summarized briefly what happened then:

"By the time Lyman Stewart died in 1923, the Western Machinery Company was in deep financial trouble. . . . Finally the company faced bankruptcy. The Bible Institute Directors were appalled. They had to save the machinery company or lose their largest endowment. To keep the company going, the Directors of the Institute voted to borrow large sums of money to pour into Western Machinery. . . . When Western Machinery collapsed just before the 1929 depression, the Institute was in trouble.

"Hard on the heels of this financial blow came the stock market crash of 1929. . . . The next ten years were nothing short of a financial nightmare. But out of this chaotic gloom emerged two pinpoints of bright hope. One was the 4,000 shares of Union Oil stock and the other was Louis T. Talbot. But for them, humanly speaking, there would be no Biola today."[1]

Just prior to Louie's arrival in Los Angeles, this was the situation: Donations to the school had dropped off drastically for several reasons. Some donors had stopped giving because of an ambiguous book, *Peter, the Fisherman Philosopher*, written by the dean, Dr. J. M. MacInnis. He resigned because of it in November 1928. With the stock market crash in 1929, many supporters of the school lost heavily; and the stocks that were held by the school or pledged as security to the banks for loans plunged in value.

With almost no income, the school found itself increasingly in debt to the banks, not only for the large sums borrowed to bolster the Western Machinery Company, but also for additional loans to pay Biola's taxes, salaries, and daily running expenses. In 1930 negotiations were started for the Temple Baptist Church to take over the institute's property, but they were not completed.

When the banks started demanding payments, the institute began selling off its assets to raise money.

The school sold its press to the Stationers' Corporation, leased the book store, contracted out the dining room, cut its employees to a skeletal staff, curtailed the expenses of all departments, and reduced its support of the school in China. Then it sold the Biola radio station, KTBI, for $37,000, and it became KFAC, the music station of Los Angeles.

Although the bank officials were sympathetic, their examiners kept criticizing them for carrying Biola's debts; and the banks seemed insatiable, for they ate up all the school's assets and any money it could raise. As a boa constrictor wraps itself around a tiger and squeezes the life out of it, so the mortgages wrapped around Biola were squeezing the very life out of the school.

In 1931 the Fidelity Savings and Loan asked for a prompt remittance of $180,407, and the Security First National asked for a payment of $20,000. The school had to default on both principal and interest. There was not enough cash to keep Biola open for another thirty days.

It was thought that the school could continue in a better environment at some less expensive location, and the board decided to sell the property for $1,650,000. The Salvation Army was interested in buying it, but the sale was not consummated and no other suitable buyer could be found.

In a last effort, all expenses were reduced to an absolute minimum, and the board tried to secure those who would teach part-time for a token payment of one dollar per year. Time and again sufficient money was not available to run the school for another month, and the institute faced the possibility of closing permanently.

When there was no way to continue, the bank gave the school a year's moratorium.

Louie had been pastor of the Church of the Open Door for six months, and the bank's moratorium galvanized him into action. Believing that the Lord would not let the testimony of the church and Biola fail, he struck out boldly, tackling the crisis like a David attacking a Goliath of debt. Startling the officials, Louie recommended

that the Church of the Open Door buy the auditorium, which it rented from the school for its sanctuary. In purchasing the auditorium, the church would secure its own permanent home, which Biola could still use, and it would solve the immediate financial crisis of the school.

Since it was already having difficulty balancing its budget, however, the executive board of the church was not ready to undertake such a tremendous step. It postponed the decision to purchase.

When Biola had no money to pay its taxes and its president had resigned, Louie was made acting president in November 1932. He accepted the additional responsibility without any remuneration from the school.

The first thing he did as acting president was to call two prayer meetings. One was for the employees, whose miniscule salaries were in arrears. Louie encompassed them in his concern as he would his own family: he brought them all closer together and explained the problems. He warmed their hearts by making the employees feel that he cared not only for Biola, but for them as individuals and for the sacrifices they were making. Causing them to feel like part of the team in saving the institute, he challenged them to carry on with faith for a brighter, stronger Biola. Their response encouraged the school's hard-pressed board of directors.

Some people felt that he looked a bit young for such heavy responsibilities.

The other prayer meeting was for the students, hundreds of eager, dedicated young people who were everyone's inspiration to save the school. They were what it was all about. With their great potential for the Lord's service, their exuberance, and their faith, they were a tonic to Louie's soul. Their attitude toward the closing of the men's dormitory illustrates their good-natured acceptance of the inconveniences of the depression.

The men and women students had been living in separate dormitories attached to either side of the main auditorium. To help the financial situation, the men's wing was leased to the Willard Hotel. The boys were moved to the lower floors of the women's dorm, and the girls were housed on the upper floors, with a large, locked, metal door on the stairway between. When the number of students increased, single rooms were made into double rooms by fastening one bed above another.

The day before the move was made, the men sang in the dining room, "We shall not be, we shall not be moved."

But the women students smilingly countered by singing "Come over on the victory side."

Louie prayed much that the Lord would help him save the school for those students and for all the students who would be coming in the years ahead.

When he first suggested that the church buy the auditorium, Louie realized that the idea was new and understood the caution of the church officials. With his remarkable ability to sense people's moods, he did not press them. Months of prayer followed; and as the year's moratorium given Biola by the bank was drawing to a close, he recommended it with an enthusiasm that was contagious: it was the time. On January 22, 1933, the church gave him authority to appoint a committee to investigate the possibilities. Louie was elated and named these men: Messrs. Billings, Evans, Myers, Nyman, Robinson, and Rose.

When the agreement of purchase they presented was favorably received, Mr. Nyman moved that another committee be appointed; that committee studied and implemented the purchase. Working with Louie on the second committee were Messrs. Bassett, Cross, Evans, Hunt, Myers, and Robinson.

After considerable prayer and consultation, Louie went to the bank with representatives from Biola and the Church of the Open

Door to present the proposition. Although they went with prayer and mighty faith, no one anticipated the surprise awaiting them.

Before they had an opportunity to mention their plan, the bank official said, "Gentlemen, I was awakened last night at two o'clock, so heavy has my heart been concerning the approaching end of the moratorium year granted the Bible institute. We do not wish to see so magnificent a work as this closed. As I endeavored to think of a way by which the bank's interests might be safeguarded and the Bible institute carried on, a plan flashed into my mind."

Then the bank official outlined the very plan Louie and the committee had come to present to him.

"We felt that this was the Lord's confirmation of the way out—His way," Louie commented, "the way that was suggested when we prayerfully waited upon Him."

As people flocked to the congregational meeting on February 16, excitement permeated the air that had been black with hopelessness.

The purchase price of the auditorium was set at $350,000, with a down payment of $25,000 and monthly payments of $2,000, including 4 percent interest. The immediate problem was to raise the $25,000 at a time when many people did not have enough money for groceries. The challenge and improbabilities of raising this sum were the greatest the church or any of the congregation had ever known.

At his best when faced with an insurmountable mountain, Louie encouraged the congregation to have faith in the living God. After other officials shared their convictions, William Nyman and Hugh Evans answered questions.

While the people prayerfully considered the matter, the Lord instilled into them a quality of greatness. Outside the church, the nation was wallowing in depression; inside the church, faith in God soared. The people decided to buy the auditorium for their church home. As they left the meeting that night, their faces were aglow and their spirits mounted up with wings like eagles.

On the following Sunday, Louie printed this message in the church bulletin:

"It is a great privilege to be stationed in the heart of a city like Los Angeles. . . . What a place to preach the gospel! What heartaches, sorrows, disappointments, broken hearts, broken homes are to be found in a great city like this. And what a tragedy it is for an individual or a church to live without putting forth the best effort to bring heaven's balm to the needy and to point men to Christ who alone can save!

"We are thankful to God that this church is anxious to do exploits for Him who has done so much for us. We accepted the challenge . . . to purchase the auditorium as a permanent church home. This step, if carried forward, will mean more to this church and to the ultimate cause of Christ than any of us can estimate. It will mean that this place, which was chosen by men of God as the most strategic location in the city for preaching the gospel and teaching the Word of God, will be maintained for this same blessed ministry. This step will also render great service to the Bible Institute of Los Angeles in this, her crisis hour.

"The Son of God calls us to follow Him in a great adventure. He says 'go forward.' Our reply shall be: 'Arise, let us be going.' "

But before the project of buying the auditorium could get started, disaster hit all of southern California. Some feared that they would lose not only the whole building, but their lives as well.

11

EARTHQUAKE!

No sooner was one crisis on its way to being solved than another struck. On March 10, 1933, just three weeks after the church decided to buy the auditorium, a devastating earthquake convulsed southern California. It measured 6.3 on the Richter scale, collapsed buildings, killed one hundred twenty people, shook loose debris that crushed cars in the streets, and caused over fifty million dollars in damage—and those are depression-year figures. Many people lost their homes, and Biola's thirteen-story building rocked until it was feared that it might collapse into a crumpled mass of concrete.

Centered near Long Beach, the main shock came at 5:54 P.M. Many schools were demolished, but the hour of the earthquake saved the lives of the schoolchildren. Roads zigzagged and broke apart, gas storage tanks exploded, and transformers flashed brilliant pyrotechnic displays.

As the Hollywood Presbyterian Hospital quivered and shook with each wave of the quake, the nurses and staff had their hands full coping with the emergency and trying to calm everyone. Louie's wife, Audrey, was a patient there for a radical mastectomy. She put on her robe, and in a quiet way walked from room to room, calming the fears of the patients and praying with them.

During the weeks that Audrey was in the hospital, Louie and his daughters moved in with their neighbors, Mr. and Mrs. William G. Nyman. Mr. Nyman had been an elder in Louie's church in Oak Park, Illinois, and when Louie moved to California, Mr. Nyman became one of the leaders at the Church of the Open Door. He had backed up Dr. Philpott's recommendation that Louie be called as pastor. During Audrey's hospitalization, Mrs. Nyman took care of the Talbot girls along with her own children, Eleanor, Mary Ann, and Bill.

They were all at the Nyman home when the earthquake struck.

Louie's daughter Audrey recalled, "We were in an upstairs room when everything began to shake. Feeling that the house was about to collapse and that there was no place to go for safety, Daddy never moved, but commented, 'Nothing can withstand this.'"

Irene Howell described what happened at the Church of the Open Door:

"The whole city trembled with fear, and everyone was living on nerves. The large quake was followed by many more, some light, some very severe. At the Sunday evening service, while Dr. Talbot was preaching, a very heavy jolt hit. About half a dozen people jumped from their seats and started to run. As that great auditorium shook, Dr. Talbot immediately took over like a commanding general. In an authoritative voice he shouted, 'Sit down! Sit down, every one of you. Brother, if you start a riot in this building tonight, in the sight of God you will be a *murderer*. Sit down! *Sit down!*'" And the people sat.

"Finally the building stopped shaking, but those in the audience still trembled. The atmosphere was tense.

"Then, just as a mother talks to a hurt child, Dr. Talbot comforted his congregation until the tenseness was gone and calm restored. He bowed his head, committing us all to the Lord's protection. Then he went on with his sermon as though nothing had happened. One minute he had the toughness and firmness of a military general, the next the quiet calm of a surgeon. God only knows what could have happened that night had the right man not been in the pulpit."

On the following Sunday the church bulletin carried this message from Louie, the shepherd, to his flock:

PRAISE FOR PRESERVATION

"We are deeply thankful to God for His protecting care over us and over this building during the period of anxiety through which we have just passed. Let us praise and exalt His holy name together. . . . Our trust for safety is not in buildings, however safe, but in the hand of God in whom we 'live, and move, and have our being.'

"If we live in the center of His will, nothing can harm us without His permissive will. The hedge that God put around Job, which the devil confessed his inability to penetrate without His divine permission, is the same one that surrounds you. That hedge is the living God Himself."

12

WILL THE FORTRESS HOLD?

GRATEFUL that the building had been spared, the congregation came to grips with the challenge of buying the auditorium for its church home.

Louie described how the Lord honored their going forward by faith:

"We felt that God had been so often dishonored in the way money had been raised for church work that we determined to cast ourselves wholly upon Him and venture out on faith. We made a covenant that we would not approach any individual and ask for money, but that we would ask God to lay the need upon the hearts of the people as that need was made known from the platform and over the air.

"The response was unanimous and enthusiastic. The choir gave over a thousand dollars, the Sunday school over three thousand dollars, and the young people's societies one thousand dollars.

"Hundreds of letters have been pouring into my office from all parts of the United States and the world. Let me share one of them with you, for its spirit is typical of them all:

> "The enclosed rings are a gift from my two daughters who are at present taking a rest cure in the Olive View (Tuberculosis) Sanatorium. They had no money, nothing to give but their high school rings, but they are heart and soul with us all in this great project and want to have some part.
>
> "They want you to know that they are praying earnestly that the money may be raised and the church and Institute continue to be a lighthouse for God till He comes. They are not able to earn any money, but they do want to give all they have, these two gold rings. May God bless you."

"Enclosed were two rings. . . . The gold itself was worth only about a dollar and a half, but the sacrificial spirit of which it was the embodiment was priceless.

"I told the story of these two rings to a Sunday morning congregation in the Church of the Open Door. Nearly three thousand people were present. There were tears as they listened. I expressed the desire to go personally to the sanatorium where these girls were confined and return their rings to them, provided two persons in the congregation would redeem the rings at fifty dollars each attaching their cards to them. At the close of the service, six persons came forward. By common consent, only two cards were attached, but each of the friends paid the fifty dollars offered.

"When I visited those girls a few days later and returned the gifts they had wholeheartedly given to the Lord, I had the joy of telling them that they had given not two rings, not even three hundred dollars, but a gift like Mary's, 'very costly . . . and the house was filled with the odour' of their self-sacrifice."[1]

Over the air and from the pulpit, Louie made "a clarion call in a crisis hour," stating that "cults of various kinds would be glad to secure this center for the propagation of error and heresies, but the Church of the Open Door has determined that, by the grace of God, this place shall be preserved for the testimony it has given out since its dedication."

Louie gave himself utterly to the cause night and day. He kept asking the church to cut his salary until it was down from $541.67 to $200 per month. Since he had a family to provide for and Audrey's medical bills to pay, and since he was using his radio program to bring in money for the church and Biola, the church set aside $100 per month on which he could draw for rent and for upkeep of his car.

His daughter Audrey told about their home life at that time:

"We lived about ten miles from the church. Many times when Mother was preparing dinner, a phone call would come from Daddy saying he had a committee scheduled or some other kind of meeting and could not make it home for dinner. Somehow Mother made Betty and me feel that we were part of the team in saving the school, and having Daddy gone so much was our part of the sacrifice. He tried to make it up to us on Saturdays by giving us the full day, and it was always lots of fun to be with him."

This message from Pastor Louie to his congregation was printed in the church bulletin on June 4, 1933:

"Last Lord's Day the sum of $8,000 was given in cash. This is a tremendous sum in view of the financial crisis through which the world is passing, and we are not unmindful that in the greater number of instances, the gifts represent sacrifice and denial. Of this amount, $700 came from the radio audience in response to an appeal given over the radio last Saturday morning.

"Our God still lives and can work in the hearts of men as He did in the days of old. The One who opened the doors of the prison that confined Peter and smote the fetters from the ankles of his servant . . . can break the financial fetters which bind this place and bring us into a new liberty in the Gospel, so that we may exercise greater influence and preach the Gospel with greater power than we have ever known. . . . Let us pray fervently to this end. . . . Let us pray, pray, *pray!*"

The first week of July was set apart for prayer. Mass meetings were held on Sunday afternoons, with well-known speakers such as Dr. William Evans, Dr. Stewart P. MacLennan, Dr. Cortland Myers, and Dr. Robert Shuler. Few people could draw music out of an audience like Dr. Herbert G. Tovey; with fellow Australian Gordon Hooker at the piano, Dr. Tovey caused the congregation to make that vast auditorium ring with triumphant songs of faith.

Louie continued the story: "A huge thermometer was placed in the main auditorium at the back of the choir loft, the rising mercury indicating from week to week the progress in giving that was being made.

"Many of God's people were so situated financially that they found it impossible to give anything in cash. At their request and for their benefit, the Joash Chest came into use. It was placed at the front of the auditorium, a reminder of the Old Testament days when the Lord's people brought of their gold and silver for the repairing of the Temple. . . .

"The chest overflowed with the love offerings of God's people. Real estate and oil stock were given, and watches, thimbles, lockets, chains, bracelets, and family heirlooms. Many of the gifts bore such messages as this, to which a tiny old-fashioned brooch was attached: 'A tiny thing, not worth much, but it's the widow's mite, just a little old relic handed down and doing no good the past twenty-five years. God bless the Church of the Open Door.'

"Not worth much! How much, we wonder, in God's sight!"

News of the church crisis spread across the country and to every

The church purchased the school's auditorium, where four thousand
people attended Biola's commencement exercises.

age level. A thirteen-year-old boy wrote, "Mr. Talbot, enclosed is
a five-dollar bill. I got a job on a farm, paying me a dollar a day.
I have to get up at three o'clock in the morning. I have worked five
days and I give you five dollars."

In a penciled scrawl came this note, "I send you these 181 pennies.
The Bible says, 'A little child shall lead them.' I am a little child."

Louie had this message printed in the church bulletin on July 2:

Fifteen Days—Thirteen Thousand Dollars! It Can Be Done!

"The bank has set the date and it will not be changed. Just two
Sundays remain . . . in which this question can be pondered, prayed
over, and decided by each member of this Church and each visitor to
this congregation.

"Around these walls is steadily rising the black tide of apostasy
and unbelief. Its dark waters are actually washing at the threshold
of our doors.

"This Church is the breakwater—the outer protection of one of
the most significant and important Christian movements in America
today. Within its encircling arms stands the great Bible Institute

of Los Angeles with its twenty-five years of unbroken testimony, its two thousand graduates, its seven hundred missionaries of whom three hundred are now in the foreign field. When you contribute to this fund, you are saving not only the Church, but the Institute as well, and preserving a movement which has had its martyrs and its saints in many lands. The failure of one is the failure of both, and the loss will have its repercussions and echoes . . . far overseas.

"Let us one and all rise to this occasion and complete this fund without delay."

People who had thought they had given everything they possibly could prayed harder and dug deeper, while Louie continued on the radio. In all the giving there was the sound of joy, not of the greatness of their sacrifice. One woman brought in a beautiful set of sterling silver, a diamond ring, and her wedding ring; she wrote: "What a joy it has been to have a part in this blessed task! How near our Lord Jesus Christ has come to us through it! I cannot tell you all it has done for me."

On July 9 the church bulletin contained these words:

JUST SEVEN DAYS REMAIN IN WHICH TO RAISE THE BALANCE
OF NINE THOUSAND FIVE HUNDRED DOLLARS
IT MUST BE DONE!

"This Sunday is our final day of decision. There can be no delay—there will be no second chance. Let us pray over it daily during the next seven days."

The people responded with deep dedication. Among the keepsakes of hallowed memories received were fourteen diamonds and a number of gold wedding rings.

Louie's radio audience sent in a total of about $4,000.

When the people entered the church on July 16, they read this in the bulletin:

VICTORY!
THE GOAL REACHED!
$25,365.47 CASH RECEIVED TO MAKE DOWN PAYMENT!

" 'I have heard thy prayer and thy supplication, that thou hast made before me: I have hallowed this house, which thou has built, to put my name there forever; and mine eyes and mine heart shall be there perpetually.' 1 Kings 9:3."

During the victory service, the big thermometer on the platform burst its tube, and the congregation stood while the choir sang the Hallelujah Chorus. Tears streamed down many faces.

As Louie watched them, he knew that more than the school and a church home had been saved; also saved was the people's faith in themselves and in their God.

The following week, the executive board of the church gave the pastor a rousing vote of thanks for his untiring efforts during the campaign. Louie summed it all up this way:

"We felt that the founders of the work had lighted a torch, and on being gathered to their fathers, had passed it to us to lift it high. From how many hearts earnest and constant prayer arose only God knows. And to Him alone belongs the glory for the answers received.

"An Armenian woman heard of our need. . . . She does not attend the church, for she does not know English. But she knows God. He spoke to her heart, and obeying Him, she brought to the church office as her gift to the work of the Lord a beautiful handmade silk moiré coverlet—rose and blue and lace trimmed. In old Armenia, it is a bride's choice possession, in which her treasures are placed to be carried away to her new home.

"The bride of Christ is getting ready. Until the Bridegroom calls, we pledge ourselves to 'preach the word,' to be 'instant in season, [and] out of season' in this magnificent location that has been given and held against the enemy by the marvelous grace of God. We give the Lord all the glory for what He has done."

Louie's position with Biola was changed from acting president to president. Again he accepted no pay from the school for these responsibilities, which he carried with his work as pastor of the church. The down payment of $25,000 had been made; he still had to raise the monthly sum of $2,000 for the banks in addition to the regularly budgeted funds for both the school and the church. Since the people's giving had been exhausted and the national depression was deepening, this was a tough assignment.

Although Dr. Charles Fuller had resigned as chairman of Biola's board of directors, he remained on the board for some time, and Hugh Evans was made chairman. As for Louie, he pressed on with lighter step; his confidence and faith in the Lord knew no bounds. He did not realize that the greatest struggle of his life was still ahead of him.

13

KANGAROO JIMMY

By the summer of 1934, Audrey seemed well again, and Louie wanted to take his wife and daughters to meet his family in Australia. His continued drive to raise money for the church and school had secured their financial condition for a time, but the heavy pressures had taken their toll of Louie's health. He was granted four months' leave of absence, with Dr. McCreery serving as acting pastor. At the farewell service, the children of the church wriggled with delight when he promised to bring them a baby kangaroo from the land down under.

Many people came to see the family sail on the S.S. *Monterey.* Because Louie was very prone to seasickness, some prankster at shipside gave him a small bottle of kerosene, saying that it would keep him from being seasick. Louie put it in his coat pocket. As the ship pulled away from the dock and colored streamers were floating in the air, a big, husky woman rushed toward the railing, waving and shouting her good-byes, and jammed Louie and the bottle against the iron railing. The bottle broke in Louie's pocket. Kerosene ran down his trousers and onto the woman's dress, making them both reek with its odor. Casting his eye at the size of this overpowering woman, Louie decided he did not want to tangle with her. He quietly moved away in the crowd, and the woman never did discover how she became soaked with kerosene. Louie chuckled whenever he saw her on shipboard.

Whenever he was not seasick, Louie led in the games on deck, and a ship's officer appointed him and a Roman Catholic priest in charge of those activities. The two of them made it a merry time for all aboard.

As he turned his face toward the horizon of the open sea, Louie rejoiced in his heart: he looked forward to a happy reunion with his family in the homeland. When the ship arrived in Sydney, there was a royal welcome from the Australian Talbots. One of the first things he wanted was a feast of prawns, and then he started out on sorties to his old haunts.

Louie took his wife and daughters to see the home he had loved. Then they went to the church of his boyhood, where he gazed ruefully with his family at the initials he had carved into one of the pews.

One day his brother Hubert accompanied him to their alma mater, Newington College, where Louie, the school's former prankster, was invited to give an address as an honored and distinguished graduate.

Invitations to speak were numerous. Feeling refreshed and rested, Louie conducted several evangelistic campaigns in and around Sydney and addressed a Christian Endeavor convention at which three thousand were present. He had the joy of seeing many lives transformed by the saving and keeping power of Christ; he also saw a number of the young people dedicate themselves to the Lord for His service.

While walking around Sydney and observing new buildings being erected, Louie was reminded of this incident from his childhood.

"When I was a lad in Australia, I observed a stone figure of a lamb atop a high building. . . . I asked my father what it meant, and he told me this story.

"When the building was in process of erection, a man accidentally fell from the scaffolding. His fellow workers rushed to him, expecting to find him dead. Instead, they saw that he was unhurt, standing and walking about. He was looking at a dying lamb, with blood oozing from its wounds.

"At the moment of the man's fall, a flock of sheep was being driven along the road near the site of the new building. One lamb took upon his body the weight of the man's fall, and though the creature gave up its life in so doing, it saved the life of another. The one whom the lamb befriended later placed a statue of a lamb on top of the building in commemoration of the event that had so profoundly impressed him and to which he owed his very existence."

As he recalled that story, Louie's thoughts turned to the Lamb of God: "Jesus Christ is God's Lamb . . . and when we were plunging to eternal ruin, He, in His own body, took the weight of our sin so that we might live. 'For God so loved the world, that he gave his only begotten Son, that whosoever believeth in him should not perish, but have everlasting life.' "[1]

One day when Louie and some of his brothers were out in the countryside, they found a wee kangaroo babe in the abdominal pouch of a mother kangaroo that someone had accidentally killed. One of the men opened his shirt and the little fellow quickly jumped in, apparently under the impression that it was another pouch. There he clung for warmth until a suitable box was made for his use. Then Louie sent this message to the children of the Church of the Open Door:

"I have the baby kangaroo which I promised to bring back. He is so small at the present time that we are feeding him with a bottle."

Among other bits of news from Louie's letters printed in the church bulletin was this information:

"Our Pastor informs us that he is in excellent health and is praising God that the trip and rest have done his body so much good. . . . Mrs. Talbot reports that she has gained five pounds in weight so far and is still gaining, so we praise God for what this rest has meant to her."

And this information was printed in a later bulletin: "Mr. Talbot and his family (with Hugh B. Evans III, who went with them), are on the S.S. *Mariposa*, scheduled to dock in the Los Angeles Harbor October 6."

As the ship carrying the Talbot party and their little kangaroo was sailing on tropical seas toward the Hawaiian Islands, Louie had this experience:

"One day, in the late afternoon, I strolled along the promenade deck. The wind was blowing gently in a westerly direction, and the great expanse of water which stretched before me was covered with millions of tiny waves. On top of each little wave was a whitecap. They were all rolling in one direction, toward the horizon. The sun, blazing in its afternoon glory, was just dropping below the horizon; and as it gradually sank, its golden beams lighted the tiny whitecapped waves, dancing there in the light of the setting sun.

"As I watched that beautiful sight, the thought came to me: 'Some day I shall see a more wonderful sight than this when I stand in the Gloryland. I shall be in the company of a great multitude which no man can number—myriads upon myriads—and every eye shall be turned in one direction. That direction will be toward the throne of God. And upon that throne shall be seated One who walked this earth two thousand years ago clothed with humility, a Man of sorrows, and acquainted with grief. But when He comes again, He will be robed in His uncreated glory; and the radiance of His presence will light the faces of the worshiping multitudes.' "

Thinking upon that experience, Louie continued: "Yes, we shall see Him in that day. The nail prints will be there—the marks of Calvary. The multitudes of the redeemed shall sing, and every creature shall praise Him 'that sitteth upon the throne.' The burden of their song will be, 'worthy is the Lamb that was slain!'

"What a prospect! What a hope! And that hope is for the weakest, the most faltering, of God's believing people."[2]

His heart thrilled anew to the words of Revelation 5:13. "And every creature which is in heaven, and on the earth, and under the earth, and such as are in the sea, and all that are in them, heard I saying, Blessing, and honour, and glory, and power, be unto him that sitteth upon the throne, and unto the Lamb for ever and ever."

As their ship pulled alongside the Los Angeles dock, Louie, his family, and Hugh Evans III, were at the railing watching the crowd waving their welcomes.

Walt Zimmermann, then an eleven-year-old boy, was among those on the dock to welcome the Talbot party, and he told how friends located the Talbots in the throng of people:

"As the ship pulled slowly up to the dock, the deck was high above us and so crowded with passengers at the railings that it was hard to identify anyone.

"One of the church members remarked, 'How in the world can we spot Dr. Talbot in that crowd?'

"But someone answered, 'He'll make himself known somehow.'

"About that time an inflated rubber kangaroo was dangled on a long string over the side of the ship. Our eyes followed the string, and there was our pastor at the other end."

Someone from the church cupped his hands and shouted up at Louie, "Which one's the kangaroo?"

Walt told what happened on the dock: "When Dr. Talbot disembarked from the ship, he took all of us kids who were there to the customs warehouse to see the real kangaroo in a crate. Then he promised us a party at his home to meet the little fellow. When the time came, his house and yard were overflowing with children from the church. The kangaroo had been named 'Jimmy.' He was very

young and small, but he hopped about the lawn, and there was great
delight as each of us shook his hand. It was a day of excitement I'll
never forget."

There was a heartwarming reception at the Church of the Open
Door for the pastor and his family, and the air was filled with antici-
pation the morning Louie brought Jimmy to church. One of his
most popular ministries with young and old was Louie's object
lessons for children in the morning services, and this one was long
remembered.

Louie told the congregation how he had found the baby kangaroo
in the pouch of its dead mother; he explained that when the mother
is well, the pouch is a place of safety for her baby. Holding Jimmy
in his arms, Louie commented that there is a place of safety for all
who put their lives in the hands of God. Then he illustrated it with
this story about another baby kangaroo.

While driving along in the countryside of Australia with some of
his brothers, he noticed a kangaroo hopping at great speed down the
road just ahead of them. To their surprise, a baby kangaroo suddenly fell out of the mother's pouch onto the road. The mother
continued speeding along. They stopped the car quickly and jumped
to rescue the baby kangaroo, but away it hopped in the opposite direction.

A man caring for his sheep saw what happened and sent his sheep
dog to help. Because he was used to rounding up sheep and other
animals, the dog soon brought the little kangaroo back.

"I lifted the baby kangaroo into my arms," Louie said as he con-

Betty feeds Kangaroo
Jimmy.

tinued the story, "and there it nestled contentedly, hiding its head under the lapel of my coat. It realized it was in the arms of a friend and was safe.

"After traveling about five miles, we were surprised to see the mother kangaroo again. . . . She had kept to the roadway after dropping her baby.

"Coming alongside of her, we slowed down and I opened the door. The baby kangaroo jumped out and rejoined his mother. I turned to look at the happy pair as we went on; and if animals have any way of expressing gratitude, I am sure that mother and baby were full of praise, in a kangaroo way, for the rescue and reunion.

"Like the baby kangaroo, . . . I was once lost and far from home, but the Lord Jesus Christ, the Friend of sinners, came to my rescue. He left His home in glory to come into this world of sorrow and sin and to die on the cross of Calvary in order that His arms of love might reach down to rescue the lost from the very jaws of death. Since the day that I received Him as my Saviour, He has been bearing me on His bosom of love, caring for me all the way. What a place of safety I have found in Him!"

Louie closed the story by asking, "Have you been rescued by Him? His loving arms are still stretched out."[3]

Kangaroo Jimmy became a great pet in the Talbot household. Betty and Audrey dressed him in fancy costumes and often took him riding in a doll buggy. One time Betty boarded a streetcar with Jimmy in her arms. The ticket collector said, "Dogs aren't allowed on this car."

"But he isn't a dog," replied Betty, "he's a kangaroo."

The ticket collector did a double take on that one and looked again. "By George, he is! Well, I guess there's no rule against a kangaroo's riding in the street car."

One time when Jimmy was a little older, Louie took him to a church for an object lesson. During the service, however, Jimmy jumped out of Louie's arms, hopped off the platform, down the aisle of the church, and down the sidewalk, with Louie chasing after him. That ended Jimmy's attendance at church.

When Jimmy grew tall and strong, the Los Angeles Zoo became his home. The Talbots often visited him there. They would call "Jimmy!," and he would come bounding over for a family visit.

Jimmy became so well known that a moving picture studio in Holly-wood courted him for a contract.

When things settled down after the excitement of Louie's return from Australia, he immersed his heart and mind in the Lord's work at the Church of the Open Door, on the radio broadcasts, and at Biola with such vigor that it generated new energy in everyone else.

14

PRIORITIES

AFTER THE AUSTRALIAN INTERLUDE, Louie returned to his pulpit at the Church of the Open Door with a renewed zeal for prayer and evangelism. These were his words:

"I return into your midst with a deep conviction that the world-wide conditions are a call from God to His people to pray. What a troubled world we are living in, and how great are the dangers that confront the church and our beloved nation! We know something of the crying needs of the harvest field and the awful and rapid increase in crime, the deplorable lack of zeal and vital piety all through Christendom, but the great remedy for this state of things is a great deal more *knee work*.

"If we, the people of God, can be stirred up so we will not content ourselves with simply praying a little more than we have done, but will live in the spirit of prayer, we shall see the blessing of God we have so much desired that shall make this place like a watered garden and a regular citadel to withstand the incoming tide of apostasy. Then there will also be great unction attending the preached Word.

"I am asking that our regular Wednesday evening meeting be made a great intercessory service. Let us enter the presence of the King together and lay all these things at His feet."[1]

The Lord moved deeply at those Wednesday night prayer meetings. Louie gave short talks on how to bring men to Christ, after which the people gave heart and soul to prayer. Many departments of the church were swept up in this momentum of soul-winning and praying. It reached even into the jails, where the team reported that by the end of that month sixty-nine men in jail had turned to the Lord for salvation.

When Louie preached one Sunday morning on "Ambassadors for Christ," the Lord's blessing swept through the congregation as hearts were stirred and commitments made. That afternoon about three thousand people heard his message, "Red Russia and the Red Shadow It Is Casting over Southern California," and many of those present went to the altar and found Christ as Saviour.

Louie continued to exhort his flock, "Pray alone! Pray in your families! Pray as you ride! Pray as you drive! Pray as you work, or as you walk!"

A spirit of worship permeated the church services, and Bob Robinson commented, "When Dr. Talbot walked onto the platform Sunday mornings, dignity and reverence came in with his presence."

On Sunday evenings Louie preached fervent evangelistic messages, which he sometimes continued through the week. The altar at the front of the church was filled at the close of those services. He was always glad he had gone forward at the Moody Church the night he had placed his full trust in Christ. He felt that when people's hearts sought God, a place where they could kneel and pray helped sanctify the moment for them.

Mrs. Gordon Hooker commented, "There were two tremendous ways the Holy Spirit worked through Dr. Talbot. One way was in drawing souls to Christ. Unsaved people just couldn't stay in their seats, as night after night for years that altar was filled with men and women kneeling in humble and earnest prayer, seeking the Lord for salvation. The other way was to inspire great sacrificial giving, with the people loving it as they gave joyfully unto the Lord."

To carry the message across downtown Los Angeles, Miss Ramage, a member of Louie's radio audience, donated a huge neon sign for the rooftop. In letters seven feet tall supported high above the roof, the words *Jesus Saves* could be seen for miles. At the close of a Sunday evening service, the congregation of nearly three thousand people streamed out of the church into the surrounding area. Three student trumpeters from Biola were on the rooftop playing, "We have heard the joyful sound, Jesus saves." As that great crowd began singing the hymn, the red neon sign was turned on and flashed its message into the night sky. Windows in nearby hotels started opening as people looked out to see what was happening.

So great was the impact of that message, that Danny Rose offered to donate a matching sign for the other side of the building. When his contribution did not cover the full cost, Ray Myers picked up the tab for the balance.

Above the rooftops burn the signs: JESUS SAVES.

Another means of ringing the message across downtown Los Angeles was the rooftop chimes that had been played for years. One day a man was walking along Hill Street; he was despondent and on his way to commit suicide. As if it were coming from heaven, he faintly heard an old hymn he used to sing many years ago. Slowing his steps, he listened as Gordon Hooker continued his daily service of playing those chimes. The man followed the sound until it became louder and louder and led him to the Church of the Open Door. He slipped in quietly and sat at the back.

Louie was preaching, and he included the way of salvation in every sermon. When the invitation was given, this man found himself walking down the aisle to the altar; tears were running down his face. He knelt and found Christ, who turned his life around.

For many years after that, he was the elevator operator in the north wing of the Biola building. Every Sunday, this emotional man could be seen sitting in the balcony of the church, often wiping his eyes with a big, white handkerchief.

Many a heartsick person was led to the church by hearing hymns played on the chimes.

Evangelism flowed through every fiber of Louie's being, whether he was speaking in churches across the land or sitting on some curbstone down the street, his arm around some man in rags, talking to him with all his heart.

Young people were always a part of his life, and Louie started teaching a Sunday school class for those aged twenty-one to thirty-one, but was asked to lower the admittance age to eighteen. He grounded them in the basics of the faith and personal evangelism. One day he said to them, "When you go to a mission or jail, don't rub in the people's present situation, but tell them there is a better life through Christ."

When a young people's group had charge of a service at a rescue mission, they decided to try their pastor out and asked him to be the speaker. "We expected him to renege because of the heavy load he was carrying, but he agreed to go," recalled Irene Howell.

"At the mission he read to the men sitting on benches, 'Come unto me, all ye that labour and are heavy laden, and I will give you rest.' He preached a sermon that would melt a heart of stone. At the close, the aisles were filled with men coming forward.

"Pastor Talbot dealt with each man in tenderness and knelt with him to pray. The sin-hardened men of skid row saw that he loved the Lord and was kind, and the young people who were with him saw it also."

It was Louie's priorities that Margaret Friant recalled, as revealed in this incident:

When the church officials were unable to placate a Christian Endeavor Society that was disturbed about something, the group requested that the pastor himself come and hear what they had to say.

The evening church service was about to start, so Louie turned it over to someone else and went downstairs to their room. After greeting the young people, he listened deeply to the heartbeat under the things they were saying, and then he talked with them until they were satisfied. It made him late for the evening service, but Louie discerned that the need of the young people was of greater priority.

Louie seemed to know how to reach each age level. Ray Killian shared this remembrance of those days: "When I was a member of the Junior High School Christian Endeavor, we were invited to Dr. Talbot's home in Glendale for an evening of fellowship and fun. This was our first visit to the pastor's house, and we were very serious and proper as we arrived.

"Dr. Talbot came to the door, and we politely started to shake his hand. We did not know that he had placed a buzzer in it, and as we each shook hands with him, the palm of our hands were buzzed.

"On the way home, the fellows in our car were making remarks like, 'Hey, he's quite a guy!' "

Louie kept up with an exhaustive schedule, but his ability to relax and fall asleep at will renewed his vigor. Herbert and Chrystal Kuester related such an incident:

"Dr. Talbot was an unusual man. As pastor and friend, he was never conceited or reticent, and as a guest in our home, he was like one of the family. He was among those invited to our home one evening to view a friend's moving pictures of our national parks. The movies were professionally done, but somewhat lengthy. Near the end of the pictures, we heard a slight snoring, and when the lights came on, Dr. Talbot's chair was empty. We looked around, and there he was—lying on the floor in front of the fireplace, sound asleep and snoring."

But as his church and radio ministry increased and his schedule became heavier, Louie decided Biola needed someone who could give full attention to its leadership. On February 12, 1935, he resigned as president of the school and recommended that Dr. Paul Rood be called as his successor. Louie remained on the board of directors and continued taking meetings in behalf of the school.

Although invitations were coming from all over America for him to speak, he limited the number he accepted. He was the commencement speaker at Wheaton College, where the degree of Doctor of Divinity was conferred upon him. His address to the graduating class was "Gibraltar Faith for Shifting Times."

He brought almost every well-known Bible teacher in America, Canada, and from across the seas to his pulpit. Mrs. Bunn recalled one Sunday morning when the sermon of a guest speaker went on

He set the standard for
priorities.

and on with no signs of stopping. As the preacher, his hands clasped behind him, leaned over the pulpit toward the people, Louie picked up a pitcher of drinking water and poured some of the water onto those clasped hands. Although Louie's trick was not visible to the congregation, the guest speaker got the point and drew his message to a close.

Series after series of Bible conferences and evangelistic meetings was held, and services took place almost every night of the week. Saturday nights, the auditorium rang with the singing of thousands at the Youth For Christ rallies. Christian Endeavor conventions filled the building; the Salvation Army, with its bands and General Evangeline Booth as the speaker, overflowed both the upper and lower auditoriums, the classrooms, and the street outside, as the sound was amplified all over the area.

In response to many requests, Louie taught weeknight Bible classes in Pasadena and other outlying cities; each class crowded out its capacity.

The demands on his time were so numerous that sometimes he had to call in substitutes on the spur of the moment. Dr. Sutherland related one such occasion:

"Dr. Talbot was the teacher of a class in personal evangelism at Biola, and one day as he was ready to go to his class, a call came from San Diego, where an emergency had arisen. He had to drive down there immediately.

"Out on the sidewalk in front of the school, he saw Mr. Cutler Whitwell, who was the new superintendent of men. Grabbing him by the arm, he took him down to the classroom. Being the prankster that he was and knowing that the Whitwells prided themselves on their background of culture, Dr. Talbot introduced him as follows:

"'Young people, I want to present to you a dear brother of mine who has just come off skid row. He was a drunk for a number of years, but his life was changed at the Union Rescue Mission, and I want him to give you his testimony now.'

"Then putting his long arm around the shoulders of the tall, lanky, and astounded Mr. Whitwell, and with a note of camaraderie and friendship in his voice, Louie said, 'You take over, Cutler. I have to leave for San Diego immediately,' and he was gone.

"Mr. Whitwell was left to explain to the students as best he could. The introduction not only captivated the young people, but as the object of one of Dr. Talbot's jokes, Cutler won an immediate acceptance into the hearts of the students. It did for him what no ordinary presentation could ever have done, and Dr. Talbot knew it would do just that.

"He was known for his unique and humorous introductions, but he did it with a distinct note of love in his voice and his arm around your shoulder, either figuratively or literally, and he just brought you to himself even while he was ripping you asunder in a joking way. Everyone enjoyed it and no one ever took offense, not even Mr. Whitwell."

Besides his class in personal evangelism, Louie sometimes gave lectures to the students studying pastoral theology. Dr. George Peek, for many years pastor of the North Long Beach Brethren Church, shared this experience of Louie's teaching at Biola:

"One day Dr. Talbot came down to our pastoral theology class and gave us three words of advice that I never forgot and always followed:

"1. Preach the Word faithfully.

"2. Fear no man (that is, be bold in the pulpit).

"3. Always preach to broken hearts.

"My admiration for Dr. Talbot as a man of God who was scholar, pastor, and administrator increases each year, for the longer I live, the more I can understand the magnitude of his ministry."

Sometimes it seemed that for every minute there were more calls on Louie's time than could be cared for in hours, and he had to evaluate the priorities when each unexpected circumstance arose. It was at such a time that Martha Hooker met him on the sidewalk outside the church. "Oh, Dr. Talbot," she exclaimed, "there is a dear old lady very ill in a rest home, and her one wish is to see you again. I don't know how much longer she will live. Could you possibly go see her?"

"Why of course," he answered. "Come on." He then took Mrs. Hooker in his car to the rest home.

She told what happened: "When Dr. Talbot entered that sick room, he was tender and reverent as he spoke so graciously to that dying woman. He read the Scriptures and then knelt by her bedside and took us into the very presence of the King of kings as he prayed. I stood at the doorway, feeling that I would trespass by walking into the room, so sacred and holy were those moments. It was one of the most blessed scenes I have ever witnessed, and I came away feeling hushed by a consciousness of the Lord's presence."

Louie's understanding of true priorities often upset schedules, but it brought blessing to many hearts.

15

THE WANDERING GOURMET

AFTER FINISHING SUPPER with his own family at the Pacific Palisades conference grounds, Louie sometimes wandered around outside and took a good sniff at the aromas emanating from other cabins. If ever he smelled fish, he rapped on the door. When it was opened, he stood there with a boyish grin and said, "I smell fish." A cry of delight went up from the family as he was invited to share their repast.

The Church of the Open Door and Biola were cooperating in a relaxed time of summer gatherings, made popular by Louie's verse-by-verse Bible studies in the informal atmosphere.

The people there soon discovered that Louie was a flexible gourmet, and when no fish was available, other pungent odors could lead his footsteps. One evening it was the scent of watermelon that drew him to the cabin of Mr. and Mrs. Gordon Hooker. A family never knew when Louie was outside their cabin testing the aromas of their dinner, and morning conversation around the conference grounds invariably included the good-natured question, "Whose supper attracted Dr. Talbot last night?" Everyone enjoyed this informal fellowship with him, and Louie loved being with the people. His wife, Audrey, accepted Louie just as he was and never tried to change him, something for which everyone was grateful.

But Louie did not limit his gourmet wanderings to the conference grounds. Whenever he made a pastoral call at the home of a church member, he soon found his way into the kitchen and raided the refrigerator. A prime target was ice cream. People enjoyed his feeling at home with them. When some of his friends knew he was coming, they put treats in their refrigerators for him.

When Ben and Marguerite Reese invited Louie and Audrey one evening for dinner, they had no idea what would happen to them.

"We were standing around the table just ready to sit down," Marguerite explained, "when the water heater exploded in the back porch. The water shot all over the walls and floor of the porch and ran onto the kitchen floor. We ran and grabbed everything we could think of to sop up the water, and Audrey was working along with us.

"On my way to the linen closet to get more towels, I walked through the kitchen. There was Dr. Talbot, standing in the kitchen with his feet in the water, and his plate heaped with food; calmly eating his supper, he was oblivious to all that was going on around him. When he finished eating, he laid down on a couch and went to sleep.

"After we had mopped up all the water and cleaned up the mess, we sat down and ate without him. It was the first dinner I had undertaken for company after Ben and I were married!"

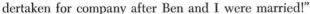

The gourmet.

But that was not the only dinner given for Louie where things did not work out as planned. He was a popular speaker during Biola's summer conferences at Mount Hermon—in California's redwoods—where Kay and Harold Gudnason had a cabin. Knowing how he loved the fresh crab he could get at the wharf in nearby Santa Cruz, Kay suggested to him one day, "Let's have a crab luncheon. You can bring the crab and invite about eight of your friends, and I'll provide the rest of the lunch."

That pleased Louie, and he went down and bought the crab. But as our wandering gourmet was coming down the trail toward the Gudnasons' cabin, he had a woebegone expression on his face.

"What's the matter?" asked Kay.

"I don't like the smell of this crab. It must not be fresh."

"We'll go on with the lunch anyway," Kay told him, "but I'll substitute fried chicken."

"What'll I do with the crab?"

"Don't put it in my garbage can, as we only have ours collected once every two weeks."

Resisting the temptation to put it under the house of Dr. Charles Fuller, who was Kay's neighbor, she told Louie, "When you walk back up the trail, stick it in the garbage can of the soda fountain at Mount Hermon, because I'm sure they must collect that every day."

Then a very potent aroma developed around the soda fountain, and Mount Hermon employees were exploring all over trying to ascertain the cause of the smell. As the wind changed, the odor drifted over toward the open auditorium and became very noticeable to the people gathered there for the meetings.

When one of the speakers on the platform kidded Louie about the shirt he was wearing, Louie told the congregation that he had sent his good shirt to the laundry because of spoiled crab, and he shared with them the whole story. It was then that people realized the cause of the odor and the discarded crab was discovered.

But what about the crab luncheon? As Kay put it: "Here came Louie along the trail with about twenty of his friends, and I had only prepared for eights guests. I scurried around and stretched and stretched the fried chicken and other food, but everyone enjoyed the fellowship; and these characteristics of Louie's endeared him to us all."

16

FORECLOSURE! BUT GOD . . . .

THE BANKS that held Biola's mortgages were becoming restless. The institute was so behind in its payment of obligations that some people were threatening to sue. In order to secure financial stability, Dr. Rood and the school's attorney suggested to the church a merging of the two institutions into one corporation.

Louie appointed a committee to formulate this merger, but while negotiations and legal technicalities were consuming valuable time, the banks decided to act.

Word reached the school's board of directors in June of 1938 that the two banks holding mortgages were initiating foreclosure proceedings. Immediate action was needed to save Biola from extinction. The possibility of the institute's deeding its property to the church was studied, but it was found that this was equal to bankruptcy and would not be keeping faith with those to whom it was indebted, especially the annuitants. They decided that such a path would not be an honorable one to follow.

A suggestion was made that Biola file under Statute 77B of the National Bankruptcy Act, through which the court invites plans for reorganization that would be satisfactory to creditors. The property would be under the protection of the court, with no foreclosures allowed and its present board of directors retained. The school's attorney, Claude Watson, also recommended this plan. Permission was reluctantly given by the board to file under this statute, providing no refinancing plan could be worked out with the banks. According to the experience of another Christian school that did file under this statute, it would have been disastrous for Biola.

There were four resignations from Biola's board of directors; some resigned because they felt that they had no acceptable solution for the school's dilemma, and others because a lawyer remarked that members of the board might be held liable for the institute's debts. "At that time," commented Mr. Allder, "hardly anyone wanted to be on the Biola board, least of all chairman." With the resignation of so many directors, it became imperative that the Church of the Open Door act immediately if the school was to be saved.

Louie felt that it was not honoring to the Lord for Biola to go through bankruptcy or foreclosure. Working with Dr. Rood and Mr. Watson from Biola, and with Ray Myers and Bob Robinson from the church, Louie said he would ask his congregation to consider taking responsibility for the $291,000 mortgage held by the Farmers and Merchants Bank. He also offered to go all out for it on his radio broadcasts. The Security First National might then refinance instead of foreclose.

As the school's attorney, Mr. Watson presented this plan to the Security First National, and the bank then made the following demands:

Foreclosure would be postponed month by month for one year providing:

$291,000 second mortgage is cleared immediately

   1,250 per month or more is paid by Biola from the Willard Hotel rent

   2,000 per month is paid by the Church of the Open Door on its continued purchase of the auditorium

   1,250 per month is paid by the Church of the Open Door for rent of other portions of the institute used by the church

  50,000 is paid by Biola within the year on the first mortgage, currently at $188,000.

That made a total of $395,000 to be paid the banks within one year, of which $291,000 had to be cleared at once. And all of this happened when the depression stalked every person, home, and business in the nation, when banks were failing, and when some educational institutions were having to close their doors.

While the church and institute were still working with the banks on the refinancing plan, they were startled to find foreclosure notices posted on the two wings of Biola attached to the auditorium. They were to be sold at public auction. Believing that the school was a sinking ship and that it would be unable to make the necessary payments, the Farmers and Merchants Bank posted August 8 as date of sale, and the Security First National set its sale date for August 5. Working against one another, each bank was trying to rescue its portion. This could have been the end of Biola.

When word of these foreclosure notices reached Louie, there was determination in his steps and a firm set to his jaw as he strode from his office down the sidewalk and stood glaring at those foreclosure signs. He did not know that Andy Billings was standing across the street watching him as he ripped those notices off the building.

Words from Scripture, "But God . . ." whirled through Louie's mind as his eyes swept that majestic building and on up to the electric sign on the roof—Jesus Saves. His shoulders squared, his posture straightened, and then his feet barely touched the sidewalk as he almost flew back to his office.

On the phone immediately to Ray Myers and to Bob Robinson, who was chairman of the church committee, Louie arranged to go with them to the Farmers and Merchants Bank to press for a settlement. The officials there listened intently as the committee outlined their plan to save the school.

"They didn't like the idea of foreclosing on the Bible institute," Bob reported, "as such foreclosures don't add any luster to a bank's reputation."

This debt of $291,000 had been building up since the 1920s, with additional loans and interest accumulating through the years. The bank held as collateral Biola's 4,000 shares of Union Oil stock; originally worth $200,000, the stock had deteriorated in value to $88,000 because of the depression.

After considerable discussion, the bank offered to accept the stock and $100,000 in cash. But Louie, Bob, and Ray were fighting for the life of their school, and they pressed for further reduction in the cash payment. The bank came down to $50,000.

Inspiring people to give was one of God's gifts to Louie, and, with Bob and Ray, the three of them made a hard team to beat. In their final offer, the officials said, "We'll take the stock and $25,000 in cash providing you'll stop bargaining." They then added with a smile for good negotiators, "If you don't, you'll be coming down here and offering us a five-dollar bill."[1]

Dr. Sutherland later commented that he felt that the reason the bank was so willing to bargain was that the officials did not think Biola would be able to raise the money anyway.

Confident that the Lord would provide the $25,000 within the time limit, Louie and the committee turned their attention to the $548,689 Biola owed to the Lyman Stewart Trust. This trust had been set up not to maintain the institute's running expenses, but to underwrite certain phases of the work, such as that of the Bible women, and to help in emergencies. It was to be used at Mrs. Stewart's discretion if the school became financially embarrassed. She had drawn from the trust to help the institute in one financial crisis after another.

As Mrs. Stewart listened to the refinancing plan, there was a moment when she was almost afraid to believe, and then relief and joy flooded her heart as she realized that the school her husband built might be saved. She offered to cancel Biola's obligation to the trust, with the exception of $100,000 to support the Bible women's work, if the sale by auction was stopped.

Feeling that God was turning disaster into victory, Louie called a congregational meeting for Monday night, July 25. But as the people poured into the meeting, they felt that it was more like going into the Slough of Despond. To have the wings of their building put on the auction block, after they had sacrificed so much to buy the auditorium, made them heartsick. They just could not cope with the inmmensity of Biola's debts.

Pastor Louie sensed their feelings as he explained the foreclosure notices. He asked Bob Robinson to tell the story of their transactions with the Farmers and Merchants Bank. An ecstatic Bob explained how they had bargained the bank down from $291,000 to just $25,000 in cash and the Union Oil stock the bank already held as collateral, and that if this were done, the other bank would refinance.

Then Louie continued, "I know some of you may feel that it's pouring money down a rat hole, but listen to this." Unable to control his excitement, he paced back and forth across the platform as he told of Mrs. Stewart's offer to cancel $448,689 of the Institute's debt to the Stewart Trust. But suddenly he stopped pacing, his right hand went up, his index finger pointed down, and that left foot kicked up as he said, "This means that we will get rid of more than $700,000 of pressing obligations by paying just $25,000 in cash."

There was a stir, a wonder in the audience. Cancel $700,000 of debts with just $25,000? The gloom that had been hovering over the school because it was reeling on the brink of extinction changed to the excitement of new life. It was as if Biola were experiencing the throes of being born again out of the ashes of despair, and the people found the dawn of a miracle glowing in their hearts. People who had been struggling with hardship in the depth and width of the depression were heard to whisper with hope, "The Lord is working here."

A few questions were asked, a resolution was passed, and the people began standing to offer subscriptions to the fund. The Lord used Louie to inspire joy in their sacrificial giving, and within twenty minutes nearly thirteen thousand dollars had been offered.

He concluded the meeting with these words, "I have just eight days in which to use the radio, and then we have next Sunday's church services in which to continue our appeal. Pray that $25,000 may be raised by August fifth."

As the meeting closed, the words of this hymn filled the night air:

> For I will be with thee
> Thy trials to bless,
> And sanctify to thee
> Thy deepest distess.

When the people started homeward, the sky held no limit to their faith.

Since he had already cut his salary to less than half, Louie gave a savings certificate as his contribution.

Some church members like Ray Myers gave large sums, while equally handsome was the dollar given by the newsboys who pooled their pennies.

Describing the school's crisis over the radio, Louie appealed for funds in his own inimitable way, and people responded not grudgingly, but with joy, as evidenced by this note from an ill and bedridden widow in his radio audience: "I'm sending five dollars as a little part in the undertaking for Biola. I can water my soup—and it will taste good, too."

A mother and daughter who had the doctor call twice a week because of their illness canceled two visits and sent his fees to help clear the debt.

The students at the Bible institute were the inspiration for much of the giving: "My heart goes out to those young students. I realize that our Lord is depending upon such consecrated young people for His future work. . . . I could not continue to pray for them if I did not help a little at this time of need."

Biola alumni also wrote: "I was graduated in June, but I hope to come back to the Bible Institute to take the medical work to prepare for service in Africa. I love the Bible Institute and want to have a part in helping to meet her present need."

And another sent a gift with this note: "I came to the Bible Institute several years ago broken down spiritually and physically. . . . I was graduated in 1937. The years of Christian fellowship there . . . have been the happiest I have ever known. It has made me utterly miserable to see the school suffer of late from lack of funds."

Two retired missionaries, who had attended Biola in Dr. Torrey's time, wrote how their daughter had dedicated her life to the Lord through the ministry of the school's Bible women just before He took her to heaven to be with Himself, and then added this word, "It would take too much time to tell you how we missionaries for forty years in China have been blessed by the Bible Institute. . . . We felt keenly that consuming desire to have a small part in meeting Biola's need." In all the more than sixteen hundred communications received, that joy in giving was expressed.

And while all this money raising was going on, Dr. Paul Rood organized a national prayer circle to surround Biola in prayer.

On Sunday, July 31, Louie announced from the pulpit that twenty-two thousand dollars was in hand. There were four days left to secure the remaining three thousand dollars. He read to the congregation some of the letters received, including this one:

"Yes, indeed, I love the Bible Institute. My one precious daughter was graduated there. I have limited strength and small salary and cannot give any money, but I am sending my engagement ring which was given to me twenty-nine years ago."[2]

Then Louie preached on "Limiting the Holy One of Israel, or Will the Bible Institute Live?"

By Wednesday, August 3, the $25,000 was in hand. When presented with the check, the officials at the Farmers and Merchants Bank were astounded, and they had to surrender the second mortgage to Biola. Foreclosure proceedings were stopped by both banks.

Just before the deadline, gifts poured in from the church, Louie's

Burning the mortgage. Photograph courtesy of the
Los Angeles Times.

radio audience, and other friends of the school until they went over the mark. The balance was put toward paying off Biola's other debts.

The mortgage burning was set for September 11, and four thousand people filled the church that Sunday morning. Representatives from the faculty, student body, and alumni of Biola, and from local rescue missions sat on the platform with officials of the church. At each of the three services held that triumphant day, portions of the papers were burned. Dr. William Evans spoke in the afternoon, and evangelist John E. Brown gave the message in the evening.

Papers representing debts of $739,689 on Biola were burned by Pastor Louie over a brass brazier, and the flames leaped heavenward and lighted the joy on his face with a glow that outshone the sun as he spoke the words, "To God be the glory, great things He hath done." Tears of joy filled many eyes as hearts welled up in praise and thanksgiving to a great God who had truly sanctified to them their deepest distress.

As Louie predicted more glorious days ahead, his words were prophetic, though he had no idea of the great things the Lord held in His hand for Biola's future.

17

HOW TO MANAGE A HUSBAND

No one could manage Louie except his wife, and their daughter Audrey told how she did it.

"Daddy was always in a good humor in the mornings when Mother brought him his toast and tea in bed. Sitting there while he ate, she would talk to him about family matters and projects. She never bothered him with problems or needs at night when he was tired, but in the morning requests were almost always granted.

"One time when Mother was having trouble with her bunions, Daddy got up and prepared the toast and tea. As he walked through the room in his pajamas carrying his own cooking, he said with a wry smile, 'This is a dog's life.'"

Louie's pet name for his wife was "Taud." Her sister Ruth told how she came by this nickname.

"Our sister Jewel tried calling her 'Sister Audrey,' which was a big mouthful for a two-year-old. Jewel shortened it to 'Staudry' and finally settled on 'Taudy,' which we all accepted, and she was never anything else to us."

When Louie arrived on the scene, he soon shortened it to "Taud."

Audrey knew just when to hold the reins and when to let them go, and she learned this early in their courtship. In those days Louie had no means of transportation except his one-seated bicycle, so he borrowed a horse and carriage to take her riding. Never adept at handling horses, Louie held a rein in each hand; he extended his hands far apart and on a level with his eyes—the carriage careened as they nearly ran off the road.

For safety as well as for her own comfort, Audrey suggested that he let her drive. A little skeptical, Louie handed her the reins. Accustomed to horses, she displayed confidence and expertise as they rode smoothly along.

117

Mrs. Audrey Talbot—her serenity was a benediction.

They both learned something that day that held throughout their marriage. Louie handled his ministry, and she took care of everything else; each had complete confidence in the other.

Louie knew nothing about building houses, so both times they could afford to build a new house, Audrey designed them, selected the lots, and watched over the construction herself. The furnishings were also in her hands.

Taud enjoyed taking care of her house and family, and she was a meticulous housekeeper. The homes she created were comfortable and tidy, though Louie could mess them up within a few minutes of his arrival.

Often he would phone that he was bringing someone home to dinner and on the way buy some fresh fish. Taking them into the kitchen, he would clean the fish. Because Louie enjoyed this, he assumed that everyone else did, too; and he sometimes made his reluctant guest help him. When they finished, Taud's kitchen was no longer immaculate, but she just let Louie do whatever he wanted, and that made it home to him.

Louie's confidence in her extended to all realms. Their daughter Betty shared these memories: "When the girls at the church first started applying makeup, I wanted to use rouge and lipstick as they did. Mother discussed it with Daddy, and after tussling with it, he said to her, 'Well, all right, but *you* put it on her.'

"We could bring girls home for the weekend any time. Our friends were always welcome, and Mother was gracious to everyone. She was not a gossip. I have never met a Christian yet who surpassed her for her genuine character.

"Sometimes she would invite missionaries to lunch, and often gave them money to help meet their needs. Without the kind of support and quiet guidance she gave Daddy, he wouldn't have been able to do the job he did. We were truly lucky to have such great parents, and they balanced each other."

"I always enjoy going home to my wife," Louie told Dr. Feinberg after a busy day, "because she rests me."

Taud's ability as a hostess, however, was often tested by Louie's forgetfulness. In the early years of their ministry at the Church of the Open Door, the Talbots filled their house with people from some group of the church almost every Friday night for a spaghetti dinner or hamburger fry. Often there were a hundred or more people filling the house and yard. One evening after speaking to a Christian Endeavor Society, Louie invited them all out for a hamburger fry and set the date. But he forgot to tell his wife and secretary, and there was another appointment scheduled for him that night.

When the young people arrived unexpectedly, Taud welcomed them with her usual grace and then scrounged the cupboards and grocery store for hamburger, hot dogs, buns, and all the fixings.

Louie at home with his family. Seated, left to right: Sylvia (niece from Australia), Betty, Audrey, Taud, and Sela (niece from Australia).

"When these things happened," their daughter Audrey commented, "Mother never scolded Daddy. She just enjoyed him and the fun and ridiculous situations he created."

At the different churches where Louie served as minister, Taud was a substitute teacher in Sunday school and played the organ or piano when there was no one else to do it. That is the story of Taud— she was always there when someone needed her.

Kathryn Mason told how Taud met her need at the Church of the Open Door. "As a young woman, I attended the missionary society in 1938 and found the members to be older women, but I was over-whelmed as I heard these women pray for the needs and problems of the missionaries. I felt that girls my age ought to have a similar group.

"I talked this over with my girl friends who also wanted to do something for missionaries, and asked Mrs. Talbot to help us. She knew just what to do and told us how to organize. I was the first president and needed her help so much. She did not take over, but was always there when we needed her."

Another member of this group, which became the Dorcas Missionary Society, commented, "Mrs. Talbot often gave the devotional messages and would help in the kitchen and sometimes wash the dishes, but during the meetings she would sit quietly in the back of the room, a woman of prayer who strengthened us."

When Louie created a problem for Doris and Herbert Cassel at the time of their wedding, it was Taud who came to their rescue.

"Since Herb was superintendent of the Sunday school," explained Doris, "we thought the proper thing to do was to invite all the church members to our wedding. However, we didn't anticipate Dr. Talbot's announcement at the Sunday morning church service with about three thousand people present.

" 'My dear friends,' he announced in his openhearted way, 'we are happy to tell you that you are all invited to the wedding of Doris and Herb on Wednesday night here in the church and then to the reception following, which will be held in the club rooms downstairs.'

"We didn't have very much money and could only manage about a hundred guests for refreshments, and he had just invited three thousand. While they were having lunch together, Mrs. Talbot ex-

Relaxing at Idylwild.

plained to him the predicament he had created for us by inviting the whole congregation to the reception.

"At the evening church service, Dr. Talbot cleared the situation by announcing, 'Now we hope you are all coming to the big wedding Wednesday night. Remember that the ones who have received personal invitations will also stay for the reception. The rest of us will all be going down to the Union Rescue Mission for a snack.'"

Taud's sense of humor surfaced one day when she was in the hospital. Mr. and Mrs. C. R. Cotter visited her, and she inquired, "Mrs. Cotter, is Louie behaving himself? If he isn't, then just put some castor oil in his tea."

When a young mother was in the hospital, Taud took the woman's two little children home and cared for them as her own.. "This was mother's kind of Christian work," observed Betty, "always there, but no banners flying."

One day at a family gathering, when Taud was quietly taking care of everyone, Betts spoke out about this: "When the awards are given out in heaven and the name 'Talbot' is called, Daddy will step forward, and the one speaking will say, 'No, the award is for Audrey Talbot.'"

' With a deep chuckle, Louie replied, "You know, Betts, I think you're right."

Audrey's secret in managing a husband? She just let him be himself.

18

"WHAT DOCTRINES WOULD YOU GIVE UP?"

NATIONALLY KNOWN PEOPLE were making a strong effort toward "the union of all churches, regardless of creed."

Standing unequivocally for the Word of God, Louie made his position clear. "Priding themselves on their broad-mindedness so-called, they rob Christ of His deity and trample underfoot the atoning blood of Calvary's cross. . . .

"I received a questionnaire, asking *what doctrines I would give up* for the sake of such a union. . . . Truly God wants a real union of all born-again souls, but that union can be realized only on the basis of the shed blood of Calvary's Lamb."[1]

In his books and to his radio audience he let his stand be known. "What we need to do is to reaffirm the great doctrines of the Word of God. Folks have fundamentals in government; they have fundamentals in science; they have fundamentals in other branches of human learning, but somehow or other they don't like fundamentals when it comes to Christianity. Fundamentals are absolutely essential, and there are great fundamental doctrines that are the foundation of the Christian church. I want folks to know that I believe the old Book and the old faith and the truth of the second coming of our Lord Jesus Christ."

Louie gave a series of seven doctrinal sermons at the Chuch of the Open Door; he entitled them, "Great Landmarks of the Faith—Can the Present Generation Believe and Trust Them?" When he finished, he had left no loose ends for his listeners to tangle with in their faith, and everyone knew that Louie believed the Bible from cover to cover.

He also continued his stand on the radio: "While some things are microscopically discerned, and some are telescopically discerned, spiritual things are spiritually discerned.

"You can never understand Calvary unless you understand who it was that was nailed to that cross, who it was that died for you. You cannot see the infinite blessedness of His atoning work until you see something of the infinite blessedness of His person.

"Do you know who it was that died for you? It was not an angel, not an archangel, not the highest created being in this universe, not even Michael, who is evidently the greatest of all the unfallen angels, but the One who died for you was not even Michael.

"The One who died for you was the Creator of this universe and the Creator of all things visible and all things invisible. And in His death He made peace through the blood of His cross.

"Some of you may have had a very ragged past. You may have done things that were grossly contrary to God's law, and you may wonder whether the blood of any man could ever wash away sins that you have committed. But my friends, such a thought as that will be dispelled when you come to see just who it was that was nailed on Calvary. Many years ago John Newton expressed it this way:

> So guilty, so helpless am I
> I dare not confide in His blood
> Nor on His protection rely
> Unless I am sure He is God.

"It was the infinite Son of God who died on that cross, and that makes the blood of the Lord Jesus Christ of value and gives the cross its meaning, 'having made peace through the blood of his cross.' No lesser being, my friends, could ever have done that. No angel in the sky, no archangel that God ever created could have come into this world to do what the Lord Jesus Christ did on the cross.

"If we cannot believe that Christ is God, we cannot believe that the cross can save or the blood can wash away your sin. Only the infinite God could bear the sins of the world and bear them away so that they never can be brought back again.

"When they were driving the nails through His hands and through His feet, the Lord Jesus Christ was nailing to the cross that which was written against every man, whether written in the Law of Moses or written in man's own heart and conscience. He nailed it there that you and I might sing:

> Jesus paid it all,
>   All to Him I owe;
> Sin had left a crimson stain,
>   He washed it white as snow.

"In Hebrews 1:3 we read, 'Who being the brightness of his glory, and the express image of his person, and upholding all things by the word of his power, when he had by himself purged our sins, sat down on the right hand of the Majesty on high.'

"Christ is the brightness, He is the effulgence, of the Father's glory, the perfect image of His person. . . . He came into the world to be the Lamb of God, to take away the sin of the world, and then after He had purged our sins by the sacrifice of Himself, by the precious blood shed on Calvary, He went up and up and up, and He went through the starry universe and sat down at the right hand of God. And as far as salvation is concerned, the Lord wants you to sit down. He wants you to rest in His finished work.

"In writing to the Hebrew Christians, Paul flooded the horizon of their souls with the glory of the person and work of the Lord Jesus Christ. And in this day of 'isms' and false philosophies, you and I, too, need to have our vision flooded with the glory of the Lord Jesus Christ."

19

THE PRESIDENCY OF WHEATON COLLEGE

WHEN DR. BUSWELL resigned as president of Wheaton College, Louie received a telegram asking him to accept the presidency of this college that had awarded him the degree of Doctor of Divinity. Much impressed with the idea of becoming president of Wheaton, he paced the floor of his office with the telegram in his hand.

About that time an old friend of his, Dr. George Palmer of Philadelphia, was holding meetings in the area and stopped by the church office. Louie showed him the telegram, "George, look at this."

After discussing it with him for some time, Dr. Palmer made a suggestion, "Louie, before you answer that, check the city from which it came."

Scrutinizing it, Louie saw that the telegram had been sent locally from Los Angeles. He looked up at George with a startled expression.

Dr. Palmer was laughing now as he said, "Jim McGinlay."

Louie accepted the incredible joke with good humor and replied, "I'll fix him."

Dr. James McGinlay was a minister from Canada who was conducting special meetings at the Church of the Open Door and was to preach there Sunday morning. As the two men sat next to each other on the platform, Louie leaned over and whispered to Jim, "I received a telegram from Wheaton College offering me the presidency, and I've decided to accept it. I'm going to announce my resignation as pastor of the church this morning and tell them I'm accepting Wheaton's offer."

Shocked at the serious turn his joke had taken, Jim whispered back, "Oh, don't make a hasty decision."

Louie countered, "I've given it a great deal of thought, and it's time now to tell the congregation."

As Jim started hurriedly to explain, Louie walked to the pulpit and said, "I have a very important announcement for the congregation this morning."

About to have apoplexy, Jim prayed in an audible whisper, "Oh Lord, stop him."

Feeling he had given him his due, Louie made some church announcement that had nothing to do with the telegram offering him the presidency of Wheaton.

Friend that Dr. Palmer was, he pulled an occasional prank himself. He shared this: "Louie and I were in his room together one day when he said, 'George, I'm going to stretch out for a while.' He did this and was asleep in no time.

"His coat was hanging on the chair. I got his wallet and took one hundred dollars out and then placed the wallet back. In the course of time, I said, 'Louie, I would like to make a contribution of one hundred dollars to the work here. You are doing such a wonderful job that I would like to be a part of it.' I'm sure he never knew it was his own money I gave him."

In the summers on the East Coast, Dr. Palmer held large tent meetings and sometimes had Louie as a guest speaker. Among those who packed out the tent to hear him was a budding young minister named Lehman Strauss. As he watched and listened, he thought, "If Dr. Talbot can put it across like that and draw such crowds, I want to know his secret."

He approached Louie after the meeting and asked, "Do you have any suggestions for a young pastor just starting out?"

"Yes," he replied, "the secret is in that Book you have in your hand. You become a man of the Word. Be a student of the Word, and in every message you preach expound something from the Word of God."

He followed Louie's advice, and many years later as a nationally known Bible teacher, Dr. Strauss was among those following in Louie's footsteps as a teacher of the Word of God on Biola's radio program.

Not only did Dr. Palmer have Louie speak at the tent meetings, but he had him at his Sandy Cove Conference Grounds whenever he could get him. "Staying at our home during the meetings," George Palmer related, "he always made himself a part of our family, and the youngsters enjoyed him so much. When they knew he was coming, they would hide their toothbrushes because sometimes he would lose or forget his. When that happened, he wouldn't hesitate to use any toothbrush he could find."

And it was not just Dr. Palmer's children who had reason to be concerned. One day at a friend's house, Louie was brushing his teeth when in walked his host. With kindly but shocked surprise, the host said, "Why, Dr. Talbot, I believe that's my toothbrush you're using."

To this, Louie genially replied, "Well, when you come to my house, you can use mine."

20

OUT OF THE DEBTS

ONE DAY Louie told Ray Myers that he could find no rest of heart until Biola was free of debt, and Ray came up with a suggestion that fired Louie's imagination.

Watching the plan develop, Russ Allder remarked, "When you gave Dr. Talbot an idea, he would pick it up and go with it. All you had to do was to keep from dragging your heels."

In 1943, the amount still due on the mortgage held by the Security First-National Bank was $110,000. Ray had two exact models of the front of the building made from plywood, with the back-up board painted red for debt. Before fastening them together, he removed the thirteen-story wings from the front model and cut them into 1,100 blocks. Their vacant places showed through in red. This model was placed in the church auditorium for all to see.

With contagious enthusiasm, Louie told the congregation and his radio audience that for each gift of $100, a block with the donor's name on it would be placed back on the model. When the wings were rebuilt with the blocks and all the red covered, Biola would be free from debt. Certificates showing a picture of the building and the amount of each gift would also be given.

Then Louie purchased the first block.

The response was immediate. A youthful airplane inspector with the United States Army spread before Louie three hundred-dollar bills as he commented, "I want the Lord to use it. When the war is over, I hope He lets me come back here as a student."

An elderly woman wanted so much to place a block on the building that she washed dishes to earn the $100. The lines of her face softened and her eyes were alight with joy as she presented her gift.

"I'll take block number eight," said one man, "because it was in 1908 that I came in touch with this place." Later he returned with

Pastor of The Church of the Open Door, President of Biola

A pioneer in Gospel broadcasting

Louie admires the headdress of the Chimbu Chief, New Guinea

Preaching through an interpreter in New Guinea, Louie tells the Gospel to some who had never heard the name of Christ.

Dressed in Shipibo costume

Peru

Language is no barrier as Louie makes friends with an Indian in Ecuador, who painted the Chancellor's face with red tribal dye.

(Below) Myers Hall of Talbot Theological Seminary

Gypsy Smith took an offering to help clear the mortgage on Biola.

another gift. "Please write my name on block number thirty-five, too, because the institute has brought blessing into my life for thirty-five years."

Several took blocks numbered according to their birthdays, while one woman gave $1,000 for ten blocks in memory of a loved one who had come to know the Lord in that building.

From Hollywood came this note with provision for a block, "We praise the Lord for the Bible school where so many students have gone out all over the world to tell the old, old story of Jesus and His love. We thank Him for our own who are now in India these five years."

Louie's evening radio class gave $3,000.

A spirit of joy permeated the congregation and the whole student body of Biola. Someone commented, "I have never seen such joy in giving." Blocks were purchased by the school's glee club, choir, dining room staff, and evening school; the student body bought a block, and each of the ten floors of students purchased one. Most of these students were working to earn their room and board.

Other blocks were taken by the faculty, employees, members of the board, and every organization of the church and Sunday school. The church choir gave $1,400.

For Louie's birthday present, the congregation gave to the fund a hundred dollars for each year of his life.

Ray Myers purchased blocks worth $5,000 and added more excitement by offering to match dollar for dollar everything given in the month of January, as the new year of 1944 rolled into place. The Navigators bought a block, Calvary Church of Santa Ana sent $100. Gypsy Smith took up an offering for the cause. Dr. W. H. Houghton, who was president of Moody Bible Institute, and Dr. S. H. Sutherland, the Dean of Biola, purchased their blocks.

A member of Louie's radio audience gave because of hearing him preach one of his most famous sermons. "I am sending a small gift as an expression of the grateful hearts of all the members of my family. Several years ago we listened to a sermon preached by the president of the Bible institute on 'Three Hells: Hell in the Heart, Hell in the Home, and Hell in the Hereafter.' We were experiencing the first two, and we were on the way to the third. But the Lord stopped us that night, and now every member of our family can truly testify that it is heaven in the heart, heaven in the home, and heaven ahead of us. May God abundantly bless the Bible Institute of Los Angeles."

Sixteen people wanted to buy the last block, and the honor was given to a sailor recuperating from wounds and shock received in action; his gift was a ring worth $100. His older brother had died in August; his had been the first gold star in the service flag of the church.[1]

The famous, the rich, and the poor; hardworking students and retired people—they all rebuilt Biola together.

"Dr. Talbot was a super salesman," commented Russ Allder, "and people bought those blocks as though they were bricks of gold." In a way they were doing just that, for they were laying up treasure in heaven.

On Monday mornings the offerings would be counted in the church office, and then Russ Allder and George King would take them to the bank. Both of these men were scrupulously honest, and because of this Louie decided to play a trick on George. He was a very conscientious man of serious mien, tall, gray-haired, and so thin one would think the wind could blow him away.

While George was sitting at a desk preparing for the trip to the bank, Louie slipped some of his own money into the cuffs of the man's trousers.

As George and Russ were leaving the church office for the bank, Louie called out, "I say, George, how come there's money falling out of your clothes?"

Startled, George looked down with an incredulous stare at the money in the cuffs of his trousers and the half dollars and quarters around his feet on the floor.

Louie let him stutter and splutter his consternation, and then, with eyes dancing with mischief, he draped his arm around George's narrow shoulders and told him he had put the money there.

George looked at Louie with dawning amazement. As he left for the bank, he was still shaking his head in unbelief that his pastor would do such a thing to him, but someone in the office saw the wrinkles in that sober face blend into a slight smile.

By the middle of January 1944, all the money to pay off the mortgage was in, and Biola was free from the manacles of debt at last. Furthermore, the school was pledged never to go into debt again so long as it should last.

Then a mighty tide of spiritual blessing swept through Biola, causing "even greater rejoicing than that which had accompanied the lifting of the burden of debt a few weeks earlier," commented Louie. Students, faculty members, and employees experienced heart searching, extended vision and deepened consecration; student after student offered life and body in surrender to Christ. "Who can estimate the outreach of such yieldedness," Louie perceived, "as these young people, being trained in the Word of God, go out to witness for Christ to the lost? Verily, Biola has been freed from its debt shackles for just such a world-reaching ministry as this."

Louie then started clearing the church debt on the auditorium. Similar blocks were given for contributions, and many will remember the five-gallon jar filled to overflowing with silver dollars that people donated.

By Easter Sunday of 1945 the church mortgage had been cleared, and Ray Myers and Mrs. Lyman Stewart assisted Louie on the platform in burning papers representing the end of debt for both institutions for as long as they endured.[2]

The Lord had inspired His people through Louie's ministry to clear nearly 1.5 million dollars of debt to banks and other creditors, in addition to increasing missionary support and carrying the general expenses of the church. And most of this was done in the grim depression years, when each dollar given meant sacrifice.

"There was wonderful harmony and fellowship between the Church of the Open Door and Biola," commented Russ Allder, "with each institution appreciating the work of the other."

Summing it all up, Louie wrote, "Above these two beautiful thirteen-story structures, the illuminated testimony, 'Jesus Saves,' now has even greater significance than before. . . . We are members of one body, and if there is any one truth that this period of financial

While the congregation sings the Doxology on Easter Sunday morning, 1945, the mortgage on the auditorium of the Church of the
Open Door is burned. Left to right: Ray Myers, Louie, Mrs. Lyman
Stewart, a military officer, and Dr. S. H. Sutherland.

struggle and deliverance has taught us it is that unity in the body of
Christ is a precious and a powerful thing."

Dr. William Ward Ayer commented, "The tremendous work that
Dr. Talbot did in preaching and teaching and raising funds to save
Biola is one of the masterpieces of church statesmanship in this century."

One day Dr. Donald Gray Barnhouse asked Dr. Sutherland, "How
much does Louie Talbot mean to Biola?"

Dr. Sutherland's reply has been quoted down through the years,
"If we think of Dr. Torrey as its George Washington, then Dr. Talbot
is Biola's Abraham Lincoln, because he freed the school from the
slavery of debt."

Louie was also free from this yoke that he had carried for thirteen
years, and it put new bounce in his step for the exciting years ahead.

21

"IT *IS* MY CAR!"

LOUIE'S LACK OF ATTENTION to his car caused many amusing incidents. After preaching at a church in Long Beach one day, he could not locate his car. He notified the police that it had been stolen and asked someone to drive him home.

Some time later the police phoned that they had found his car right where he said he had left it.

Louie had someone drive him there, but when the police pointed out the car, he said, "I saw that one, but it's not mine."

"It has the license number you gave us, and it's registered in your name."

Louie went over and inspected the car more closely. "My hat!" he exclaimed. "It *is* my car! I forgot that I had it washed and didn't recognize it."

The policeman took a dim view of that explanation and went away looking at Louie out of the corner of his eye.

When Louie's mind was on his sermons, he seemed to live in another world from everyone else, and it often made him absent-minded. One morning Elmer Olson was talking informally with a group at the church when Louie walked up laughing, "On my way to church," he explained, "I picked up a man and gave him a ride. But when we arrived here, I was thinking about my sermon, got out of the car, and said to the man, 'Thanks for the lift,' and started walking off.

" 'Wait a minute,' the man called out. 'This is *your* car. You're the one who gave me the ride!' "

Louie was not a good driver, and one day when Eugene and Helen Poole were following Louie home in their car, they noticed that he was driving more erratically than usual. Watching to see what was the matter, they saw him raising his right hand as though he were

133

preaching, and that index finger would jab toward the windshield as though making an important point.

As the Pooles continued to follow him, they realized that each time his index finger stabbed forward, his foot jabbed on the gas, causing the car to spurt forward and slow down, jerk forward again and return to normal speed. As he was rehearsing his sermon, he visualized his congregation and forgot momentarily that he was driving a car—to the menace of everyone else on the highway.

Apart from thinking of it as a means of getting from one place to another, he hardly gave his car a thought and seldom had it repaired.

After Irene Howell had spent the night at the Talbot home with young Audrey, she rode with Louie in his car the next morning to Biola. On the way, however, the car broke down and had to be left for service. The rest of the trip was made by streetcar.

"As soon as Dr. Talbot boarded the car," Irene reported later, "he started to entertain all the passengers within hearing distance by mimicking some Burns and Allen routines. By the time we disembarked, the whole car was in a hilarious mood."

The church board passed a motion that the pastor's car be taken to a garage and put in first-class shape!

A sea of troubles engulfed almost everyone when Louie purchased a new car and sold his old one to Lucille Cooper. His new car was stolen, and Louie reported it to the police and gave them the license number.

After choir rehearsal that evening, Lucille and a friend were driving along when a police car pulled them to the side of the road. "You're driving a stolen car," they said.

"No, we aren't."

"Yes, you are, and if you can't give a plausible reason why you're driving it, you'll have to come with us."

At the police station, Lucille told her story, and the police phoned Louie.

After some conversation, it turned out that when reporting the theft of his new car, he had in the excitement of the moment given them the first license number that came to his mind—that of his old car he had sold to Lucille.

The police gave Louie the scolding of his life and told him the penalty for causing false arrest. But his friends chuckled as news

spread throughout the congregation that the pastor's absentminded-
ness had landed two church members at the police station. The one
who laughed the hardest was Louie himself.

The next time he saw the two women, all their frustration and
exasperation vanished. They found themselves laughing with him
as, with that magic twinkle in his eyes, he said, "When I heard that
you two girls had been hauled into the police station, I thought it
was the best news I had heard for years." Louie was unsinkable.

Arriving at a church in New Jersey, Louie drove up behind a man
parking his car and asked, "Are you going to that church?" When
the gentleman nodded, Louie said, "I'm the preacher. I'm late. Here
are my keys. Back my car into that space, and drop my keys into the
collection plate." Then he ran down the sidewalk and into the church
without even asking the stranger's name. The astonished man was
Mr. Charles Ruth, who later commented, "Dr. Talbot was a great
preacher and played a part in my entering the ministry."

22

LEADER OF MEN

ONE NEVER KNEW what to expect when Louie gave his object lessons for the children in church each Sunday morning. One of his most popular series was on the Bible zoo, when each Sunday he brought some live animal mentioned in the Scriptures. Few people ever forgot the lion cub, but perhaps the best remembered is that of two pigeons representing Christians. Each had a scripture verse attached to one of its legs. The fantail strutted around, enamored with its own appearance and fine feathers, but with no thought of its message.

But the other was a homing pigeon. Taken to an exit on the balcony, the bird winged its way into the blue sky on its missionary journey. Before the service was over, the phone on the platform rang, and the sound was amplified for all to hear. The owner of the homing pigeon said it had returned with the message, "Christ is risen."

Biola graduates Eric and Syvilla Horn recalled the balloons Louie used. One represented a person who never took time for prayer, and it quickly gravitated to the floor. The other depicted a Christian who prayed and read the Word, and it floated up to the ceiling; but something went wrong, and soon it began descending, catching every eye in the church. Never at a loss for words, Louie exclaimed, "Now that fellow's run into a little trouble and he's started backsliding already!"

The children had a big place in Louie's heart, and some quality of warmth and gentleness in his personality drew them to him. He had a platform built for the children's choir Sunday mornings and for the evening's orchestra.

On the way to the pulpit one Sunday morning, he stopped long enough to leave a lifetime blessing on a little boy named David Hill,

Man of strong convictions.

who grew up to become a public school teacher. "He began talking to my parents and to me. I was only about six years old at the time. Dr. Talbot placed his hand down on my head and said a little prayer for me. The memory of it has remained with me through life."

But it was unusual to meet Louie just before church. Ben Reese told why, "Many times I saw him pacing up and down on the fourth floor just before the service, concentrating on his message, preaching it to himself. No one talked to him at that time."

Whether by using lions, pigeons, balloons, the radio, the pulpit, or any other means he could think up, Louie preached the Gospel with deep intensity, and his preparation was thorough. Although he could be fun and nonsense in social groups, when he was in the pulpit, he was a different man, preaching with penetrating power. Louie never let an opportunity to reach someone for the Lord go by, and an example of that fervency was told by Betty Bruechert.

"I remember the great days of evangelism in the Church of the Open Door, when the altar was crowded every Sunday night with people on their knees. And often Dr. Talbot left the pulpit when he had fiinshed his message and knelt with men who came forward, although there were many church workers designated to do this.

"One night a man in obvious distress of mind came forward. The personal worker said, 'Dr. Talbot, come and talk to this man. I can't get anywhere with him.'

"The man's conviction for his sin and serious domestic difficulties had driven him to despair, and he kept saying, 'It's no use; it's no use!'

"Then suddenly he leaped to his feet with the words, 'I think I'll just end it all,' and he walked rapidly down the aisle toward the door.

"Calling an assistant to take over the meeting, Dr. Talbot pursued the man, who increased his pace. He started running down the street, with Dr. Talbot running after him. They ran for several blocks, past Pershing Square.

"Finally the man gave up, and Dr. Talbot brought him back to the church. There they talked and prayed until the man came to know Christ as Saviour. Later he joined the church and became one of the most aggressive soul-winners there."

Louie was not only fervent in evangelism, but he preached fearlessly against Communism and the various cults. Showing on a large screen quotations from their writings, he would contrast them with the truth of the Scriptures. In his series entitled "What's Wrong With . . . ?," he published many pamphlets exposing their false teachings.

While many people had their eyes opened to the dangers of Communism and the cults, his teaching fired up the zealots in those causes against Louie. The police gave him a special badge to use in case anyone caused public disturbance in the church.

Those were the years of World War II, and Louie was a strong supporter of the war effort. He had become a naturalized citizen in 1940, and he wanted to do his part for America. Movie stars and other celebrities sold war bonds from a platform in Pershing Square, and it was reported that when Louie was on that platform, with all the skill, enthusiasm, and charisma of his salesmanship, he outsold most of them.

On Sundays men in the armed forces came by the hundreds to the Church of the Open Door. When Louie gave the invitation at the close of the evening services, hands would go up all over the auditorium. Many of those young men walked down the aisle to the altar, where they found a Saviour who would be with them in the war zones.

Dr. Sutherland told what was done for them after church: "Dr. Talbot arranged for a fellowship hour to be conducted for the men in the military after the evening service. We had a time of singspiration, fellowship, and refreshments for them, and they were joined by students from Biola and young people from the church. Dr. Talbot would come down after he had finished dealing with individuals in the main auditorium; and it was thrilling indeed to hear him tell those military men how much we appreciated what they were doing for our country. He would urge them to get right with the Lord before they went overseas. Some who had not made definite decisions at the church service made them there at the fellowship hour. The young people would talk to them individually and present each one with a Gideon New Testament."

Louie's concern for the men in the military ran deep. Another program he arranged for them was described by C. R. Cotter: "As servicemen poured through Los Angeles, some needed a place to stay overnight. On Saturdays we provided sleeping accommodations in the club rooms downstairs. In the morning, Mr. Kliewer, of the Biola dining room, provided fresh doughnuts and coffee, and then at 7:00 A.M. there was a special Bible class for them. There were from sixty to a hundred men there every Saturday night, and some would stay for the Sunday church services."

During those war years, Dr. Sutherland was dean of Biola and director of Christian education at the Church of the Open Door. He gave his impressions of Louie as a leader of men:

"Although I was not a board member, I had the privilege of attending the board and committee meetings of both institutions, and I watched Dr. Talbot at work. The subject of psychology was not included in the curriculums when he had his schooling, but he was a master psychologist. I used to watch in amazement at the power he had in convincing men, and tried to study how he did it. I came to the conclusion he didn't have any method. He just did it.

"I've seen groups of men waiting for his appearance at a board or committee meeting. Although they loved and admired him and had tremendous loyalty to him, sometimes they felt that he needed their direction and were all set to guide him when he arrived.

"Then Dr. Talbot would come into the room, and it was like the noonday sun melting the snow. He would greet them, and the men would be respectfully quiet as he started to speak. He would come up with an idea or two of which everyone approved, and then he would move on into his whole plan and program with all the force of his personality and persuasiveness. The men would see the reasonableness of his suggestions as they began to understand the mind of the man. Before the meeting would be over, they were as enthusiastic as he was.

"On the other hand, I've seen him go into a meeting where he sensed before a word was spoken that there was strong opposition to an idea the men knew he had in mind. He would back away from it. Then a few months later when he felt the time was right, he

The Church of the Open Door became a center for evangelism and
Bible teaching.

would come at it from a different point of view. Because the men
had come to see the wisdom of it, that program was adopted."

Somehow he was able to put his finger on the pulse of a meeting
and sense the thoughts and emotions of those present.

Bob Robinson described the board meetings of the Church of the
Open Door: "When Louie came in, his presence filled the room.
There was an atmosphere; and when he spoke, there was a silence
filled with deep regard and respect. He understood parliamentary
procedure very well, and there was a certain solemnity as we considered official church business."

Dr. Sutherland told what it was like to work with Louie: "Dr.
Talbot knew when to be harsh and when to be tender. Although the
moments of harshness appeared at very rare instances, once in a
while there were flashes of what was either temper or righteous in-
dignation. He really could cut a man down to size on rare occasions.

"There was only one time that I was greatly upset at what Dr.
Talbot and the Biola board decided to do. They let someone go that
I thought should be kept on the staff. Feeling that Dr. Talbot de-

served to be told exactly how I felt, I lectured him for five or ten minutes on what I thought of him and the board for making that decision. I fully expected that by the time I finished, he would say, 'Sam, you can prepare your resignation, and we'll accept it at the next board meeting.'

"But instead, he paused a moment, put his arm around me, and said, 'Sam, what you've just said is absolutely right, but this is a controversial problem. If we take the action that you feel we should take, we'll be defending our position for the next twenty-five years. If, on the other hand, we continue on the course we have chosen, the problem will fade away and we'll be able to go ahead.'

"I couldn't argue against that, so I kept quiet, and his decision was correct. But I'll never forget the love that he showed when it could have been just the opposite. His love, devotion, and keen insight into human personality were revealed in a magnificent manner to me on that occasion.

"Another time, while I was directing the young people's activities at the church, there were seven Christian Endeavor societies, and I felt that our program was in a rut. I had some innovative ideas, but soon found that what I said didn't carry much weight with the leaders of these groups. I decided to go directly to Dr. Talbot.

"Whenever it was humanly possible, he would take the necessary time to discuss these ideas with me. A few times he said, 'Sam, I suggest that you postpone this. It might not work just now.'

"But most of the time he would reply, 'We'll put it over,' and those were joyous words to my ears indeed. And he was as good as his word. With the force of Dr. Talbot's backing up these programs, the young people readily implemented them, and we had a wonderful working arrangement together."

But like a finely cut diamond, Louie's personality had many facets. Ralph Davis, a member of the church board for many years, showed a warm, human side of Pastor Louie:

"I worked in the sales department of a national meat packer, and one day a phone call came from Dr. Talbot: 'I say, Ralph, I've been thinking of having the church board over some Saturday afternoon for dinner. To do something different, I want to serve them suckling pigs roasted.'

"He was so excited about the idea that I didn't have the heart to tell him that suckling pigs were just not available in California. But

I checked with our livestock procurement department, and we finally found a place in the Midwest where we could get some suckling pigs. When I phoned Dr. Talbot this news, his joy and excitement knew no bounds, and when they arrived, he rushed over to see them. I believe that he was probably the proudest man in town when he saw those pigs.

"They were sent to a cafe for roasting and then delivered to the Talbot home, where large serving tables had been set up. The pigs were displayed in a spectacular manner, with a red apple in the mouth of each one.

"The chef came along to carve and serve the roasted pigs; but before he did, each person in attendance was escorted to the table by Dr. Talbot, where every detail of the masterpiece was pointed out. Dr. Talbot remained at the serving table to be sure that each guest received a generous serving, along with his enthusiastic proclamation that truly this meat was fit for a king."

Louie also enjoyed taking members of the board on fishing trips, even though he invariably became seasick.

But such treats became rare, as more and more he was speaking across the nation in churches, Bible conferences, and men's groups and giving expositions of the Word of God, messages on prophecy, and hope in Christ to men in penitentiaries and rescue missions. Sometimes he was away from the church for three months at a time taking meetings in behalf of Biola.

Louie would go anywhere to reach a person needing the Lord and take time to talk and pray with anyone who was hurting and came to him for help. He often put the individual at ease by saying, "Now tell me what's on your heart,' and the person had Louie's full attention. Being a keen reader of human nature, he could discern whether gentleness or strong exhortation was needed. One day a Christian young man began making excuses for his bad habits by saying, "I inherited these weaknesses from my father."

"But you have another Father," Louie countered, "a heavenly Father, and it's time you inherited something from Him."

On rare occasions Louie would reprimand a person in no uncertain terms.

A member of the church who came before the board of elders told them he was trying to improve his witnessing. In order to do this, he was leaving his wife and baby because he felt that his testimony for the Lord would be better if he were single.

Louie and the board listened for about five minutes, and Mr. Allder recalled how Louie then let loose on that man. "He told that fellow he was insulting the Lord's work by saying he could have a better testimony by leaving his wife and child than by staying with them. He accused him of using the Lord's work as an excuse to be rid of his responsibilities, and really gave him a dressing down, calling him among other things a coward.

"After the man left the room, the board of elders sat there stunned. Although we all felt exactly the same as Dr. Talbot, and he had said for us what we all felt like saying, we had never heard him tell anyone off like that."

The board members went home realizing anew that although their pastor was usually gracious, he was no Milquetoast.

In the midst of his demanding schedule, Louie felt a strong urge to visit his family in Australia once again. He did not know that his oldest brother, Jack, was very ill there. Gordon Hooker had not seen his family in that land for twenty years, and Taud suggested the two men go together. They decided to make a quick trip by plane.

The farewell was observed by two Biola students, Sam and Dorothy Gallagher: "The entire student body and faculty turned out on the sidewalks for a hearty send-off. As they were about to leave for the airport and cameras were clicking, Dr. Tovey pulled up his car and opened the door for the travelers. To our utter delight, Dr. Talbot lifted his wife off the ground and twirled that little brunette around with her skirts flying, as he said good-bye to her. Oh how we students loved that!"

When they arrived at the airport, Louie discovered he did not have his passport. Dr. Tovey was chaplain of the Montebello Police Department and had a special police badge. Stretching its privileges a bit, he and Louie sped back to town. When they arrived, they discovered that the passport was locked in the safe and everyone had gone home. Phones rang, people scurried, and Louie's secretary, Lela, rushed from her home to the office.

As time for departure drew near, Gordon was on pins and needles at the airport; he was trying to decide whether to go on without Louie or wait for him and miss the plane. When it was almost too late, Louie came running, waving his passport.

When Louie arrived in Australia, he found Jack dying of stomach cancer. Their niece Jean told of Louie's ministry to the family: "Uncle Jack was a fine Christian man and a gentleman. Uncle Lou spent most of the time with him, and he stood by the family as a tower of strength at the time of death and during the days that followed."

Louie knew then why he had felt that urge to wing his way to Australia. When preaching a sermon on the four men who brought a sick man to the Lord, Louie said, "It took four of us brothers to bring my father to the Saviour." Jack had been one of the four.

When Louie returned home, he found plans under way for a missionary conference that was to be unique and long remembered.

23

ALL ABOARD THE S.S. *GLAD TIDINGS*

MISSIONS WAS a burning fire that never dimmed in Louie's soul. In addition to the Lord's commission to go and teach all nations, there was his own burden for the land of China. He often said, "If I had my life to live over again, I would spend it telling the Gospel to those who have never heard the name of Christ."

Among the first things he did as pastor of the Church of the Open Door was enlarge the missionary conference, increase the number of missionaries supported, and have a large map of the world painted on the alcove in back of the choir loft. Small lights in various countries represented missionaries of the church and Biola graduates on the mission fields. And under his ministry, a compound of cottages was purchased for the use of the missionaries when they were home on furlough.

Perhaps the most thrilling service at the church each year was the

The S. S. *Glad Tidings.* Louie (wearing a white suit) is seated in the foreground. His officer's hat is on the chair near the pulpit.

closing night of the missionary conference, when hundreds of young people went forward to offer their lives to the Lord for whatever He asked them to do, wherever He called them to go. In his heart, Louie stood right there with them. It was a sacred, life-changing night of spiritual depth. The passing of years found many of those young lives being spent in the nooks and crannies of distant lands; the men and women went over land and sea, mountain and desert to tell the good news of salvation in Christ.

During the conference, phone calls, amplified for all to hear, were often made to missionaries in foreign lands, many of whom had received their commission from the Lord in one of those earlier meetings.

Picturesque display booths representing many countries filled the club rooms during the conference, and the church platform was decorated with a striking missionary theme. Suggestions were invited some years for its motif. A Biola student, whose father was a sea captain, submitted the idea of making the curved platforms of the church into a ship with missionaries aboard arriving at a tropical island. This was refreshingly different, so the committee called the student for an interview.

Having been familiar with ships most of her life, she enabled the committee to visualize members of the choir dressed in costumes of different lands and seated on the upper deck. On the main deck would be the pastor and his staff as the ship's officers. And the passengers would be missionaries dressed in costumes of the countries to which they were bound.

The lower platform would be transformed into a tropical island at which the ship had arrived, with a gangplank reaching from the shore to the main deck.

Much impressed, the committee decided to adopt this plan, and David Isaac did a masterful piece of work in carrying it out.

The vessel was named the S.S. *Glad Tidings*, and Louie, wearing the hat of the commanding officer, was called "The Admiral." Whenever he wanted to emphasize an important announcement, he sounded the ship's bell. Through the years that followed, people often commented on the striking effect of the ship and how Louie enjoyed ringing that bell.

It was not until eighteen years later that he discovered who the student was who had designed the ship.

But it was more than the young people who went forward at that missionary conference who were headed toward the mission fields of the world. Louie was going to China!

In a Mongolian outfit at a missionary display booth.

24

REACHING CHINA AT LAST

LOUIE'S EYES glowed with excitement as friends from Biola and the church bade farewell to him and Russ Allder at the airport. They were flying to China, a land that had been on Louie's heart for many years.

Biola's branch there was the Hunan Bible Institute in Changsha. It had survived World War II better than most buildings in the area, but was in a somewhat battered condition from the Chinese-Japanese conflict. Not only was a conference to be held regarding the future ministry of the school and the deepest needs of China's millions, but Louie was to bring messages of evangelism and strength in Christ to all who gathered.

He experienced emotions that ran deeper than his words could express. "It is difficult for me to describe my feelings as for the first time I looked upon the great mission field of China. When I gazed into the faces of Chinese men, women, and children making their way along the narrow, crowded streets, I realized as never before something of the appalling spiritual, moral, and material needs of that country."

They spent three days in Shanghai, where Louie preached five times, two of which were to great Youth For Christ gatherings. Thousands of Chinese youth attended those meetings, and in one service alone one hundred came forward to accept Christ in response to a very simple Gospel message. "The rising generation of Chinese, especially the students, have . . . two great rival forces which are battling for their souls—Christianity and Communism. . . .

"Our hearts were deeply moved as we for the first time beheld that great citadel for God, the Hunan Bible Institute."

The Bible conference was in progress when they arrived, and it was a great sight to behold the crowds of Chinese Christian workers.

Louie and J. R. Allder
leave for China.

They listened intently to the expositions of the Word of God, prayed together, and counseled together over their problems, and they all had a good time in the Lord.

Mr. Allder and Louie enjoyed renewing fellowship with those in charge of the school: Dr. and Mrs. Charles Roberts, Mr. and Mrs. Russell Davis, and the Edwin Coreys, and they also enjoyed becoming acquainted with Chinese brothers and sisters whom they learned to love.

"It was my privilege to bring a Bible message each day, which of course had to be interpreted. . . . Many conferences were conducted at which vital plans for the future of the school were discussed."[1]

Louie and Mr. Allder missed an important dinner engagement that had been arranged by Mr. Hollington Tong, the minister of information. Invited guests included Madame Chiang Kai-shek, topnotch generals of the generalissimo's army, and the American ambassador.

When the two men had to cross the Yangtze River to reach the plane, a storm was raging. They engaged a little sampan to take them over that tempestuous river. Waves tossed the fragile skiff about, drenched Louie and Mr. Allder to the skin, and covered them with yellow mud. By the time they reached the other side, the plane had gone.

In an effort to make it up to the two men, Mr. Tong flew to Shanghai and entertained them there.

As Louie flew over the countryside of China, he noted its checker-

board of rice paddies and watched the Chinese villagers. His heart
yearned for the people of that land. "The doors are open to the
Gospel now," he commented. "Only God knows whether a year
from now they will still be open."

On the journey home, Russ Allder and Dr. Duncan McRoberts
were with Louie on the plane. Russ shared this story. "We were
sitting on the front seats of the plane when Dr. Talbot wanted something from his luggage. He opened it all up and dumped everything
out on the floor. As he rummaged through it, I managed unobtrusive-
ly to pick up a jade-decorated jewel case he was taking home as a
present for his wife, Audrey.

"Confiding in the oriental stewardess, Duncan and I included her
in the plot. When she came through the plane offering refreshments,
Dr. McRoberts said, 'Dr. Talbot so appreciates the fine service you
have rendered us that he wants to present you with this little token
of his esteem,' and he gave her the jewel case. She bowed with the
courtesy of the far east, thanking him profusely for such a fine gift.
As she walked away with the prized gift for his wife, Dr. Talbot's
face became red, and I thought he was going to choke. It was the
only time I've seen him speechless.

"We let him stew about it for a while, and then he said, 'My hat!
That was my wife's gift. The next time you fellows get overcome
with a wave of generosity, take one of your own presents.'"

The Chinese at the Hunan Bible Institute conference were eager
and earnest.

"After about ten minutes, the stewardess returned with the gift in her hands and said to Dr. Talbot, 'I have wanted a box like this all my life. It is a most beautiful present. But my! I just can't bring myself to accept this, because I understand it is a present for your wife. I wouldn't think of taking it—unless you want me to have it!'

"At this point Dr. McRoberts and I could no longer keep a straight face. Dr. Talbot realized then that for once we had outpranked him, much to the merriment of everyone, including the stewardess, who gave the gift back to him."

When Louie returned, there was great urgency in his plea to reach China with the Gospel while there was still time. His fears that the door would soon close were well founded, for Communists swept the land, and the Hunan Bible Institute fell into their hands. Although Dr. Charles Roberts was able to continue a ministry for the Lord in Hong Kong under Biola's sponsorship, only prayer warriors could help the Chinese Christians who fell into the hands of the Communists.

This fueled the fire in Louie's soul for evangelism in other distant lands before doors closed, and it set the pattern for the rest of his life.

25

A SHEPHERD BIDS HIS FLOCK
FAREWELL

Louie was not feeling well. When he had gone to Mexico in 1943 as the guest of W. Cameron Townsend, his heart had been thrilled with the work of the Wycliffe translators, many of whom were Biola graduates. But the wandering gourmet had sampled unwashed fruit and various foods in the market, and soon he had been flown home ill with fever. A specialist in tropical diseases had been called in for consultation.

In February of 1948, he was in pain again. His brother Jack had died of stomach cancer, and Louie wondered whether this was also his problem. On February 23 he was taken to the Hollywood Presbyterian Hospital, where Dr. Herbert Movius diagnosed a duodenal ulcer and removed two-thirds of Louie's stomach.

Just five days after he was released from the hospital, and at a time when no one else was watching, Louie was given his heart's desire, a can of shrimp, by his friend Danny Rose. Louie devoured all the shrimp and drank the juice in the can. An ambulance returned him to the hospital for another stay of twelve days.

After recovering, he watched his diet a little more carefully and often went into a coffee shop for a bowl of soup. Dr. Kenneth Fischer shared what happened. "One day while I was a student at Biola, I went to a nearby restaurant, and Dr. Talbot came in and sat down next to me. We both ordered just soup. When our bowls of soup arrived, we bowed our heads for a word of silent grace.

"Feeling a bit overwhelmed at sitting next to the president of my school, I said a long prayer, thinking it would make a good impression. At the conclusion of it, I looked up, and Dr. Talbot had his soup half finished.

"Then he put his arm over my shoulder and said with a twinkle

It was the flash of his smile, the twinkle in his eyes.

in his eye, 'Brother, if you take that long to pray over a bowl of soup, you'll *never* get anywhere!' "

Another place that Louie frequented near the church was a barber shop. One day the barber was giving him a shave and had him lying back in the chair; he had a warm, damp cloth over Louie's face. Then a customer took the Lord's name in vain.

"Sit me up," Louie told the barber.

"Is anything wrong, sir?"

"No, just put me up."

Sitting upright and removing the cloth from his face, he said to that customer, "My name is Louie Talbot. If you need to use someone's name in profanity, then use my name, but don't you ever again profane the name of my Saviour and the Saviour my mother loved. The Lord Jesus Christ died on Calvary's cross for your sins and mine. And, brother, don't you ever take His name in vain again in my presence."

Then Louie signaled for the barber to lay him back down in the chair. For a few moments there was complete silence, and then the customer answered, "I'm sorry. My mother loved Him, too."

Although calls continued coming from across America for Louie to speak in Bible conferences, he accepted fewer and fewer, for his physician told him he must cut down on his heavy program. One time he decided that instead of taking the plane to a conference, he would travel by train in order to have a little time for rest and relaxation.

After breakfast the next morning, a man with a beard went through the train distributing pamphlets. When he came to Louie, the man said, "When you have a little spare time, here's some literature you might like to read."

When Louie looked at the pamphlet, he recognized it instantly as that of a well-known cult.

In relating the story, Louie said, "I got hot under the collar and felt like tackling that fellow. And then the Lord seemed to say to me, 'What are you getting so upset about? All you've been doing on this train is sleeping and going to the dining car. At least that man's sharing with others what he believes.'

"Then I went through that train twice. First I walked the length of the train picking up all the pamphlets that man had distributed and got rid of them. Then I took some Gospel tracts out of my suitcase and went through the train again giving them out. And when I came to this bearded fellow who was now relaxing in a seat, I handed him one of my tracts and said, 'When you have a little spare time, here's some literature you might like to read.' Then I went back and relaxed in my seat."

Louie returned home in time for the annual picnic of the Church of the Open Door. The wandering gourmet visited each table looking for fried chicken and other goodies, but no one would give him anything to eat for fear he would become ill. However, resourceful Louie soon solved that problem. Securing a piece of cardboard, he wrote on it in big letters, "My stomach is OK," hung it around his neck, and made the rounds again. Who could resist him?

Art and Ruby Enns, who often sang duets for Louie before he preached, recalled how Louie would be out in the foyer wanting to shake hands and talk with everyone on Sunday mornings at the conclusion of the church service. "He would ask in a way that made us feel he truly cared, 'And how is it with you folks today?' It was the tone of his voice, his arm over a shoulder, or sometimes a twinkle in his eye, but he always left us with a warm glow in our hearts.

"He was a true shepherd to his flock. When our place of business burned to the ground and we were in the dumps, the doorbell rang at our home. There was Dr. Talbot with a large group of our friends from the Church of the Open Door to cheer us up."

When Mrs. Enns's father was ill in the hospital about two hundred miles away at Reedley, Louie took off from his busy schedule and went with them to visit him. Art told what happened after the visit to the hospital.

"We then drove over to Dad's ranch for a jackrabbit hunt. A little after we arrived, we saw [Louie] watching the hogs in their pen. There was a persimmon tree nearby, and he was feeding the hogs green persimmons and laughing as the mouths of those pigs puckered up." Louie always enjoyed life wherever he was, even at a pigpen.

He also took time for the children. When a little boy named Harold Jacobs sent him a special valentine, Louie wrote him a letter.

> My dear Harold:
>
> These few lines are to thank you for your valentine and the kind remembrance of me. It was very kind of you to do this.
>
> I would like to own a dog that looks as cute as the one that is on the valentine.
>
> When you are in Los Angeles, come in to see me. May God bless you.
>
> Ever yours in Him,
> Louis T. Talbot

No one knows the many times Louie quietly helped those in financial difficulty: sometimes he gave his own money; other times he gave gifts that had been handed to him. Bob Pierce, who was to found World Vision and take the needy and hungry of the world into his heart and ministry, was in need himself one Christmas before he was so well-known. It was Louie who showed up on his doorstep with financial help.

Eugene Poole of Biola's stewardship department shared this experience: "During the crucial days of the depression, our salaries at Biola were low and often late in payment. We had serious illness in our family that called for doctors, hospitals, and rest homes. There was a bill for a hundred dollars that we did not have the money to pay. However, we didn't mention it to anyone but the Lord.

"One day Dr. Talbot left word that he wanted to see me. After his customary warm welcome, and with his way of understanding situations and saying just the right words, he remarked, 'Gene, I hear you and Helen have been having some unexpected medical bills lately. I was handed this seventy-five dollars by a member of the church yesterday who told me to use it wherever needed. I want you to take it. Just thank the Lord and put it on your doctor's bill or wherever you need it most.'

"I thanked him and wiped aside a tear or two. He put his arm around me and reminded me that he had little to do with it. He said the Lord had spoken to some church member, and it was His way of being a Friend in need. We shall never cease to thank our God upon every remembrance of Dr. Talbot."

He was also aware of the needs of those who worked with him.

Viola Fowler, who was the church secretary for many years, remembered what it was like in the office. "He worked hard and had a very heavy schedule. It kept all of us going to keep up with him. But once in a while, when he realized we were tired and had been pushing ourselves to get everything done, he would say, 'I think it's time we had a party around here.' While we cleaned off his desk, he would give someone money to go out and buy cake and ice cream or Coca-Cola. Then we would enjoy a few moments of fun and relaxation, after which we went back to our work refreshed."

But Louie's physician told him it was imperative that he give up part of his work. As pastor of the Church of the Open Door, president of Biola, conference speaker across the nation, radio Bible teacher, and author, Louie was inundated with work that was not too heavy for his spirit and soul, but more than his body could stand.

He had struggled with this decision on other occasions, but among those who had urged him to stay as head of both institutions was a man whose friendship dated back to his days in Chicago. This man was A. M. Johnson, who built Scotty's Castle for his home in Death Valley and who was a generous donor to the Lord's work.

But everyone realized that a choice had to be made. While sitting on the platform Sunday morning and looking over the members of his congregation, Louie felt that they were a vital part of his being. They were his flock. He had seen the little children grow to adulthood, had married some of them and dedicated their children. His eyes dwelt long on the stalwarts of the faith who had stood by him in the battle to save the buildings from the auction block. He thought of the people numbering in the thousands who had knelt at the altar and found the Saviour during the last seventeen years.

But as he watched the students of Biola with all their potential for Christian service, he said, "The greatest investment a person can make is in a life that is being prepared to carry the Gospel of our Lord." Those young people were excitement in his veins, and their future challenged his deepest depths. As president of Biola, he decided to dedicate himself and all his time and energy to the school as long as God gave him life.

At the church board meeting on April 19, Louie informed the members that his physicians had told him he must unburden himself of part of his heavy work. He asked the board to be in prayer regarding his successor as pastor of the church. A spirit of sadness draped itself over that meeting like a pall. Although they had twice been able to talk him out of resigning, the board members realized that because of Louie's health, this one had to be final.

It was on July 27, 1948, that Louie handed in his handwritten resignation to the church he loved.

> To the Members of the Church of the Open Door:
> My beloved Friends,
>
> It is with great regret that I tender my resignation as Pastor of the Church of the Open Door to become effective December 31, 1948.
>
> The reason for this step is that the work of both Bible Institute and Church has grown to the place where a separate head is required for each.
>
> It has been my conviction that, generally speaking, long pastorates are not for the good of any congregation and certainly seventeen years is long enough for anyone. The termination of my pastorate with the Church of the Open Door will enable me as the President of the Bible Institute to minister on the Pacific Coast and the Middle West in behalf of the school. I feel that a great future is before the Church and the Institute and that now is the time for plans to be laid. . . .
>
> I shall carry blessed memories of my association here, and will find it a great joy to speak highly of this ministry wherever I go. I am happy that I will be leaving the Church a united people in a prosperous state spiritually. I trust that this will ever remain so and that my successor will lead the congregation to greater heights of usefulness and service.
>
> With much love to you all.
>
> > Ever yours in Him,
> > Louis T. Talbot

The executive board of the church accepted Louie's resignation "with profound regret" and only because of his insistence. When the church officials did not know where they could find another man of such stature to fill their pulpit, Louie recommended Dr. J. Vernon McGee. The church extended a call to him, and he became the new pastor on January 1, 1949.

At a congregational meeting held August 25, a motion was unanimously passed making Louie honorary pastor of the Church of the Open Door.

The farewell services were held on December 26, 1948. Louie's friend, Dr. Bob Shuler, preached in the morning, and Dr. John Brown gave the evening message.

The bulletin carried this message with Louie's picture:

FAREWELL TO OUR PASTOR, DR. LOUIS T. TALBOT
FAITHFUL AND BELOVED

"It is with very deep sadness in our hearts that we . . . announce the farewell services for our pastor. . . . After many attempts on his part to resign, we were finally obliged to accede to his request to be released.

"The need for him to lessen some of his activities was impressed upon us when . . . he underwent a serious major operation. Then, too, his responsibilities as president of the Bible Institute of Los Angeles were increasing to the point where a choice between the two positions was inevitable. So, after a completely satisfactory association of seventeen blessed years, we must say good-bye, and there is not a member of the church who will do so without tears and heartache.

"One need only look at what Dr. Talbot, under God, has accomplished these years to realize how completely *faithful* he has been. Clearing our building of . . . debt, . . . he has built a national reputation as a prophetic preacher and evangelist. . . . Under Dr. Talbot's ministry thousands of souls have been saved; the church membership has increased from 1200 to 3500. . . .

"But it is not only because Dr. Talbot has been so faithful that this parting is so hard. It is also because he is *beloved*.

"In spite of his concentration upon almost insurmountable tasks for God, he has taken the time to express a personal interest in us, advising us in our problems, and comforting us in our sorrow. It is a well-known fact that Dr. Louis T. Talbot is the 'most approachable' of all the great preachers—humble, and human, and humorous.

"Ever a real friend to us, he has become so much a part of our lives that it hurts to sever the ties that bind. The spiritual impact of his life upon ours and our families will last through all eternity. He has literally poured out his life for God and for us.

"May God bless you, Dr. Talbot, in discharging your great responsibilities as president of the Bible Institute. . . . May God continue to multiply you in the lives of thousands of lost men and women. . . ."

Louie felt a great sadness of heart as he left the people he loved at the Church of the Open Door. He did not know that the most colorful part of his life was still ahead of him, when he would dwell with the African pygmies, go four thousand miles up the Amazon, talk with the spectacular Chimbus of New Guinea, and have the thrill of walking onto a beautiful new campus with the Biola students.

26

FATHER OF THE BRIDES

WHEN THE TWO GIRLS, Audrey and Betty, were growing up, Louie kept them in line by going to the radiator in their home and reporting their deeds to Santa Claus, but later he had other methods.

Although he was traveling and taking meetings, he managed to keep an eye on his two daughters. "Daddy was away a great deal speaking at conferences," recalled Betty. "But when he was home, it was a quality time and he was all ours."

During World War II, Audrey was a nurse in the navy, and Louie kept in touch with her by letter. Addressing her as "Ariel," he signed himself "Caliban"; the names represented the beautiful spirit and the monster in Shakespeare's *The Tempest*.

When young men started calling on his daughters Louie watched them with an eagle eye. When one of them would stay too long, Louie might stroll into the living room with his famous red fan and give the young man an object lesson. The red fan had to be turned in the right direction or it would fall apart, and the right direction for that suitor was out the front door.

One evening a young man wore thin his welcome, and Louie called out, "Has that lounge hound gone home yet?" Fortunately, his daughter was beginning to feel the same way about her visitor.

The first time a handsome Marine officer named Gerald Foster called on Betty, Louie met him at the door with a collection basket. But he won Betty for his bride. It was during World War II, and they were married in the Naval Academy Chapel at Annapolis on the same day that his ship brought home troops from overseas. Gerald (Jerry) became a professor at the University of Denver.

When Audrey was married, in 1949, her mother chose the Wilshire Christian Church as the place for the wedding. The peaceful

Louie escorts his daughter Audrey down the aisle. He was still recovering from surgery and commented, "I look like a fossil dug up
from the La Brea Tar Pits."

times lent themselves to more lavish arrangements than were possible
for Betty's wartime wedding.

Audrey's bridegoom was the Reverend Charles Svendsen, pastor
of the Montrose Community Church. Audrey's sister, Betty, was

among those in the wedding party, as was Jean Talbot, from Australia, the daughter of Louie's brother Hubert. There are touches of the Talbot humor in Jean's letter to the Australian clan. Describing the wedding, at which there were over a thousand guests, she wrote:

"Uncle Louie was in very high spirits at the rehearsal, so much so that I do not think Audrey gained very much by rehearsing. I tell you we just laughed all the way through it.

"Uncle Louie was in and out all the next day just like a big kid, and at 5:30 P.M., when we were dashing to get ready to snatch a bite to eat and go to the church to dress, he said, 'Well Jean, how are all the folks back home? Sit down and tell me. . . .'

"Audrey in her magnolia satin gown and fingertip veil, which fell softly over her face, was beautiful as she gracefully walked down the aisle on Uncle Louie's arm. He looked very distinguished and quite handsome.

"After the reception, we went back into the church where pictures were taken, with Uncle Louie looking as if he had just received his income tax bill. We tried to get him to smile, with Betty saying, 'Hi, Daddy, you look as if the collection plate came in empty.' With this he smiled and the photograph was snapped."

After the reception, Caliban said good-bye to Ariel as she left on a honeymoon with her bridegroom.

Picking up the idea of the wedding on his radio broadcast, Louie said: "When a young woman is about to be a bride, she has a hope chest. I guess all of you women remember when you had a hope chest, and you made little things, and embroidered towels, and you put them into your hope chest. And when the marriage took place, the hope chest was put on display.

"There is going to be a marriage in heaven, and you are going to be a part of the Bride. And everything you do in the name of the Lord Jesus Christ is just putting something into your hope chest. And I ask you, what are you doing about *that* hope chest? Did you put anything in there today—some little thing that you did in the name of the Lord Jesus? It would be a very embarrassed bride if she came right up to the wedding day and the hope chest was empty.

"God does not forget any little thing that has been done for Him. The Lord said that not even a cup of cold water given in His name shall be forgotten."

27

LOUIE AND THE MICROPHONE

"AND GOOD MORNING, my radio friends. This is Louis T. Talbot greeting you and welcoming you to another broadcast of Bible study in the wonderful name of our soon-coming Lord."

It is eight o'clock in the morning, and Louie is broadcasting live from the platform of the Church of the Open Door. The vast auditorium is empty save for Louie and the radio technician, who has Louie tucked safely into the curve of the grand piano so that he cannot pace back and forth or get too close to the microphone.

But as Louie warms to his subject, he leans closer to the mike until he almost swallows it. The technician, trying to keep the mike a proper distance from Louie, gradually pulls it toward the other side of the piano. But it is as though his listeners are in that microphone, and Louie, in his enthusiastic preaching, bends toward them. The mike is pulled farther away until it is at the far end of the piano and Louie is lying on top of that grand piano trying to stay close to the mike while preaching at full speed:

"When I was in school in Australia, there was a prize day at the end of the term. All the students gathered together in the assembly hall, and then the faculty walked in and sat on the platform, and with the faculty there was some notable person. It may have been the governor of the state or the mayor of the city.

"And then names were called—those who had passed examinations, those who had done well—and the prizes were presented. Some were given medals, and then scholarships were won by others to universities. And we call that the prize day.

"My dear friends, do you know that something like that is going to take place when the Church is translated and we are caught up to meet the Lord? The Lord says, 'Behold, I come quickly; and my reward is with me' (Rev 22:12).

"You cheer up, my friends, the prize day is yet coming. Salvation is not a reward at all, for salvation is a gift, but crowns are to be given for service. Now the crowns are these. . . ."

He almost swallowed the microphone.

The manager of a radio network described Louie's broadcasting: "He is the most fantastic radio personality I ever encountered. He does all the wrong things; he breaks every rule of broadcasting: he sits too close to the microphone; he holds onto the mechanism and rattles it when he gets excited so it sounds like a sonic boom; he shouts when he gets excited, which emphasizes his Australian accent; he has little musical accompaniment and no 'props'; his teaching broadcast is longer than good programming indicates. Yet he is loved from coast to coast and his ratings are among the highest. He comes through to the radio audience as if indeed it were his own family or congregation; apparently he visualizes the hundreds sitting enrapt before their radios, open Bibles on their laps, and he takes them all in and brings them right into the presence of God."[1]

When Bob Smith was Louie's radio technician, he accompanied Louie when he showed a silent moving picture of Biola. Part of

Bob's work was to synchronize live music to the film as Louie spoke. Bob commented on what it was like working with Louie:

"Dr. Talbot asked you to do impossible things to accomplish certain results, and you went to any ends to do what he wanted. You might even feel like giving him a little kick for getting some of his ideas, but if he asked you to, you would jump over a cliff for him.

"One time before the days of tape recorders, Dr. Talbot had an important engagement that conflicted with his broadcast time, so we decided to record on a disc. But while he was going strong right in the middle of his message, something went wrong. I stopped him and asked that he start all over again.

"It broke his train of thought, his concentration, and his momentum; and since he was speaking without any written manuscript, he couldn't get started again. That was one time his usual good nature deserted him, and he walked off and left me. I saw to it that it never happened again."

If a person happened to meet Louie just before radio time, he might find himself drawn unexpectedly into the broadcast. Dr. Sutherland told what happened to him when Louie's priorities deemed a certain interview more important than being on the radio:

"I wanted to see Dr. Talbot after his evening broadcast was over and went down to his office to wait for him. Although the program was about to start, I could hear him talking very earnestly with a member of the church board. His signature song came on the radio, so I opened his office door and said, 'Dr. Talbot, you have to be on the radio in thirty seconds.'

"'I say, Sam,' he called out, 'you take the radio. I'm busy.'

"By that time the announcer was saying, 'And now from the office of the Church of the Open Door, here is Dr. Louis T. Talbot.' I didn't have a Bible with me, and without any time to collect my thoughts, I had to speak for twenty-five minutes on his radio program. I offered a quick prayer that the Lord would help me, and He must have answered because I received several gracious letters."

When Al Sanders joined the radio program, the technicians were still baffled about how to keep Louie a proper distance from that microphone. Al told how he solved the problem.

"I'm sure that in Dr. Talbot's mind each one of those microphones represented an individual person. He would practically crawl inside of the microphone, trying to convey the message of the Gospel.

We got to the place where we put a dead mike at Dr. Talbot's desk which he could get as close to as he desired, but then we also had another microphone on the floor about twelve or eighteen inches away from the desk. The one on the floor was live. The one close to Dr. Talbot was not even plugged in and was a dead mike. That was the best kind of a pickup that we could possibly get for the program."

Al tried to explain that indefinable quality that reached through Louie into the hearts of his listeners. "Although he had an Australian brogue and his voice did not have the dulcet tone of a good broadcaster, he had something that God gave to him and to him alone for a specific purpose—the gift of communicating his message in such a way that people applied it to their own lives. He touched the heart chords of his listeners. He could take a little story and bring out of it a truth from the Scriptures that penetrated the depths of his listeners.

"A lump still comes into my throat when I think of those great days under his preaching at the Church of the Open Door. The whole front of the church would be filled with people kneeling at the altar seeking the Lord; and I treasure the Bible where I wrote the names of those I counseled at that altar during those years."

Here are a few excerpts from the thousands of letters Louie received from his radio audience.

"Now listen to this—"

IN THE WILDS

"I have but a small battery set, but your message comes in clear and plain. I believe there is a Power greater than radio that brings your message to my humble shack here in the wilds of Curry County."

IN A POTATO PATCH

"I have just heard your broadcast. I was backslidden, and cursed with almost every breath. As you preached this morning, the Lord came in His glory, washing me clean from every sin and forgiving me my many sins. I can hardly write for the tears of gratitude to my dear Lord. We are camped out here in a potato patch, and I was one of the most miserable women in the world."

IN A JEWISH HOME

"I do love to listen to your broadcast. I am a little Jewish girl nine years old. . . . I am sending 25¢ to help keep the gospel on the air."

IN NERVOUS COLLAPSE

"I found myself on the verge of a nervous collapse and just knelt beside my radio to rest a minute. Some way my hand reached out and turned on my radio and found your broadcast. My mind was just too weary to grasp your message, but just to hear your voice expounding the Word of God brought relief. God gave me much needed strength . . . I now teach a class of women and recommend your radio program to them."

IN A SHOE SHOP

"Every day at 11:00 A.M. the customers of our shoe shop hear your booming but impassioned voice sending forth the Word of Life."

IN A LARGE DEPARTMENT STORE

"Yesterday I was in one of our large stores where I heard your theme song come on the air, and then your message followed. I am unable to express in words how much good it did me to think that a great store like this one would tune in to your message."

IN THE WAR

"May, 1943—For years I have been attending your church faithfully until evacuation came. You have been one man I highly admired because of your sincere endeavors in preaching Christ. Every time things seem dismal and hopeless, and evil seems everywhere, I think of you as a real inspiration and a bulwark Christian. I am a boy of 19."

IN THE NAVY

"I have a brother in the Navy who is in the Radio Room, and he tells me that every morning he tunes in to your broadcast and turns on all the loud speakers throughout the ship, so that your message is carried all over his ship. He says the fellows listen to every word you say."

IN A MILITARY CAMP

"In five wards this morning I heard Dr. Talbot's broadcast. One Jewish boy had his chair as close to the radio as he could get it and he seemed to be very eager to hear the Bible expounded."

IN OPPOSITION

"I thank God for your bold, fearless, clear-cut testimony over the radio. There is opposition in the home. . . ."

IN THE CULTS

"I was so happy Sunday night when you told of the conversion of the Communist . . . I want to tell you that your radio messages have cured me forever from all cults and philosophies, and I know how to handle them when they come to me with their false literature."

IN A CAR

"We women of this church had an echo meeting of our conference at a large home. A number of us did not wish to miss your morning broadcast, so we sat in our car to get it by radio. We were discovered, and it was the unanimous wish of the group (of over a hundred) for our hostess to tune in to your message and let our meeting follow."

IN CHEWING TOBACCO

"When you finished broadcasting the book of Daniel, I got down

on my knees and asked Jesus to forgive my sins, and He did. I then
threw away the greatest pleasure I had in my life—that was chewing tobacco. Cussing has left me. I am saved and thank God."

One day Louie received a phone call from Walter Wesbrook, the
tennis pro at the Huntington-Sheraton Hotel in Pasadena. He had
been listening to Louie over the radio and wanted to tell him that
he "loved his clear teaching of the Word."
When he heard the man's name, Louie almost bolted out of his
chair. "Are you the Wesbrook who was a tennis champion?"
"That's right."
"You were one of the heroes in my life."
The two men became great friends, and Mr. Wesbrook often accompanied Louie to his evening preaching engagements. He had a
talking myna bird, and one time Mr. Wesbrook took it with him to
a meeting. He had a problem, however, making sure the bird would
say things suitable for church.
After preaching on the wonderful change in the life of Nebuchadnezzar, Louie received a telephone call asking him to take a cab to
the palatial home of a man whose name almost everyone had seen in
electric lights. When Louie arrived, he was ushered to a bedroom
where the man was recovering from a night out on the town. Louie
told what happened:
"'I heard you on the radio this morning,' the man said. 'You were
talking about a man named Nebuchadnezzar. Mr. Talbot, what God
did for that man, I want Him to do for me. Where does Nebuchadnezzar live? I want to get in touch with him.'
"He felt a little sad when I told him that Nebuchadnezzar had
lived several thousand years ago, but I said to him, 'My dear friend,
it isn't Nebuchadnezzar that you need to know. The One you need
to know is the One who is living now, the One who changed the
heart of Nebuchadnezzar.'
"I got down by his bedside, and I'll never forget how that fellow
cried to the Lord."
In relating that story, Louie asked his listeners these questions:
"Have you ever humbled yourself and taken your place as one in
dire need of sovereign mercy? Do you know what it is to have fled
for refuge to the great God? Have you found in His Son, our Lord
Jesus Christ, a hiding place from the judgment of all your sins? I

beseech you, my dear friends, do not turn these questions to one side."

Louie was receiving letters and contributions from a Roman Catholic priest who was listening to his Bible studies over the radio. When this priest heard Louie announce that he would be speaking in a certain church in the San Francisco area, he wrote him that he would be in the congregation dressed in a regular business suit.

After the service, the priest introduced himself and invited Louie to accompany him to the place where he lived. He had dinner with the priests there and talked earnestly with them about the Lord.

The Bible studies Louie gave over the radio were published in eleven books and hundreds of booklets. (Books he wrote are listed in the appendix.) His most widely read book, *God's Plan of the Ages*, has become an authoritative classic on the subject. A stirring testimony concerning this book came from an American in Korea who had been cast off by his family. In writing to Louie, he signed himself *Harabuji* (Grandfather):

"I, an alcoholic, mired in sin and on my death bed, cried out in agony to the God that I had ignored most of my life. And with that wondrous love of His, He gave back that life to me that I might use it to serve Him and glorify Him. What a wonderful, wonderful heavenly Father."

A missionary loaned Harabuji a copy of *God's Plan of the Ages*, and he marveled at the Bible teaching it contained. When he wanted a copy for himself, the missionary mistakenly told him that it was out of print, so Harabuji copied every word of that book by hand. When Louie heard of this, he sent him a printed copy and another of his books. In the last letter that came from him, Harabuji wrote that he was teaching English and Bible to high school and college young people in Korea.

It was November 16, 1932, that Louie began his weekday radio programs in Los Angeles with a series of prophetic messages on the book of Daniel. He paid for the broadcasts himself until they became self-sustaining. The bookkeeping was handled through the Church of the Open Door, but by 1943 the broadcasts were being extended all along the Pacific Coast. When Louie was away, he would arrange for other speakers to take his broadcasts, and sometimes they had no connection with the Church of the Open Door.

The radio mail and personnel overflowed the church office; and it was felt by both organizations that beginning July 1, 1943, it would be better for Biola to handle Louie's weekday programs and for the church to be responsible for the Sunday services.

Louie's broadcast became known as "The Biola Hour," which continues to this day as the school's official radio program. Although most of his broadcasting was on Pacific Coast networks covering California, Oregon, and Washington, for a time it was carried on 185 stations extending from coast to coast on the Mutual Broadcasting System. When the work was at its heaviest, Dr. William Orr assisted with the details. From 1959 to 1971, Biola had its own FM station, KBBI.

"Dr. Talbot could have been a millionaire," said Dr. Sutherland, "but he gave the income from his radio and books to Biola."

Louie often remarked, "I want to die a poor man," but in the meantime some of his most glamorous, humorous, and famous ministries were still ahead of him.

28

A CHALLENGE FROM GENERAL MacARTHUR

ONE OF THE GREATEST THRILLS of Louie's life came to him in Japan. His zeal for missions was an unquenchable flame, and Biola granted his deepest wish when the board sent him on a missionary journey to great mission fields of the world.

With Paul Bauman as his photographer, Louie landed in Japan; and what a refreshing time of rejoicing in the fellowship of glad reunion it was for him and the Biola graduates serving there.

On September 23, 1949, Louie wrote: "I am amazed at the splendid work General Douglas MacArthur has done to restore order and to inspire the people with a hopeful spirit. People are learning to appreciate the American way of life and what true democracy is. The spiritual need is very great, and the opportunity is correspondingly great because the people have open minds for the Gospel message. I am thankful for the part Biola graduates are having in the molding of the future of this great nation by their missionary endeavors."

In conversation with General Whitney, Louie found him very cooperative, and he arranged an interview with General Douglas MacArthur, supreme commander of the Allied forces in Japan. Louie had long admired him, and the interview became one of the most treasured moments of his lifetime.

When Louie and Paul arrived at General MacArthur's headquarters, a military aide said that they had been allotted twenty minutes and that he would come for them when their time was up.

As they walked into the room, General MacArthur was seated at a large desk. Louie and Paul stood immobile in the presence of that impressive general, who was known to be autocratic, brilliant, and supremely dedicated.

Louie described that tense moment: "He put us at ease with the

Louie and Dr. Paul Bauman on their way to the Far East.

gracious words, 'Welcome to Japan! Come over and sit on the davenport, and we'll have a talk about the Japanese problem.'

"As we started walking toward him, somehow the distance seemed to get longer and longer. But soon we began to converse as though we had been friends for years.

"I'll never forget the direct impact of the General's first question, 'What brings you to Japan?'"

As Louie described Biola and its students in training for Christian service, the general's eyes kindled. "I stated that twenty of our graduates were laboring as missionaries in Japan, and hundreds more all over the world. He was greatly interested to learn that the board of directors of our schools had commissioned us to visit these mission fields to photograph our graduates in action, and to acquaint ourselves at first hand with the needs of these lands in order that we might better equip our students to serve the people. . . . Then I asked

General MacArthur: 'What is the very best equipment we can give our students to fit them for service in Japan?'

"To this he replied that it was his conviction that the only permanent solution for Japan's problem was to put the Bible in the hands of the people. In order to accomplish this, he has called for 3,000 missionaries and for 10,000,000 Bibles for Japan within the next three years. Later he will ask for 8,000,000 more copies of God's Word, or a total of 18,000,000. Never in the history of any land has a top-flight general, or any military power, ever made such an astounding request! But I heard it with my own ears from his own lips. What a challenge!

"About this time the door opened, and there was the military aide indicating our time was up.

"But General MacArthur said to him, 'I want to spend more time with these gentlemen.'

"I was deeply impressed with the General's unequivocal declaration that he believed the Bible to be the Word of God, the foundation of all lasting government.

" 'It is my firm conviction,' he said, 'that there is power in that Book, for it has never failed. Now is the time to strike. The Church has the greatest opportunity of her career right here in Japan; and if she fails to rise to it, history will write it down as the greatest tragedy since the beginning of the Christian era. God will hold us responsible.'

"As we were leaving, I said, 'General, when you return to the United States, the people will give you a great welcome.'

" 'I have a job to do and I must complete it first. I long to see my homeland again,' he replied. 'My eleven-year-old son has never seen his country, and it is hard, but my job is yet unfinished.'

"We assured the General of our prayers and cooperation, and promised to convey his challenge to the Christian youth of America. We shook hands heartily, and with a parting 'God bless you,' we went on our way. We had been with the General a full hour."[1]

Louie and Paul next turned their faces toward Borneo, where Louie was astounded at what he found.

29

GOD'S WONDERS IN BORNEO

THE REASON Louie was sitting in the cockpit of the Catalina flying boat when it splashed down at Pontianak, Borneo, was that he knew the pilot. It had been a delightful surprise to discover that he was an old boyhood friend from Australia. He had attended a rival school when Louie was at Newington, and they had battled it out many times on the football field.

Standing among the bronze-skinned people at the wharf to welcome Louie and Paul was Biola graduate Arthur Mouw, a missionary serving under the Christian and Missionary Alliance. Something else also greeted them in that town straddling the equator—a Borneo cloudburst. After assembling the necessary provisions, they loaded them into a launch.

As the travelers chugged two hundred and fifty miles up rivers to Balai Sepoeak, the weather felt to them "like a Turkish bath," and Louie frequented the improvised shower. It was supplied with buckets of river water, which he poured over himself with a can.

Coolness came with sundown. The moon turned the river into a yellow ribbon. With the folds of night came a change.

"The skies grew dark and the silence deepened," wrote Louie.[1] "I had always heard you could cut the jungle quiet with a knife, and now I believe it. . . . All we could discern along the river banks were deep, dark thickets." The sultry stillness was only broken by the chattering of monkeys in the tops of the trees, the chug-chug of the motor, and on occasion the call of some wild bird.

His sixtieth birthday was the next day, and he requested a sample of monkey meat to celebrate. The next morning Mr. Mouw shot a monkey high in a tree, and it was skinned, cleaned, and cooked for the birthday dinner. Such kidding and apprehension accompanied the ceremony, and Louie was laughing so hard, that he had to postpone the blessing.

Christian Dyaks in front of a longhouse.

"I managed to get some of the meat down," he said, "but I never seemed hungry enough to try it again."

Later, they arrived at the mission station, where Mrs. Mouw's delicious meal helped prepare them for a long trek to a Christian Dyak church deeper in the jungle.

They traversed a twelve-inch-wide footpath that had been gouged out of the jungle. A tangle of roots beneath them kept tripping their feet, and on every side were tough grasses, moss, vines, and ferns. Overhead hung the impenetrable thicket of trees and vines that shut out light and occasionally struck them in the face. Louie peered anxiously from time to time to the right and left, and wondered when the lurking snakes, spiders, or insects would attack.

"It had rained heavily the night before. We walked in ooze, occasionally sinking to our hips and once to our waists in the water. . . . It was unbearably hot and humid."

Finally, the first village! Before Louie and his group stretched a two-hundred-fifty-foot longhouse built on stilts six feet off the ground and ringed by ladders of notched logs. Inside the longhouse the Dyaks chopped their wood, wove their baskets, made their knives, reared their families, conducted community gatherings, and celebrated feasts.

After refreshing themselves with rice balls, tea, and coconut milk

at the first village, they set out for Rasa Terbang and reached the
Dyak longhouse at 5:30 P.M. There the local custom had been to
put the nose against the visitor's cheek and then smell him all over.

Louie was glad he was spared that—he felt that he needed a bath
more than anything else.

Even though the travelers were bone weary, the approximately
five hundred Dyaks insisted on shaking hands. And after supper they
would not leave until the visitors took off their shirts and shoes and
slipped beneath the mosquito netting.

At four o'clock in the morning a loud flapping awakened the men
with a start, as an "old rooster began to blow his horn. This was the
signal for the greatest bedlam I ever heard in my life. All the other
chickens, dogs, pigs and ducks joined in the chorus."

The Dyaks gathered for prayer at 5:30 A.M. at the longhouse,
where they related their needs in detail to the Lord; they included
prayer for sick chickens and pigs.

Louie, then sixty years old, had aching muscles, stiff joints, and
blistered feet, but he pressed on to Bethel. There a Sunday school
choir sang a welcome song, followed by hymn after hymn memorized
perfectly. The group had committed to memory nearly three hundred hymns.

He reflected on the influence of the Christian Gospel. Years ago

A converted witch doc-
tor points to the sky,
indicating his faith in
God. A Dyak church
is in the background.

these former "wild men of Borneo" would have been taking the visitors' heads instead of shaking their hands, and Louie ranked the work of the missionaries with that of David Livingstone. He prayed that as people at home saw the pictures, they might realize the power of God available to them to change their own lives.

The church service in the Dyaks' bamboo sanctuary, which looked something like an American park pavilion raised high off the ground, lasted for what seemed like half a day; those who came from outlying regions had spent too much time on the trail to hurry home. The Dyaks had built the church themselves with no cost to the mission. The bamboo was fastened by rattan. It had no nails, and it had no seats except two benches for the elders who assisted in prayer and personal work. Bethel Church had a membership of six hundred, and the membership of all the churches totaled four thousand.

Dyaks whom Louie met on the footpaths would report to friends at the next village, "On the trail he is very weak, but he is really mighty and powerful in preaching."

In the following days Louie preached with a variety of handicaps: a streptococcus infection in his ankle, blisters on his heels, and insect bites all over his body. He took quinine to fight off malaria. "It was worth it all just to see those trophies of the grace of God in those jungle churches," he said.

Louie's enthusiasm and lively preaching stamped its mark on the Dyak church. When he left the jungles where thousands had heard him preach, many of the national pastors adopted the mannerisms and voice modulation of their visitor from America. Mr. Mouw was amused to see Dyak pastors stabbing the index finger for emphasis while kicking up the left foot, or using other characteristic gestures in an attempt to capture the dynamism that marked Louie's sermons even when translated into another tongue.

Mr. Mouw commented, "He preached with the same power that he does at home, although the Dyaks could not understand a word until I put it into their language. When he used his red Gospel fan, and through me explained its meaning, they understood all: If you go the Lord's way—to the right—your life falls into a useful, orderly pattern, but if to the left, all is confusion and chaos. We thank God Dr. Talbot came our way."

After Louie left that tropic isle, he plunged into the multitudes of India.

30

"INDIA–UPON MY HEART"

WEARY TO THE POINT of exhaustion, Louie and Paul reached their hotel in Calcutta, and in no time at all Hubert Mitchell was pounding on their door to give them a hearty welcome to India.

Soon they witnessed a Mohammedan parade, in which young men, to demonstrate their devotion to Mohammed, stripped themselves to the waist and beat their breasts until the blood flowed.

Louie felt he was on holy ground as he stood in the pulpit where William Carey had preached, and he pondered over that man's translations of the Word of God into forty languages and dialects.

Two hundred missionaries and Christian workers gathered that evening to greet Paul and Louie, and the next night about a thousand young people assembled for a Youth For Christ open-air meeting. Louie preached on 1 Timothy 1:15, and at the close about thirty of them made decisions for Christ.

The next day they flew to Benares, where Louie was burdened by what he saw. "It was the sight of the multitudes at the sacred Ganges River that I shall never forget: . . . thousands of people . . . turning their eyes to the sun in a sort of a trance as they entered the filthy waters in an attempt to wash away their sins and to find peace of heart!

"We saw the bodies of the dead carried to the burning ghats, clad in white cloth, immersed in the river, and then placed on the wooden pyres, and burned. Then the ashes . . . were tossed right into the water where the living went on with their futile ablutions."

India penetrated the depths of his soul. He stood with missionary Jantzen as lepers came for treatment. Some had dreadful ulcers, and others were without fingers or toes, all showing ravages of this disease.

"If this one sight of such misery so tugged at my heartstrings that

Children kneeling in prayer at the Ramabai Mukti Mission touched Louie's heart.

I felt I could bear no more, what must be the strain on the missionaries . . . who spend years ministering to them? . . . The most touching sight I saw was that of lepers putting their stumps of hands together and singing, 'Thank You, Lord, for saving my soul.' "

Louie wrote that he was "proud of the fortitude" of the Biola graduates he met everywhere on the mission fields of the world. One of them, Don Hillis, welcomed him and Paul to Poona, where another Youth For Christ meeting was scheduled.

I was among the Biola missionaries from the Ramabai Mukti Mission attending the rally, after which we drove the Talbot party to Mukti. On arrival there, he said, "I'd like to have a bath."

"We'll try to find some hot water for you," I answered.

In my room was a large, water-filled brass container on a bed of red coals. It was too heavy for me to lift, so Ruth Bollman helped. Half carrying, half slopping that water down the long row of guest rooms, I called, "Dr. Talbot, here is the hot water for your bath."

Then a sleepy voice drawled, "I've gone to bed now. I don't think I'll bother."

We hauled that hot brass container about a hundred and fifty yards as we sloshed it back to my room. Our hands were scalded, the skirts of our best dresses were wet and spotted with soot, our shoes were sopping, and our backs felt as if they would break. But at least I was able to enjoy a hot bath, which was more than he had.

The next morning when Louie was introduced to the Mukti family of about seven hundred women and children, he said, "I am your grandfather come to visit you," and the children climbed into his arms and into his heart.

"It was hard to believe that each of those charming, clean, well-cared-for, happy little Indian girls had a tragic story," he commented. One "tiny girl was found in a dreadful thorn bush by some of the mission children who heard her crying and thought she was a kitten.

. . . It was most touching to see the little blind girls. But in spite of their sightless eyes, they had radiant smiles."[1]

He preached in the church, a spacious building constructed in the form of a cross. There villagers joined the Mukti women and children; they made a large congregation. "The singing was wonderful," he wrote. "During the prayer you could have heard a pin drop. Even the littlest tot bowed reverently with clasped hands." The children were like a refreshing spring to him.

During his stay there, he spoke at four services; he amused and won the congregation by having the Indian pastor imitate his gestures as he interpreted, and at the baptismal service Louie presented each of the twenty people baptized with a New Testament in the Marathi language.

Some of the missionaries took the men to see the evangelistic work in the villages. It was a dusty journey, and as soon as he arrived back, Louie took off the only shirt he had with him and washed it. Just at that moment he was called for dinner. He came into the dining room with his dark blue nylon shirt dripping water all over the floor.

Before leaving, he wanted to see the grave of the founder of the mission, Pandita Ramabai, who is considered to be among the ten greatest Christian women the world has known. I was reluctant to take him there, because at that time the cemetery was overgrown with weeds, but he insisted.

As we stood looking at the marble cross marking the grave of that devout woman of God and at the other white crosses, I said in a rather self-pitying tone, "Well, if I should die out here, this is where I'll be—among the weed-shrouded crosses."

But Louie was not aware of the weeds. He saw only cross after cross bearing the names of missionaries. With a look of another realm in his eyes, he answered me, "When the Lord comes for His own, I

Louie presents New Testaments in the Marathi language to those just baptized at the Ramabai Mukti Mission.

can imagine no more glorious place to be than here on the battle-front with these fallen warriors, who laid down their lives in spreading the Gospel to those who have never heard."

At that moment, I felt lower than the dust under his feet, and I turned away to hide the tears that welled up in my eyes at the shallowness of my own perception.

As we walked back from the cemetery, Louie said, "Dr. Sutherland is pushing to make Biola into a college granting degrees. While traveling around, I've been talking to some of our graduates about it. What do you think?"

"I'm all for it. The time may come when only missionaries qualified in certain fields may be granted visas; and because of this, I'm going to complete the work on my degree at an accredited college during furlough."

Louie was quiet for a moment, and then remarked, "Some missionaries have told me that a college degree gives them a position of strength in their community and in dealing with government officials."

"Then why don't you go ahead?"

"If I could be sure it wouldn't weaken our teaching of the Bible. . . ." His voice trailed off for a contemplative moment, and then he continued, "So many colleges that started out as Christian institutions have ceased to stress the Word of God, and as a result they have not been true to it. That must not happen to Biola."

"Then safeguard it by requiring the same amount of Bible as you have today, but add the other subjects necessary for a degree. Otherwise, our young people will have to attend secular schools for their degrees."

Louie was thoughtful as he answered slowly, "Yeah, I guess that's right."

"Why don't you encourage Dr. Sutherland by writing him a letter today, telling him how you feel and what the missionaries have been saying to you?"

When Louie reached his room, he sat down and penned that letter. While its consequential message was winging its way over the seas to Biola, the Talbot party left Mukti. The children came out to wave them farewell; but Louie later commented, "They will always be upon my heart," and he became their international representative.

Don Hillis, Louie, and
Paul Bauman at Banga-
lore, India.

The men traveled on to Madras, and Don Hillis told what it was
like to accompany Paul and Louie: "Dr. Bauman kept kidding Dr.
Talbot about his tendency to leave things behind, and suggested
he was just a valet picking up Dr. Talbot's things so he would have
clothes to wear by the time he arrived home.

"It was obvious many times that Dr. Talbot was thinking of the
spiritual applications of things around him, seeing an object lesson
in almost everything. His desire to see world evangelism accomplished and souls won was continually evident. His unwavering faith
in the Word of God, and his zeal and pleasure in preaching the Word
were all a challenge to my own heart. He was one of the finest servants of the cross with whom the Lord allowed me to have fellowship."

In southern India, Biola graduates Elmer and Gloria Fricke drove
them into the villages, where the poverty distressed Louie's heart.
When they visited the Hindu temples, it was the idolatry that burdened him.

After seeing the magnificent palace of the maharajah, Louie could
not resist a ride on one of the elephants, from which he promptly
tumbled.

Then their trip took the men far to the north, and in one of his
letters Louie wrote of the awesome view. "At Darjeeling we saw
the most magnificent scenery my eyes ever have beheld. When the
sunrise and sunset turns the snowy peaks of Mount Everest into
rainbow hues, it fairly takes one's breath away."

Louie left India carrying a lifetime burden for her people. In the
meantime, the letter he sent from the Ramabai Mukti Mission
reached Dr. Sutherland and caused excitement as it rekindled his
hope and vision for Biola's future.

31

THE LETTER FROM INDIA

WHEN DR. SUTHERLAND received the letter Louie wrote after visiting Pandita Ramabai's grave, hope and excitement flooded his heart. He told what it was like before and after that letter came.

"One of the most thrilling experiences I had when I was dean of Biola, and Dr. Talbot was president, occurred in 1949 when I received a letter from India.

"I had felt it essential after World War II that we enlarge our academic horizons at Biola, maintaining thirty units of Bible and doctrine, but incorporating a far wider curriculum. This would meet the needs of the postwar era, even as the Bible institute had met the needs of former years.

"I did my best to get the board of directors to enlarge their vision, but my recommendations fell on deaf ears. I pled with them to expand the curriculum, suggested we change the name to Biola Bible College, that we offer more degrees, and that we upgrade our whole academic curriculum. At every board meeting I urged some facet of this program about which I had strong convictions.

"Then one day after a board meeting, Dr. Talbot called me into his office. In a very quiet, deliberate, and tender manner, he said, 'Sam, I want to caution you. You're not getting anywhere with the board in this idea of turning Biola into a college. All that you're doing is hurting your own stature. It's getting to the point where the board members instinctively rebel at whatever you have to say because they know you're leading up to this degree program.' He paused for a moment or two and then continued, 'I would counsel you not even to raise this question for the next number of months. Then we'll see what happens down the way perhaps a year hence.'

"That was just about my darkest hour as dean, and I was totally discouraged. But I didn't feel led to resign, so I kept quiet, and went on doing my job as effectively as I knew how in my disheartened condition.

"A few months later Dr. Talbot left on a missionary tour, and his itinerary included India. Since there were a number of Biola graduates serving at the Ramabai Mukti Mission, he was scheduled to visit there.

"All along his journey, he had discussed with Biola missionaries the idea of making our school into a college, and had found that almost everyone felt more academic training was needed. At the Mukti Mission, Miss Carol Terry climaxed what others had told him, provided pen and paper, and recommended that he write me what he had heard and how he felt about it.

"When I received his letter, I knew something good was going to come, because it started out 'My beloved Sam.' It was his custom to address me 'Dear Dr. Sutherland' when writing a memo that did not contain good news, and to address me 'Dear Sam' when it was just a matter of information; but I always knew something good was about to happen when he began 'My beloved Sam.'

"In the letter he told me something of his travel experiences, and said he had been talking with Biola missionaries who felt the need of academic degrees and the training they provided. Then he wound up with these thrilling words that I'll never forget, 'When I return, we'll implement the program that you have been trying to put over in the board of directors. I wish I had gotten your vision earlier.'

"I tell you that was good news to a weary heart, and was the happiest moment of my years as dean, even as the previous conversation with him had been the saddest.

"When he returned from his trip, he was absolutely true to his word. He told me, 'Sam, I want you to tell the board what you want us to do as a Bible institute and where you want us to go; and when you have outlined your program, I'll see that it's put over.'

"He did just that. It changed the course of the school's history and led to the Biola College of today."

32

AT CALVARY

LOUIE'S HEART was hushed as he trod sacred ground. "It is impossible to put into words the feelings that came into my heart as I set my feet upon the streets and fields where the Lord Jesus Christ had walked, and looked upon scenes which must have met His eyes daily for thirty-three years."

The two historic spots that made the deepest impression upon his heart were Golgotha and the tomb where the body of the Lord was laid. He shared his reactions on seeing the place of the crucifixion, which in English is "skull," in Greek "Calvary," and in Hebrew "Golgotha."

"I climbed to the top of the north wall east of the Damascus Gate, and there it was. A hush fell upon my heart. The top was bare, smooth, scalplike, with deep cavities clearly resembling eyes, a nose, and a mouth. . . . One's entire attention is riveted upon that grim place where Christ was lifted up between earth and heaven as the atoning sacrifice for the sins of the world."

It seemed to Louie as he stood there that he could see the three crosses laid upon the ground. He thought of how they stretched the Lord Jesus upon that implement of torture, placed huge iron nails in the centers of His palms, and drove the nails into the wood with their mallets. As he pictured them raising that cross with the Lord upon it, he felt that every movement irritated the holes in His feet and hands. Louie could almost hear Him praying, "Father, forgive them; for they know not what they do."

"Surely crucifixion is the cruelest and blackest of punishments," he wrote, "for it gives the greatest torture for the longest time. It includes all that pain and death can have that is horrible and ghastly —dizziness, cramp, thirst, starvation, helplessness . . . , publicity of shame, long continuance of torment . . . , untended wounds, all intensified just up to the point at which they can be endured at all,

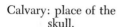
Calvary: place of the
  skull.

but all stopping just short of the point which would give to the sufferer the relief of unconsciousness. But only once in all the hours at
Golgotha did the Lord make reference to His suffering, when He
cried, 'I thirst. . . . '

"I thought of my own sin, and the part it had in nailing Him to
that cross, and I thanked Him again for dying in my stead, to obtain
my eternal salvation."

Louie was swept back in memory to when he was a young man on
his way from Australia to the Moody Bible Institute. While in England he had gone to hear Dr. F. B. Meyer, and now he seemed to
hear his words again:

"One day I was reading in the Word of God where Paul wrote,
'I am crucified with Christ,' and I said, 'Lord, I want You to take
this pride of mine and I want You to nail it to the cross. And I want
You to take this censorious spirit that I have toward my fellow pastors and the way that I look down on them. And that superior air
that I have, Lord, I want You to take that away. I want that to be
crucified. And my love for money. I want You to nail that to the
cross, and this pride of place and pride of face, and this love of all
my accomplishments. I want You to nail them to the cross so that
I'll really be able to say with the Apostle Paul, "I am crucified with
Christ." ' "

And as Dr. Meyers's words flooded his mind again, Louie said,
"I stood at Calvary that day, and as I thought of the nails going
through His hands and through His feet, I saw instead those nails

Where the Lord was
laid.

going through my hands. I said with the apostle Paul, 'I am crucified with Christ: nevertheless I live; yet not I, but Christ liveth in me.'

"Blessed was the hour when the Lord Jesus Christ cried, 'It is
finished' and the price of our redemption was fully paid."

Then Louie turned his thoughts to where the Lord was laid.

"When General Gordon was seeking evidence that this was indeed
the genuine site of the crucifixion, he had the entire area investigated
for graves. He found what he was looking for in a monolithic
tomb. . . . It seemed to him that the words of John 19:41 were thus
corroborated, 'Now in the place where he was crucified there was a
garden; and in the garden a new sepulchre, wherein was never man
yet laid.'

"I approached the ancient garden at the foot of the hill. A huge
door opened to admit me. . . . There in front of me was the Garden
Tomb. What awe filled my heart as I walked over to it, and stooped
to enter the low door, even as the disciples had on that first Easter
morning. . . .

"Along the wall at the far end was a crypt about six and a half
feet long and two feet wide. I said to myself, 'Was that where they
laid Him?'

"One of the things about the Garden Tomb that most impressed
me was the square window above the unfinished section. As I gazed
upon it, I could see how readily it would let in the rays of the morning sun, which would immediately shine upon any body lying in

the farther crypt. Now at last I understood how John could tell at once by looking into the dark tomb, without even entering, that Jesus had risen indeed, leaving His grave clothes, and the napkin that was about His head in a place by itself (John 20:7).

"As I had thought of the death of my Lord at Calvary, so now I allowed my mind to dwell upon the resurrection. I walked about the Tomb, seated myself on the ledge where perhaps a white-robed angel had once sat, and considered the 'infallible proofs': the broken Roman seal, the disrupted stone, the orderly grave clothes, the fearful earthquake, the angel visitants, the terrified guards, the frightened women, the dumbfounded disciples. . . . Jesus made seventeen personal appearances after His resurrection before and after His ascension to various persons individually and in groups. In addition, 'He was seen of above five hundred brethren at once' (I Cor. 15:6). God so multiplied the evidence that the resurrection of Christ has become one of the most thoroughly attested facts of history.

"So I rejoiced that day as I stood in the Garden Tomb that it was an empty tomb, that we do not worship a Saviour still hanging on a cross, or lying in a sepulchre.

"As believers, our own resurrection is guaranteed by Christ's. . . . 'Because I live, ye shall live also' (John 14:19). 'Jesus said unto her, I am the resurrection, and the life: he that believeth in me, though he were dead, yet shall he live.' "[1]

33

PETRA–CITY OF MYSTERY

As Louie sat astride his small Arabian horse heading toward a pink sandstone mountain called "Petra," he still had not fully recovered from the emotional impact of his visit to the sacred sites of the Holy Land farther to the north in Palestine.

As the horse took him nearer to the rose-colored eminence sliced by the canyon of *Es Siq* (a cleft), it appeared to him as if God had by His own hand split in two the sandstone mountains of Petra to open a conduit into the rock-hewn city of the dead.

In the distance he saw Mount Hor, on which Aaron was buried, and the Wilderness of Sin nearby.

Presently he was riding downhill into the stony, almost circular valley called *Petra*, which is a Greek word meaning "rock."

In the eerie glow of pink shadows from an early sun, Louie was captivated. The craggy pinnacles changed by turns to pink, rose, deep purple, and ruby red, giving the impression of being filled with strange shadows of bygone generations.

Surely, he thought, God had preserved this unique place, carved so majestically from the mountains, for some purpose that would be made clear in the future.

Blinking incredulously at the most entrancing structures their eyes had seen, Louie and Paul moved slowly through the abandoned wastes. They were face-to-face one moment with "an incomparable Grecian temple carved out of the rock mountain," and the next moment they were struggling to absorb the impact of Citadel Rock, a crusader's castle, the unfinished tomb, a columbarium, a Roman amphitheater, giant obelisks, and traces of temples, bridges, and walls.

Louie stared with horror at the Great Place of Sacrifice, throne of the god of the sun, with its two altars and the provisions for disposing of the blood of sacrifices.

"It was not difficult to imagine the dreadful scenes that must have taken place on this rocky hill—the ghastly offerings . . . and the filthy immoral rites which characterized worship in the 'high places.' "[1]

He turned away with a shudder as Paul and his camera ground out footage.

Viewers of his film later gasped when they saw Louie leaping chasms, slipping and sliding on his ascent to Petra's highest promenades, and pursuing each intriguing bit of lore.

In the front of his mind always were the prophecies of the Word of God, especially the words of his Lord recorded in Matthew 24: 16: "Let them which be in Judaea flee into the mountains" and in Revelation 12:6: "the woman [Israel] fled into the wilderness, where she hath a place prepared of God."

The Grecian temple. Photograph copyright by The Matson Photo Service.

Dr. W. E. Blackstone believed that here were the "chambers" of Isaiah 26:20, "God's hiding-place for the Jews during the tribulation."

It seemed to Louie that this could be the prophesied place of refuge for the Jewish remnant, that "no more appropriate spot on earth for harboring these outcasts from the Satanic wrath of Antichrist and his hordes could be found."

On returning home, he told people, "I wouldn't have missed seeing Petra for anything."

Louie's films, technically perfected by Paul Bauman and Virgil Wemmer, made a smashing impact on pretelevision audiences in churches of America. When his film *I Saw Petra* premiered in the Church of the Open Door, the four thousand seats were filled and there was no room for the hundreds remaining outside. His booklet in color on Petra had large sales.

Everywhere Louie showed his pictures, the response was overwhelming. He felt the call of other lands saying "Come over and help us!" His next trip took him four thousand miles up the Amazon.

Louie leaped a chasm to reach this urn on Petra's heights. Photograph copyright by The Matson Photo Service.

34

FOUR THOUSAND MILES UP THE AMAZON

BY THE SPRING of 1951 many thousands of people had swarmed into churches, city auditoriums, and conference grounds to view the captivating Asian footage of Louie's missionary movies. He recognized that God had handed him an extraordinary tool to kindle in the hearts of North Americans support for missionary outreach to earth's remotest ends.

Biola had many missionaries south of our border, and Louie asked the board to send him to that harvest field. He invited J. Russell Davis, formerly with the school in Hunan, China, to serve as cameraman-cohort during the ten-week sojourn in South America. From Russ's comprehensive diary, colorful circumstances of the trip emerge.[1]

In Colombia, Venezuela, Brazil, Peru, Bolivia, and Ecuador Louie

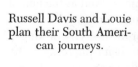
Russell Davis and Louie plan their South American journeys.

found ways to entertain, to serve, to express his astonishment about the manner of life among primitive peoples, and to get the movies he wanted. From the cockpits of many airplanes flown by Missionary Aviation Fellowship, he prayed repeatedly for the jungle people—unknown, unseen, without anything to read, and with no way to hear the Gospel of redeeming grace.

He walked amid the ruins of the Inca civilization, where beautiful virgins had been willing sacrifices to the Inca gods in rituals of sun worship. The hearts had been cut out of the victims and placed in a cavity in the chest of a stone image.

His particular delight was meeting Biola graduates scattered everywhere. In Peru, he was on hand to witness the arrival of the Wycliffe Translators' new Catalina aircraft. Louie officiated at a ceremony dedicating the Aeronca *SMU '51*, named for Biola's Student Missionary Union of 1951, which had raised the money for the aircraft. Marjory Nyman, first woman graduate to receive a degree from Biola, christened the plane.

The mighty Amazon River intrigued him completely. He kept reminding himself that he was in the heart of an unbroken jungle larger than the entire United States.

In the oppressive heat, Louie one day purposely fell off the missionary's launch into the river to cool off. On shore that day he followed a group of people and found himself at a national sporting event—cockfighting.

On another trip the plane rose to twenty-four thousand feet over the Andes. The passengers' shirts were soaked with perspiration as everyone boarded the plane. In minutes the temperature in the cabin was below zero and everyone had to breathe oxygen from a tube. The passengers would occasionally scrape the ice from the window and peer down on the snowcapped Andes. And at the end of the trip, in Lima, Dr. Cameron Townsend, founder of Wycliffe Bible Translators, met them and took them on a tour of this "city of kings," which has the oldest university in the western hemisphere.

As the journeys continued, a constant parade of strange and wondrous sights came into the camera's view: Indians with bright red paint over their bodies and hair . . . quaint market places . . . ancient ruins . . . broken-down trains and donkey carts . . . a blowgun fired with deadly accuracy . . . desert sands and rain forests . . . wild orchids clinging like mistletoe to trees . . . missionaries fatigued in their

Dressed in Shipibo Indian costumes, Louie and Russ put on a comedy for the missionaries.

labors and taking time for fun . . . and trophies of grace from among disadvantaged peoples.

Marjory Nyman, a Wycliffe missionary, shared with Louie her apprehension and fear when it came time to fly to her assignment. His words of comfort have remained with her through the years: "The safest place in the world is to be in the center of the Lord's will."

While in Peru, he decided to produce a comedy for the missionaries, and Marjory described it: "Dressed in a Shipibo Indian costume, Dr. Talbot strode down to the lakeside; and at that moment Russ appeared in Shipibo costume, carrying two ceremonial canoe paddles. Dr. Talbot gave a whoop and grabbed a paddle. That started a circular dance with more whooping and hollering as the men landed blows on each other.

"Dr. Talbot gave his companion many more wallops than Russ dared to give the honored doctor. But to us, the funniest angle of this farce was that the men had unknowingly chosen to wear Shipibo women's costumes with men's headdresses!"

Louie wanted to ride on an alligator, but had to settle for the back of a large turtle. Before leaving that area, our gourmet suffered through a feast of monkey given in his honor.

An Indian, Louie, and Marjory Nyman at the christening of the
airplane given by Biola students.

To Louie's Andes and Amazon experiences were added those of
the Orinoco River basin in Venezuela. Hosted by Dr. and Mrs. Van
Eddings of the Orinoco River Mission, and shuttled by MAF avi-
ators Jim Truxton and Hobey Lawrence, the travelers moved among
the Panara Indians and ministered at the Chapel of the Good Shepherd. They also visited the Bible Institute at Las Delicias, which is
directed by Mr. and Mrs. Harold Tuggy.

"Dr. Talbot was tremendously impressed by Mary Olvey's concern for the salvation of the Panara Indians," recalled aviator Jim
Truxton. "He encouraged her to press on toward the goal of evangelizing this tribe. We talked about it late into the evening."

Finally the twenty thousand feet of film was all exposed, the ten
weeks gone. Each farewell was difficult on the frontiers.

They flew back to Los Angeles, and soon Louie's hands were full to
overflowing with the showing of his colorful, challenging films and
with ministering the Word of God. But the cost of all his missionary
journeys to his health had been higher than he realized, and it was to
lead to his resignation as president of Biola.

35

LOUIE BECOMES THE CHANCELLOR

It was Louie's delight to show his moving pictures of India, Petra, and four thousand miles up the Amazon. Everywhere he went people crowded out the churches and auditoriums.

Although excellent musical backgrounds and narrations had been added to the films, he was often requested to narrate them live because of his humorous comments and the depth of his impassioned burden for the people he had filmed. It also added the warmth and force of his personality, which no recording could convey.

Here are two examples of the humor he wove into the pictures:

"See how this hippopotamus is enjoying eating that grass. I've seen men and women in church chewing gum just like that. . . .

"And look at the face of that wild boar. All the women in the congregation who are grateful they don't have a face like that should put five dollars in the collection plate."

The colorful and spectacular pictures mixed with Louie's humor attracted the young people, and the Lord used the stirring scenes to call many of them into His service in lands of great need. The training of such dedicated, motivated men and women at Biola College was very much on Louie's heart; and he watched with deep interest the development of the graduate school, a theological seminary.

Dr. Charles L. Feinberg was dean of that school, and he related what happened when he first came from Dallas to help develop the seminary:

"One day I came to Dr. Talbot to inform him I had found a suitable home in Altadena and needed money for a down payment to hold the property. The only surprise he expressed was the great confidence of my wife in my judgment to make a choice for the family without her seeing the house.

"Immediately he took a number of bills from his pocket, went

The chancellor.

Dr. Charles Feinberg
and Louie discuss the
verities of the faith.

with me to his office where he obtained the remainder from his desk,
and unceremoniously handed me the money. Recovering from my
astonishment, I asked him, 'But, Dr. Talbot, is that all?'

" 'What do you mean?'

" 'You have just loaned me $1,000 of your own money. I appreciate
it deeply, but don't you think I ought to sign some statement, indicating I received this money?'

"Now it was his turn to be surprised as he asked, 'What for?'

"His famous finesse in taking offerings (even two and more in one
meeting) for God's work at home and abroad has obscured this won-
derfully generous side of his character. His self-forgetfulness and
humility were real, not playacting. When the time came for the
three-year seminary to be named, in 1952, it was the undoubted conviction of Dr. Samuel Sutherland, president of Biola, and a number
of us that it should be called the 'Talbot Theological Seminary.'

"Dr. Talbot's uneasiness over the matter was manifest and expressed. One day in the lobby of the downtown building, he cor-

nered me and asked pointedly, 'Why should the seminary be named after me? What was the reasoning that went into the decision?'

"I told him those were not difficult questions to answer. It was because he had under God freed Biola of an unbearable and crushing burden of debt, and, even more, his name was synonymous worldwide with orthodoxy and fidelity to the Word of God.

"Having clear-cut, well-defined convictions, there never had been a shadow of doubt where he stood on the verbal, plenary inspiration and the undiminished infallibility and inerrancy of the Word of God. He believed the Bible implicitly, and the seminary is the length and shadow of his useful life.

"He had no rebuttal and never again asked me why the new seminary should be so named."

An illustration used by Dr. Charles Mayes at a Talbot Seminary banquet so delighted Louie that he used it frequently, adding many colorful embellishments not given here.

Over a fish market a homemade sign read "Fresh Fish For Sale Here."

One day a man came along and said to the owner, "Why does your sign read 'Fresh Fish For Sale *Here?*' Anybody would know that this is the place. Why don't you take off the word *Here?*"

So the owner did that, and the sign read, "Fresh Fish For Sale."

A few days later another man came along and asked, "Why do you say 'Fresh Fish *For Sale?*' Everybody knows you have them for sale." So the owner changed the sign to read, "Fresh Fish."

Several days had passed by when another customer said, "Why do you have a sign 'Fresh Fish'? You wouldn't sell any other kind. If I owned this place, I'd take off that word *Fresh.*" The owner complied, and his sign read "Fish."

In due time another man remarked, "I don't like your sign. Anybody that passed within a block of your place would know that you sell fish because he can smell them." So the owner removed the last portion of his sign.

"This reminds me of what has been going on in some of the theological seminaries in America," Louie commented. "As soon as anyone questions some important truth or doctrine formerly taught by the seminary, the doctrine is removed."

That this might never happen to Talbot Theological Seminary was the passionate prayer of Louie's heart.

It was becoming obvious, however, that the years of heavy responsibilities and the ruggedness of jungle travels had taken their toll on his health. This portion of a letter he wrote while he was in Borneo reveals something of that cost:

"We will reach the end of our water route tonight at 11:00 o'clock. We shall then tie the launch to a tree and walk for *ten hours* through the jungle to Mr. Mouw's station where the Dyaks live. Am wondering how I'll be able to stick out that ten-hour hike. I'll be wishing for my Nash before I've gone a mile. However, I'm *going* to stick it out, even if as a result I'll have to spend the rest of my days in an old people's home."

Louie slogged through that ten hours of jungle almost to the point of exhaustion. When he set his mind on a goal, some kind of steel entered his soul, and he let nothing stand in his way; he never counted the cost to himself.

But it all caught up with him, and in May of 1952 he wrote Dr. Sutherland from Paso Robles, where he was holding special meetings. "I have a real case of shingles. They are sore! . . . Having good meetings. I rest during the day and speak at night. Will be home about May 24. Would write more but my back and side are kicking up."

In his reply, Dr. Sutherland wrote, "I have just received your letter from Paso Robles. . . . I can imagine a little something of what you must be suffering, which all adds up to the fact that we are genuinely concerned about your health. . . .

"I'm satisfied in my own mind that if you do not take a few months' rest pretty soon, you will be taking a permanent rest very shortly, and we certainly do not want you to retire yet.

"Why not forget speaking dates, photographic trips, and everything else that requires any thought, strain, and physical effort, and get away for a time of rest and relaxation? . . . Those are as strict orders as one of your subordinates can possibly give."

Louie reached the point where he realized he must lighten his heavy load somehow. While not wanting to stop preaching the Word or to sever his connection with Biola, he did feel it was time for the administration of the school, with its multiplied responsibilities, increasing academic program, and its future, to be in the hands of a younger man who could give the school his full attention, vigor, and strength.

Louie as chancellor and Dr. Sutherland as president of Biola College
and Talbot Theological Seminary.

After much prayerful consideration, Louie, as president of Biola,
sent in his resignation on June 25, 1952. He wrote in his letter to
the board, "I do not wish, however, to be altogether severed from
the school. . . . It has been a wonderful joy and privilege to be
associated with you individually and collectively in this great ministry of training young men and women for Christian service at home
and abroad. I certainly want to have some part in the future ministry of this institution."

On the same day he resigned, Louie submitted a recommendation that Dr. Sutherland be made his successor.

At the board meeting of September 11, 1952, Louie's resignation
was accepted with deep regret, and Dr. Sutherland was appointed to
succeed him as president. Louie was given the lifetime title of
chancellor.

The inauguration was held in the main auditorium of the Church
of the Open Door, with the faculty and school officials in academic

attire. On his robe, Louie wore the colorful hood of blue and orange satin with red velvet presented to him by Wheaton College when the Doctor of Divinity degree was conferred upon him.

In an impressive ceremony, and with representatives from many educational institutions in the large audience, Louie was installed as chancellor and Dr. Sutherland as president. Both men were presented with engraved gavels.

In his response, Louie said, "When I attended the Olympics in Australia, I saw a runner bring in the torch that had been lighted in Greece. Today, Dr. Sutherland, I hand you a torch that was lit by our forefathers in the faith, and I trust that when it is time for you to hand it to your successor, it will be burning even brighter than it is as I hand it to you today."

And then with his unfailing touch of humor, Louie added, "And by the way, Dr. Sutherland, I want you to note that the gavel given to you is not quite as large as the one that was presented to me, so I can still keep you in line."

With the weight of the presidency lifted from his shoulders, Louie's health began to improve, and he took meetings up and down the Pacific Coast and across the country in behalf of Biola.

Nothing could keep him from preaching the Gospel, "neither snow nor rain nor heat nor gloom of night" nor ice. Dr. Lloyd T. Anderson told what happened in Oregon.

"When I was pastor of the First Baptist Church of Salem, Oregon, we were on the radio every day and twice on Sundays. We used to have Dr. Talbot come up and hold meetings for us as often as we could. One morning the ice set in, and it was impossible to climb the hill to the radio station. I phoned the station and asked, 'Is it possible for us to broadcast over the telephone?'

"They said that could be done, so I phoned Dr. Talbot and told him we would put the program out over the air from his hotel room.

"When I arrived there, Louie was still in bed, and we had to be on the air in three minutes.

"As long as I live I'll never forget the spectacle of Louie pacing back and forth across the room in his B.V.D.s and preaching the Gospel fervently over the telephone." His concentration was so intense that he was totally unaware of how ludicrous he looked. He was conscious only of the Word of God and the hearts of his listeners.

One of Louie's greatest joys was speaking in churches pastored by Biola graduates. Dr. Roy Kraft shared his experience with Louie.

"I know of no man who more profoundly affected my life than Dr. Talbot. When I first met him, I was a student at Biola and looked upon him as a truly great man of God. This realization never faded, but my appreciation of him grew with the years. I used to introduce him to our people as 'A great man who doesn't know it.' His humility made an indelible impression upon me.

"One Sunday evening after a great day of his ministry in our church, we had gone home and had a bite to eat. Before going to bed, he and Jeannette and I stood in the living room, and he put his arms around us and prayed, 'Dear Lord, before we go to bed, we want to tell You again that we love You. We're so glad we don't have to be great or important, but we can love You and You bless us.' I have never forgotten that sacred moment.

"He loved the ocean. When he came to Santa Cruz, he would go to the wharf and buy crabs, and then sit down on the wharf, dangle his legs over the side, and eat away.

"He used to ask the man in the fish market if he had any fish heads. I asked him, 'What are you going to do with them?'

" 'Take them home and boil them to get the jelly out.'

"I questioned the advisability, but the man behind the counter said, 'That man knows what is really good.' We bought the fish heads, brought them home, and he boiled them and relished the prized 'jelly.'

"Sometimes we would go fishing. Taking the boat out in the bay, we caught fish until he had enough and would say, 'Roy, let's chase sharks.' So we put one man in the front of the small boat and gave him the gaff. Another man held the front man in the boat, and one man ran the motor. We would spot the fins above the water and go for them. The front man would gaff the shark and hold on, and we would cut off the motor and go for a shark ride. Although it was wet in the front position, he always enjoyed being the man with the gaff.

"In our kitchen he would sample any food being prepared, and it seemed to be a delight of his to take a knife and carve the roast or bird in the most unusual and fantastic design.

"His ability to relax was amazing. Anytime and anywhere he could turn some kind of switch and go to sleep. It might be on the

Bible teacher beloved in many countries.

living room sofa when the room was filled with those who counted it a privilege to be in his company, or in a chair in the midst of a boring conversation.

"I can never remember once when he was a disappointment to me. Every time I heard him speak, he got hold of the old Gospel Bell and rang out the message."

When Louie was holding meetings in Minneapolis, in March of 1953, he was asked to take the presidency of Northwestern Schools. During the years he was pastor of the Oliver Presbyterian Church, he had taught personal evangelism at Northwestern, and the founder, Dr. W. B. Riley, had been a close friend of his. There were many people in that area who loved Louie.

Here is a portion of a deeply moving letter Louie wrote to Dr. Sutherland. It gives a rare glimpse inside Louie himself:

"For some time now, I have had a growing conviction that the work—all the work—the Lord had for me to do for Biola is finished, and the word 'Finis' has been written to the last chapter.

"It is not easy to write this, I assure you. However, church history shows that the Lord's servants come and go, but His work still goes on, and that has and always will be true of Biola under God. I have deep assurance for Biola's future because you are at the helm. I want to say, Sam, that you have been a peach of a friend and as loyal as anyone can be. I shall always appreciate this all through my life.

"I have been in conference with the Northwestern Trustees at their invitation, and the situation . . . challenges me tremendously. . . .

"Now the urge being pressed is that I take over (Northwestern) in the fall. . . . However, I want to be dead sure before I give the final word. . . .

"Sam, I hate to write all this to you, but I am sure it is best for you, the school and everyone. When a man's work is done, to remain is only to mark time. . . .

"The Lord seems to be saying, 'Now I want you to take one more mountain.'

"You know, Sam, that I'll always be a 'Booster' for Biola and would never think of leaving if I did not feel that the Lord is leading in another direction."

Louie received a telegram from Dr. Sutherland on behalf of the board:

YOUR LETTER RECEIVED   WE ARE SHOCKED BEYOND
WORDS   PLEASE DO NOT MAKE ANY HASTY MOVE UN-
TIL WE CAN TALK FACE TO FACE   RATHER DISAS-
TROUS COMPLICATIONS WOULD ARISE IF YOU CARRY
OUT YOUR DECISION

In a telephone conversation, Louie told Dr. Sutherland that he had
received word from Billy Graham to the effect that if he would become the president of Northwestern, he could count on his support
one hundred percent.

Writing again to Sam, Louie penned these words: "I thank you
for your desire to keep me as part of the Biola family. . . . However,
I have felt for some time that I am a millstone around your neck.
While I feel that this is so, I don't think you share this viewpoint.
However, I am waiting on God for the cloud either to remain still or
move."

A telegram came right back from Dr. Sutherland:

I AM ALMOST POSITIVE YOU WOULD LOSE A HOST OF
THE BEST FRIENDS YOU HAVE IN THE WORLD IF YOU
GIVE ANY FINAL COMMITMENT BACK THERE AT LEAST
UNTIL YOU HAVE TALKED WITH US HERE AT BIOLA
THIS PROBLEM IS VASTLY BIGGER THAN YOU MAY RE-
ALIZE   PLEASE UNDER NO CIRCUMSTANCES MAKE
ANY COMMITMENTS THERE AT THE PRESENT TIME
HOPE TO SEE YOU AROUND EASTER

Louie did not want to hurt Biola by leaving, so he finally left the
decision up to its board of directors and said that he would do whatever they felt was best. Their unanimous decision was that he should
stay with Biola, and he remained the school's chancellor for the rest
of his life.

God had made Louie a mountain climber, and he was happiest
when the Lord gave him an impossible mountain to climb. A whole
range of mountains was to challenge him, but in the meantime the
school sent him to film the coronation of Queen Elizabeth II, an experience that excited his heart.

When the coronation was over, his hosts in England, Eric and
Syvilla Horn, took him to see the Martyrs' Memorial, the gilt-tipped
arrows of which depict the flames that enveloped those who were
faithful unto death. And out of this experience came Louie's state-

ment, "It would be wonderful for a martyr to die with tears in his eyes, only to open his eyes and find the hand of the Lord Jesus wiping those tears away."

Through the years Louie had spent much time studying the lives of great heroes of the faith. Going to Wesley Chapel, he pondered over the family Bible on display there. Then he went to Scotland. "When I was in seminary," he recalled, "I heard a godly professor say that no person should enter the ministry until he had read the life of Robert Murray M'Cheyne." Louie was reading that life again in memory as he sat meditating and looking at the old pulpit of that devout man of prayer.

All through his ministry he studied the lives of men God had greatly used during the centuries. By his bedside he kept *Foxe's Book of Martyrs*.

The visit was for him a pilgrimage into the depths of the lives of men God had greatly used for His glory, a time when Louie sought renewal in deep communion with his God. He felt the Lord strengthen the sinews of his body, soul, and spirit; and later, while standing by the tomb of David Livingstone in Westminster Abbey, he knew he must follow Livingstone to Africa. That journey was to take him to New Guinea and to some of his most colorful experiences. He soon found his feet climbing again.

36

NEW GUINEA CALLS "COME BACK!"

ARMED WITH CAMERA and determination, Louie next followed the sun westward to steaming New Guinea, "the very last outpost to civilization." He called it a "land of mystery and of darkness, where the people still live in the Stone Age and practice cannibalism when they can escape the eye of the government."

Because Australia patrolled large areas, Louie and a cameraman named Murdock were relatively free to penetrate regions where primitives romped and warred in the buzz and heat of the insects' domain.

On the very day Louie made application to enter this colorful realm, seven white people had been killed by a New Guinea tribe. Reluctantly, the officials approved Louie's application to enter certain areas; they warned him that he would be obliged to follow strictly the directives of government officials. Louie carried with him an impressive letter of introduction bearing the beribboned gold seal of the state of California, and it opened many doors for him.

"I attended several road courts," Louie wrote. "They are just what the name implies. The jeep stops and the officials hear and judge their cases. The majority of complaints center about their most valuable possessions—their pigs. Occasionally it has to do with women, dowries, thefts from their little gardens, etc. Those found guilty of murder or cannibalism are put into prison."

"I saw a poor widow obliged to smear her body and hair with hideous gray clay which she was required to wear for a long period. Others had covered their bodies with pig's grease and charcoal, making their skin shiny and black. Many of the men wore boar-like tusks through their noses."

Louie had with him Mr. Colin Simpson, anthropologist, author,

209

Louie meets the chief of the Chimbus.

and authority on New Guinea, and a wonderful help in communicating with the people.

"One of the greatest thrills of my life," Louie reported, "was giving the message of salvation in the Lord Jesus Christ to these people who were hearing it for the first time. I would speak to my companion, Colin Simpson. He would put it into Pidgin English so that one of the tribesmen who was a patrolman could then interpret into the language of the people. I did not depend upon words alone, but pointed to the skies, made a cross of sticks, and in other ways tried to make clear the story of God, the great Creator, who loved them and sent His Son to die for their salvation. I never tried harder in any sermons I ever preached to get the message across as I did in that land."

Eager as Louie was to reach as many tribes as possible, he became ill with what was diagnosed as sunstroke, and he had to stay in Goroka until he was better. One day when a cluster of distant tribesmen came to that center for trade, they encircled him and pointed repeatedly to his head and its scarcity of hair. The natives had an abundance of hair. As Louie attempted to reply, he pointed to a native woman, then to himself, then to a distant mountain to the east, indicating that he had a wife a long, long way off. Then he put two fingers together and pretended to jerk out various hairs one at a time—he was indicating that his wife had denuded his dome by plucking out his hair. The natives stared at each other for a few seconds and then roared with laughter.

"They are like children," he noted, "and they all chew betel nut, which makes their teeth and gums, including their tongues, blood red."

Louie visited the Wabaga wigmen, who collect hair from dead relatives and weave it into huge wigs of bizarre shapes and sizes. He was also near the Kukukuku tribe, where sporadic killings had taken place.

But the tribe that won his heart for all time was the Chimbus. From Nondugl, he had a hard three-hour walk in the blistering sun—most of it uphill—to reach those colorful Chimbus. "It was certainly rough going," Louie reported, "and to make matters worse for me, my heavy boots were too large for my feet and created the worst crop of blisters I have ever had."

"On the way we met two painted, highly decorated men carrying a smoked pig on a bamboo pole. The more decorated of the two told us very enthusiastically that it was part payment for a girl he wanted to marry."

The chief of the Chimbus was very tall and slender, with a dignity that was unmistakable. It took Colin Simpson and another interpreter for Louie to communicate with him. Bypassing the seeming futility of words, Louie tried to impress the chief by removing his false teeth and showing them to him. The startled tribesmen pulled at theirs but shook their heads that their teeth would not come out. Whatever the chief thought, his facial expression did not change. Colin warned him not to do it again.

Overnight accommodations were necessary, and Louie described his hotel room:

"I spent one night with the Chimbus, and the chief used his spear to drive ten pigs out of the small grass hut where I was to sleep."

An open sesame among the Chimbus was the coveted gift of a sack of salt and some paint for their faces. The bestowal of such riches yielded in return a fantastic dance. The participants beat out the rhythm with their fingers on small drums as they whirled and

Two great friends part as Louie tells Mr. Myers, "I'll bring you back
a tiger skin, Ray."

stamped and danced for approximately two hours. Their faces were painted with unique designs. The headdresses they wore for the dance held gorgeous, long, delicate, feathery, sometimes iridescent plumes from the bird of paradise. Those and other colorful feathers formed a kaleidoscope of rioting crimson, yellow and orange, saffron and violet, and brilliant green edged with shining blue, all swaying back and forth in rhythm with the movements of the dancers. The tail feathers of the king of Saxony bird of paradise looked like strips of celluloid tape to which streamers were attached.

Louie had charmed the Chimbus as much as they had fascinated him. As a farewell gift, the Chimbus piled his arms high with pineapples, yams, sugarcane, peanuts and other produce, calling out "Stay with us! Stay with us!" It was a moving sight, and Louie said that he would tell young people in America to prepare themselves to bring them the Gospel, to which the people roared, "Then come back! Come back!"[1]

Louie's heart ached for those unenlightened people. New Guinea had been called "the Land Time Forgot." He prayed it would not be "the Land the Church Forgot." While grateful for the oversight Australian officials had given the country, and for some fine missionary work reaching New Guinea's heart, he longed to see dedicated Christians bringing more of its plagued and impoverished people with them to heaven.

Before leaving New Guinea, Louie wanted to phone his wife; but since he could never remember his unlisted phone number, he had the operator call his daughter Betty. The call roused her out of her sleep:

Operator: "I have a collect call from New Guinea from Louis Talbot. Will you accept the charges?"

Betty: "Well, yes."

Louie: "Hello, Betts? I say [pronounced *sigh*], what's my phone number?"

After calls from all over the globe kept waking her in the middle of the night—her father was usually in a different time zone—Betty thought of a solution to the problem. For his birthday, she bought him a handsome leather belt with his phone number engraved in gold letters on the inside. On the accompanying birthday card, she wrote these lines:

Each time the phone rings, I reflect,
Is Paris calling me collect?
Or is it London, or Quebec?
I'm wakened from my peaceful slumber
To hear, "What's Dr. Talbot's number?"
Then a "Will you accept the charges?"
Into my subconscious barges.

That's why your number, I've long felt
Should be imprinted on your belt,
Where it is Johnny on the spot
Snuggled right around your pot,
'Twill go with you from town to town
And keep your pants from falling down.

Having found that everything was all right at home, Louie turned
his steps toward the jungle warfare of the Malay.

37

RED TERROR OVER MALAYA

CHRISTMAS AT SINGAPORE in 1953 was unusual for the missionaries there because Louie was in their midst. Because he was to visit the sultan of Johore, the group gave him a sultan's outfit, which he promptly donned and became the "sultan of the day." There was even a snake charmer to entertain everyone that afternoon on the lawn. In the evening Louie gave a Christmas message to the English soldiers.

While waiting in Singapore for a visa, he was among the thousands of people who watched a tremendous bonfire flare and then simmer down. After that, barefooted young Hindu men walked through the red-hot coals and ashes. There was agony of pain on the faces of some of the men, while others seemed to be in a trance. The anguish in Louie's heart was that they felt this rite would help them in eternity.

And then he saw the human pincushions, Hindu men who had scores of huge pins and spikes stuck into the upper part of their bodies and even their tongues. He longed to tell them that they had only to accept the sacrifice made by the Son of God on a cross to attain what their hearts unknowingly sought. Sleep would not come to him that night.

Places that were impenetrable opened to him whenever he showed his gold-sealed, beribboned letters from the mayor of Los Angeles and from California's governor and secretary of state.

The sultan of Johore welcomed Louie to the palace and granted all his requests. He was even allowed to enter the enclosure of tigers in the private zoo. Holding a rather narrow plank of wood for protection, Louie joined the tigers from the jungles of Malaya for a little spree.

It was just a few months before the French yielded to the Com-

Human pincushions in Singapore.

munist Vietminh in 1954 that he headed for the war zones. His car zigzagged through military barricades and roadblocks. When the brigadier general saw Louie's golden letters, he granted him permission to go with the army into the guerrilla-infested area of Malaya, but he had to sign this disclaimer of rights:

Military Headquarters, Kuling

I hereby agree to the following conditions:

1. If I should be shot and killed,
2. If I should be shot and wounded,
3. If I should meet in any other way with bodily harm, sickness, etc., while journeying with the military forces of the Malaya, neither my relatives, friends or any organization with which I am associated will bring suit for damages or any other method of recourse against the military forces operating in the Malay.

Louis T. Talbot.

Both Louie and his Chinese photographer signed, and they were outfitted with jungle green uniforms and guns. Then their tank moved along a rough road to a thick part of the jungle, where they dismounted quickly with the soldiers and crept quietly through thick growth as they searched for terrorist guerrillas. The heavy trousers and thick boots kept out leeches, ants, and other insects.

"At times I was covered with ants," Louie related later, "and some of them and other creatures did get to my neck where I did battle with them." While trying to keep his gun ready to shoot on a moment's notice, Louie slogged through thick jungle and swamps. He often stumbled, but he did his best at the age of sixty-five to keep up with the young soldiers.

There were about "10,000 terrorists operating in the jungles, fighting a 'hit-and-run' war in an effort to break the morale of the people, smash the government and pave the way for the whole country to be taken over by Communism," Louie reported.[1]

He witnessed the horrible tyranny and violence of godless Communism, and his heart cried out that Communism never gain control in America and sweep away personal freedoms and all that is held sacred. He hoped that his picture "Red Terror over Malaya" would open the eyes of multitudes in the United States to the dangers and cause them to pray that what he saw in Malaya would never happen in America.

After he left the war zones, he became the guest of the Gordon Smiths, who took him to see the "loincloth people of the jungles" of Indochina. "These are the most superstitious people in the world," he wrote. "If one sneezes in a group, no one may leave the room for some time or the spirits would be angry." They believe turtles bring death to their children, and they will not live in a house if a crow alights on it.

One night Louie witnessed a village sacrifice. About three hundred almost nude people crowded into a two-hundred-foot longhouse, where the glow of little fires built on mud floors revealed huge jars filled with rice alcohol and fetishes such as the horn of a buffalo, the foot of a chicken, the tooth of a dog.

The weird sacrifice commenced when the sorceress began incantations with a bowl of pig's blood, which she smeared on the fetishes to appease the spirits. Gong beaters began their incantations and swayed from side to side with the muffled and syncopated beat.

This lasted all night and ended with people sprawled on the floor in a drunken stupor. "It was the worst orgy that I had ever witnessed," Louie commented, as his heart cried out in prayer that in their darkness they might know the One who said, "I am the light of the world."

Before leaving Indochina, Louie wanted to get a tiger skin for Ray Myers. Ensconced on a platform in a tree that had bait tied at its base, Louie waited alone for his tiger in the midst of the jungle.

In the dense darkness of the jungle night, he heard "weird sounds from birds, insects, animals such as the barking deer that barks like a dog, and the big sambur deer that bells out 'payo,' birds that hammer and knock and others with voices like a flute." It could make one feel that the place was haunted. Louie sat quietly waiting. In his hand was his high-powered gun, to which a strong flashlight had been attached.

At about midnight he heard the approach of the tiger. When the tiger started crunching the bones of the bait, Louie turned on the light. "All I could see were two balls of fire looking up at me." He took aim and shot. "Because of a tense feeling that came over me, I

Frolicking with three tigers in the zoo of the sultan of Johore.

Louie is outfitted by the army for jungle warfare in the Malay.

missed . . . , and the tiger roared off into the jungle." He went back the next day for another vigil, but the tiger knew better than to return.

As Louie continued his journey, he had to change planes at Bangkok. Among the young people who had responded to his previous pictures of mission fields were Biola graduates Norman and Florence Allensworth. They had gone to Bangkok to spread the Gospel among people living there on boats. Norman went to the airport when Louie was first scheduled to come, but Louie did not arrive. About ten days later Norm spotted him sitting in a hotel that had windows facing the street.

"I rushed into the hotel," Norman said, "and after exchanging greetings, I asked him how long he would be staying in Bangkok. He was leaving the same evening.

"We took him to our home, where Florence prepared a meal, and he rested on our divan. He gave us some wise counsel that we sorely needed, and we greatly appreciated everything he told us."

At the airport Louie took some film out of his suitcase for Norman to mail to Biola. Norm was astonished. "Why, Dr. Talbot," he said, "you didn't have your suitcases locked."

"Well," he replied, "I've lost my keys so many times and had to break the locks, that I find it much better just to leave my suitcase unlocked."

"As I watched him depart," said Norman, "I was conscious of a deep love for this great man of God who was the first to tell me of Christ."

On his way to Africa, Louie made a brief stop in India to get pictures of a stirring service held at the Ramabai Mukti Mission after Christmas. For the service, sacrificial gifts are brought to the altar. A farmer brings his best goat; others carry chickens, while some of the widows and elderly women bring wheat or rice saved by fasting.

Each gift is something a person gives up. The orphan children lay their candy or even a treasured doll on the altar. Lines on wrinkled faces soften, dull eyes light up, and the little ones almost skip with joy as each brings a sacrificial gift to the Saviour, manger born.

Feeling his heart warmed by those hundreds of children who called him their grandfather, Louie flew on to Livingstone's Africa, and to a hippo hunt.

38

HIPPOS AND PYGMIES

ORAN SMITH was waiting for Louie at the airport in Cairo. Bad feelings against Britain had arisen in 1954 over England's heavy hand at the Suez Canal, and Louie's Australian brogue made him sound to the Egyptians like an Englishman. This resulted in hostilities, and a large crowd gathered, shaking fists at them and shouting threats to the "Britishers."

After viewing the pyramids, Louie went to the Valley of The Kings, where he was intensely interested in the tombs of Rameses I, II, III, and Tutankhamen. He thought of the selfishness of those men, who tried, but failed to take their gold with them.

When Louie and Oran reached Kenya, the gold-sealed letters helped them pass roadblocks on their way to visit Biola missionaries; and they were thrilled to see the work at Kijabe, where the church seated one thousand people and was thriving amid persecution.

Traveling in a dusty jeep toward the village of Kandora, they found the smoke of battle still clinging to the atmosphere. "The Mau Maus had just attacked the village. . . . By our stopping at the roadblock," Louie wrote, "we had just escaped being caught in the cross fire between the Mau Maus and British soldiers who were attempting to defend the village. . . . We saw over thirty bodies of Mau Maus lying

The hippo hunt. Front to back: Oran Smith, his son David, Louie, and Richard Dilworth.

221

along the road . . . [and] . . . witnessed schoolhouses which had
been burned and demolished [and] in which were charred remains of
little children."[1] The scenes moved Louie to prayer for Kenya.

He visited Biola missionaries at Khartoum, Doro, and every place
he could get to them; he refreshed their hearts and his.

In Tanganyika he dedicated a forty-five foot launch named the
Biola, which had been purchased by the students for the Africa
Inland Mission. During the ceremony, a choir of nationals sang, Biola graduates Richard Dilworth and Hamilton Morrow spoke, and
Louie officially presented the launch and led in a dedicatory prayer
that it might be the means of evangelizing many along the banks of
the river.

Louie wanted to provide meat for the nationals of the area and decided to shoot a hippopotamus for them. That led to one of the
funniest and most exciting experiences of all his journeys.

Dick Dilworth recounted that watery, mixed-up, hippo hunt. "Dr.
Talbot, Oran Smith, and I were in a dugout canoe, and they held the
two guns. The rest of the men were in the launch *Biola*. Although
they were supposed to keep at a distance, they found themselves
near the hippos, and Dr. Herbert Movius took a shot at them. One
of the hippos came toward us through the water, and Dr. Talbot
and Oran shouted, 'What'll we do?'

" 'Shoot!'

"Dr. Talbot shot my 375 Magnum rifle and hit about halfway between our canoe and the hippo. His second shot wasn't much better.
The hippo veered off about twenty feet away from us. I grabbed the
gun from Oran's frozen arm and shot the hippo as it headed into the
reeds.

"Dr. Talbot and Oran were then stationed in the canoe near where
the hippo disappeared. While Dave and I began cutting our way
through the reeds, we saw the hippo heading toward Dr. Talbot and
Oran in their canoe.

"I shouted, 'It's coming!'

"Dr. Talbot leaped out of the frail canoe toward a sturdy rock,
but missed. Holding his gun high, he tried desperately to scramble
up that slippery rock, splashing vainly in the water and tearing a
large hole in his trousers and scraping off some of his skin.

"The hippo had only gone out far enough to be deeper in the

With the chief of the Pygmies.

reeds. Dave, who was Oran's son, and I later located it, and he stepped on its back. The hippo raised up a bit, and then died.

"In the meantime, Louie had to clamber back into the canoe without tipping his fellow passenger into the water. After a while another hippo appeared and Oran, who now had his gun back again, got it with one shot.

"A rope was attached to the *Biola*, and both hippopotami were towed ashore. It was a happy occasion for the nationals who were hungry for meat, and a local subchief took charge of distributing it. We took home four fillets six feet long, three inches thick and six inches wide. What steak and hippoburgers!"

Louie had wanted to see Africa "in the raw," and with one leg of his soaking-wet trousers torn open and his flesh scratched by the rock, he was having part of his wish fulfilled. At the missionaries' bungalow, he took off his ripped trousers and handed them to Florence Dilworth. "These are for you to fix," he said. "I don't have another pair."

That evening as they were laughing over the events of the day, Louie said, "I've preached at the Church of the Open Door hundreds of times on brotherly love; but when you are in a canoe and a hippo's charging toward you, one certainly forgets all about brotherly love. At that moment, I didn't even know Oran was around."

Another day Louie was being filmed when a tsetse fly landed on the bald spot of his head. Because a carpenter at the station had died six months earlier from a bite, the missionaries became very concerned. Dr. Movius, who had been asked by Louie's wife to look after his health on the trip, ordered him to get into the car, but he replied, "Why not die with African sleeping sickness rather than from some civilized American germ?"

The tsetse fly continued its assault, and Louie must have given his guardian angel a headache that day.

There Louie also filmed shots of witchcraft; the shots have been called the most remarkable documentary movies of the subject ever taken. It was arranged for a witch doctor to reenact a typical ceremony, and Dick Dilworth described what happened:

"Supposing a little child to be ill, the witch doctor attempted a cure by making a sacrifice and incantations to the spirits of the child's ancestors. A ram, which ordinarily would have been brought by the child's parents, was slain by a spear and then skinned. A few pieces were roasted in the fire, and the rest was cooked and distributed to all present for a kind of feast. Meantime, the witch doctor built a little house for the spirits of the ancestors to appease them and make them stop tormenting the child. His expression was fearful as he worshiped before this little grass hut, setting the roasted bits of food before it.

"Then he said to the ancestral spirits, 'Laugh now. Accept our gift to you. Let the child get well.' Looking at the liver of the ram, he supposedly could tell by it whether someone living was responsible for the illness of the child. Usually the blame is fixed on someone living, and in this way thousands of people, especially elderly ones, have been driven away or killed."

Elephant dance of the Pygmies.

Louie makes a cross out of sticks as he presents the Gospel to a tribe in Nigeria.

Mr. Dilworth seized the opportunity to preach the Gospel to the gathered crowd of Africans. Taking the head of the ram in his hands, he told the people about the Lamb of God, the Lord Jesus Christ, who had shed His blood on Calvary for their sins.

"Never have I seen a sermon illustrated like that! I shall remember it to the end of my days," commented Louie.

Traveling onward, he described the landscape: "Africa is a beautiful country with its towering mountains, tumbling waterfalls, and blue lakes. It was not far from the gorgeous Congo Falls that I had the thrilling experience of 'shooting the rapids' in a dugout canoe. Although sometimes the boat would spin around in a circle, and my stomach with it, the young man managed to keep it under control."

At Adja, Louie met Biola graduates Mr. and Mrs. Harold Amstutz; their work among the lepers, their school, and a church filled to capacity every Sunday with two thousand people deeply moved Louie's heart.

"Some of our missionaries are performing labors which rank with those recorded in the book of Acts. . . . It is not a life full of thrills to be a missionary. It is more likely to be filled with heartaches, disappointment, sickness, and smells. Nevertheless, God has a wonderful reward laid up for those who at His command go into all the world to preach the gospel."

Louie and Oran hiked through dense forests to reach a village of pygmies. What a welcome they gave the two men! Like children the pygmies scampered about, and they soon asked Louie to take his gun and bring down some monkey meat for them. That day he killed fifteen large monkeys, which they immediately roasted, and Louie poured relished salt into each outstretched hand.

"They kept insisting that we stay with them forever," Louie wrote. "Of course, they were thinking of more monkeys! However, I found a great delight sitting around their fires until all hours of the night, talking with them through an interpreter about the things of God. . . . When we get to heaven, I trust that we'll have the privilege of introducing you to some of the dear little people of the jungle."

In a town of mud huts on the border of the Sahara Desert, Louie kept soaking his clothes and then putting them on wet just to keep cool. "I take off my hat to these missionaries," he commented. "These are God's *big* men and women."

Before leaving Africa, his gold-sealed letters opened for him the doors of the majestic palace of the sultan of Nigeria. "Beautiful oriental rugs and lion skins on the floor," he wrote, "reminded me of Arabian Nights. . . . It was worth the heat and sand just to be with this old boy. He and I became real pals."

Then Louie boarded a plane for Spain and home. He had spent four rugged months filming some of the most compelling and primitive scenes in the world. When Louie's pictures were shown in the Church of the Open Door, Mayor Poulson was among those who crowded out the auditorium, and three showings were necessary. Hundreds of churches were motivated, while many young people responded, "Here am I, Lord, send me!"

39

A CAMPUS FOR BIOLA

BIOLA STUDENTS were the springs in Louie's feet. He was a popular speaker at other colleges, and received the degree of Doctor of Laws from John Brown University. But as he saw the spacious campuses of other schools, he thought of the Biola students crowded into that downtown building with no campus but the streets of Los Angeles. For their health as well as their training, he felt that they needed better facilities.

On February 5, 1952, he wrote to Ray Myers, who was chairman of the board, and recommended a campus for Biola.

"I suggest that a committee be appointed consisting of yourself, Mr. Isaac, Mr. Allder, and Dr. Sutherland to look around for a suitable acreage for moving the Bible Institute. I have been impressed lately with the movement of other institutes to suitable quarters outside of the downtown area. . . . I recognize that there would be some difficulties in making such a move, but there would also be great and important advantages. I want us to do some real preliminary work in assembling information relative to such a move."

Ray put this suggestion on the back burner of his mind to simmer and made a note to look into the agreement with the Church of the Open Door, with whom Biola shared the building. Mr. Allder noted some vacant lands, but the matter was not pursued.

A few months after Louie had become chancellor and Dr. Sutherland president in 1953, they were having lunch with Ray Myers at the Jonathan Club. The men were discussing the new building to be erected on the parking lot owned by the school.

"What do you have in mind for the new building?" Ray asked Dr. Sutherland.

Dr. Sutherland then gave his suggestion for each of the thirteen floors, which, because of earthquakes, was the limited height at that time in Los Angeles.

At a Biola chapel ser-
vice, Louie officially
opens the campaign for
funds to develop the
new campus by pre-
senting Dr. Sutherland
with a savings certifi-
cate.

"Do you know how much you're talking about?" Ray asked.

"About one and a half million dollars."

Ray figured a bit and said, "Sam, you're about right. It would
cost a hundred thousand dollars a floor."

Ray was silent for a few moments as what Louie had suggested
about a campus came to mind, and he began figuring on the paper
doily in front of him. "Do you know, for one and a half million
dollars I could build a campus with all of the facilities and then
some that we could have in the downtown location."

Dr. Sutherland nearly shot out of his chair. "You could?"

Ray was emphatic: "Yes, I could."

"Let's go!" Dr. Sutherland almost shouted.

Louie had been silent during all the figuring, but this brought
him to life, and in his deep, sonorous tone he answered, "Yeah, let's
go!"

"That was the beginning of the campus," Dr. Sutherland commented. "We talked more about it and figured; and Dr. Talbot persuaded Russ Allder, and then he talked to other men on the board.
Then Dr. Talbot went out to the home of Mrs. Stewart and discussed it with her."

Mrs. Stewart had been very gracious and generous to the school,
and the board would hesitate to move ahead with such a tremedous
change without her approval.

Louie explained the crowded conditions in the downtown building and mentioned the lack of athletic facilities, and told her what
it would cost to put up a new building on the school's parking lot;

Contemplating the
school's future on the
new campus.

and she realized how true those things were. Then he suggested the
idea of a campus, what it would mean to the students, and how it
could develop into a tremendous future for Biola and fulfill in a
greater measure than ever before the vision and purpose of her
husband for Biola.

Mrs. Stewart was very interested, and then she replied, "I wonder
why we haven't done this before?"

Everyone was then united in the project. After viewing many
prospective sites, the board selected land in La Mirada, and the mon-
umental venture of the new campus began.

Back in 1945 when Dr. Sutherland had recommended that Biola
buy the parking lot across from the school, the board members had
hesitated. But Ray Myers had told them, "If you don't buy that lot,
I will, and a few years from now I'll sell it back to you at a much
higher price."

The school purchased the lot for $70,000, and it more than paid for itself in rentals. In 1954 it was sold, bringing in $500,000 to start the campus fund.

And then one of Louie's radio fans, who did not attend church, left to Biola an estate of four hundred thousand dollars.

Some of the acreage purchased in La Mirada was resold at a profit, and the thrilling process of turning groves of lemon, orange, and olive trees, a hay field, and two swamps into a beautiful college campus began.

Dr. Sutherland walked with Louie through the hay field, pointing out where they hoped to erect certain buildings; Louie answered, "Ah, Sam, this is great, this is great! Let's do it."

The three who had the vision and courage for the new campus: Louie, Ray Myers, and Dr. Sutherland.

Ray Myers and Mrs. Lyman Stewart watch as Louie turns a shovelful of dirt at the groundbreaking service for the new campus.

And Louie broadcast this over the radio: "While we are expand-
ing and going to have a greater Biola out there in La Mirada, let me
tell you that the doctrinal position of Biola stands today and will
continue to stand until the Lord Jesus Christ comes. You have a
part in this, my dear friend, and you will be doing something that
will meet the great need of making an impact for God in this day
when Communism and rationalism and spiritism are attempting to
take over.

"I pray God will let me live to see that campus in La Mirada completed."

Returning to Biola between his speaking tours, Louie felt that it
was a sacred privilege to turn a shovel of dirt when the ground
was broken for the new campus on May 26, 1957. Ray Myers and
Dr. Sutherland also took the shovel in hand in that hay field that
was to blossom with buildings, grass, and walkways for the thousands
of dedicated young people in the years to come.

The California sun sent down its rays of benediction on the three
thousand five hundred friends of Biola who gathered to consecrate
the ground. Among those who addressed them were Louie's long-

time friend Dr. Bob Shuler, who represented pastors, and missionary Dick Hillis, who spoke for the alumni. Louie reviewed what God had wrought for Biola, and Dr. Sutherland outlined the future development and the challenge of future days.

Although the founders of Biola were with the Lord, everyone was thrilled to see relatives representing them. Mrs. Lyman Stewart was there, and T. C. Horton and Dr. R. A. Torrey were represented by their daughters.

Louie closed the groundbreaking ceremonies with prayer, "Our God and Father, we want to thank Thee for the privilege of holding for a little while the torch of testimony for Christ that was once held by such great men. We pray that this torch may burn brighter over the years, and we ask that the erection of these buildings on this campus may prove to be a greater testimony for the Lord Jesus Christ than Biola has ever known."

As building after building raised its red brick walls toward the skies, some called it "the miracle campus." Funds came for buildings in memory of dedicated servants of the Lord, more bequests of estates came in from Louie's radio listeners just as the money was needed, and with it all, there were smaller gifts that molded together into God's provision, as Biola remembered its pledge not to go into debt. Louie gave a five thousand dollar savings certificate and had the board cut his salary by $424 per month. And there was a gift of $16.44 from the children of the Calvary Baptist Church of Whittier who wanted to have a share in training missionaries.

Louie was glad to leave the developing of the campus and the structuring of Biola's academic program in Dr. Sutherland's efficient, capable hands; he himself continued his radio ministry, speaking engagements, and film showings in churches across the country.

During that time Louie attended the Billy Graham crusade in New York City at Madison Square Garden. Planned for six weeks starting in May of 1957, it lasted for sixteen weeks; it filled the Garden, jammed an open-air meeting on Wall Street, overspread Yankee Stadium with one hundred thousand people inside and twenty thousand outside, and crowded Times Square with from one hundred sixty thousand to two hundred thousand people. Over two million attended the crusade, with 61,148 decisions for Christ.

While he was there, Louie spoke over the radio: "This is Louis T. Talbot greeting you from New York City, where I am the personal guest of Billy Graham at the greatest evangelistic crusade ever held in modern times. . . .

"At a luncheon in the Commodore Hotel, the special guests included New York's leading businessmen, industrialists, bankers, newspaper editors, senators, congressmen, and several ambassadors from foreign countries. Billy Graham spoke on the significance of world movements in the light of prophecy and presented Christ as the only hope of the world. He concluded with a terrific appeal to those leaders of New York's industry and political life to link their lives with Christ and use their influence for Him. I'm sure that company present never received a greater challenge.

"Then last night at the Madison Square Garden, I had the honor of sitting on the platform with Billy Graham, and Cliff Barrows introduced me to that great multitude of people. The singing of the choir made one think of heaven, and Billy's message on Satan and his approach to the people of the twentieth century solemnized

Daniel Rose accepts Louie's invitation to provide for the building of a library for the school.

every heart and every life. At the close of the message literally hundreds of people, young, middle-aged, and those advancing in life, just streamed down the aisles to accept Christ.

"I got to bed at 3:00 A.M. because I met so many old friends and graduates of Biola at the close of the service. I'll be on the radio again Friday morning and will tell you more about it, so until then God bless you all."

Upon Louie's return to California, he took meetings up and down the coast; he delighted his audiences in many ways, but never more than at the North Long Beach Brethren Church, of which Biola graduate, the Reverend George Peek, was the pastor.

The new sanctuary seating eleven hundred people was packed, and Louie was the dedicatory speaker. "He was really fired up that day," recalled Dr. Peek, "and about fifteen minutes along in his message, when he was pouring it on for all he was worth, Dr. Talbot suddenly stopped, and there was a brief moment of silence. His dentures had flown right out of his mouth."

Quick as a wink, Louie grabbed them in mid air, slipped them back into place, and commented, "Babe Ruth couldn't have done a better job than that." While the congregation gasped and chuckled, he went right on with his sermon as if nothing had happened.

But he noticed that all the youngsters in the front rows were staring up at him in awe and expectation. Pausing for a moment, he smiled down at them, "Now you boys and girls might as well relax because I'm not going to do it again." Laughter rippled through the audience, but Louie went right on with his sermon; he caught them all up in the fervor of his message.

Traveling by train to a meeting in San Jose, Louie slept in an upper berth. When he arrived early in the morning, he quickly dressed and disembarked, but while walking along the street, he realized that his shoes felt a bit sloppy. Looking down, he said to his host, "My word! These are not my shoes."

In the meantime, the man in the lower berth, who was on the way to his wedding, struggled in vain to put on shoes that were too small. His bride-to-be met the train, and he had to greet her in his stocking feet.

The cooperative railway official arranged for each man to get his own shoes back, and Louie sent the embarrassed bridegroom a wedding present.

Looking over the campus grounds, Louie comments, "I say, Sam, this is great!"

Eugene Poole often drove Louie up the Pacific coast on his speaking tours and took care of necessary details. But one day when Mr. Poole was fussing over keeping things in order, Louie commented, "Gene, if you always put everything in order, after a while you get in a rut!"

The ocean fascinated Louie when he was not seasick on a boat. He held some meetings in San Luis Obispo, so he drove over with Eugene Poole to watch powerful waves excavate caves in the fortresslike Morro Rock. There were large signs warning people not to go on the north side, where people have been dashed against the rock or thrown into the caves by the rushing water.

Although Gene pleaded with him not to go out beyond the signs, Louie pressed onward, saying to Gene, "It thrills me to see how God pours so much power and thunderous sound into those waves."

An eager Louie and a reluctant Gene ventured toward the forbidden north side, only to see coming a huge wave, which looked to them "about thirty feet high." They moved away as fast as they could, but became soaking wet.

When Gene woke up the next morning, Louie and the car were gone. Gene did not have to guess; he knew where Louie must have gone. After a while, a dripping Louie with a glowing face returned. He had made it around the north side of Morro Rock. The evening's newspaper carried a front-page story of a couple who had done just that, but a wave had swept them under the water into the caves, and life was over for them.

The tremendous force, majesty, and power of those waves exploding against that forbidden rock did to Louie's soul something that drew him back a second time in spite of the danger.

What was it that made him seemingly fearless in facing those killer waves on the north side of Morro Rock? Was it the same thing that took him into the guerrilla warfare of the Malayan jungles, where some soldiers feared to tread?

In regard to his deepest feelings, Louie could sometimes be a very private man. One reason may have been his unshakable belief, which he expressed many times, that man is immortal until God's time to take him. That time had come for his Taud.

40

"IS ALL MY WORK DONE?"

WHEN TAUD first realized the seriousness of her illness, she cried a little and then said to her daughter Audrey, "Daddy and I have been preaching Romans 8:28 for over forty years, and now is our opportunity to show that we believe it, 'And we know that all things work together for good to them that love God, to them who are the called according to his purpose.'" •

Having settled that, Taud accepted her condition with the same serenity that characterized her whole life. Cancer crept through her body, causing two major surgeries, hips that broke, two years in a wheelchair, months in the hospital, and pain that pierced the hearts of her family.

She had loved her home and had always filled it with the best of life. Hospitality clothed her like a generous garment. When the Talbots lived in the Midwest, Taud's sister Sammy and Louie's sister Gladys lived with them; in Taud's more spacious California home, the visiting nieces from Australia, Jean and Sylvia, found a place of happiness, fun, and refreshment. During some of the time that Louie was away on speaking tours or missionary journeys, Taud's mother, father, and brother shared her home. Someone said she never had a selfish thought in her life.

Delighting in helping her grandchildren appreciate and create good music, she taught Elisabeth piano from a wheelchair right up to the last time she went to the hospital.

Taud wrote in a family memory book, "These years of my life have been full of work, play, sacrifice, peace, joy, and blessing."

When friends came to comfort her at the hospital, they found her cheerful and left with a benediction in their own hearts. Too weak to hold a book in her hands, she used a thin, paperback hymnal to read her favorite hymns.

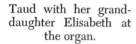

Taud with her grand-
daughter Elisabeth at
the organ.

Her acceptance of the pain that racked her was like a comforting blanket around the family she loved and the grandchildren to whom she was "Mammer."

As she lingered before the gates of heaven, one last act of thoughtfulness was asked of her in a letter from Mrs. Collins, a member of Louie's radio audience.

"A little over a year ago my five-year-old son, Monty Collins, went home to heaven. I know by the sure Word of God that he is with the Lord, happy and real, and I surely will go to him some day.

"But since you will be there so soon, will you please just look him up and tell him who you are and what a wonderful thing it is for him to be in heaven, and give him my love.

"Whenever his playmates came to the house at eleven o'clock, Monty would say, 'Don't you go in there because Mummy is listening to Mr. Talbot' (on the radio)."

Louie came back from Taud's bedside that evening and read chapters twenty-one and twenty-two of Revelation. His eyes paused on the verses, "And God shall wipe away all tears from their eyes; and there shall be no more death, neither sorrow, nor crying, neither shall there be any more pain: for the former things are passed away. And he that sat upon the throne said, Behold, I make all things new. . . . And they shall see his face."

Taud's last words to her daughter Betty were, "Is all my work done?"

And when that time came on February 22, 1960, the Lord took Louie's helpmate of forty-four years to her heavenly home.

When he was able to share it with his radio audience, Louie spoke these words:

> The Bride eyes not her garment,
>   But her dear Bridegroom's face;
> [She] will not gaze at glory
>   But on [her] King of grace.
> Not at the crown He giveth
>   But on His pierced hand,
> The Lamb is all the glory
>   Of Immanuel's land.
>
> [ANNE R. COUSIN]

41

LOUIE WALKS ALONE

WITH HIS WIFE and home gone, Louie seemed to be at loose ends and drew closer to his daughters and their families. When his grandchildren were tiny, Louie often greeted them with a humorous facial expression and a "Boo." Hearing his voice over the radio, they would point at it with puzzled faces and ask, "Boo?" It became the family nickname for him.

Betty's husband, Jerry, had been studying for his doctorate at the University of Southern California and was asked to teach at the University of Karachi. It was decided that "Boo" should go with them.

The travelers stopped en route for a family reunion, and the Australian clan felt caught up in a whirlwind when Louie arrived with Betty, Jerry, and their lively children, Shirley and David. Leaving Boo there to enjoy his favorite prawns for a few months, Jerry and his family went on to get settled in Karachi.

But after six wonderful weeks in Australia, Louie sent Betty a cablegram.

> HAD MY FILL OF PRAWNS   AUSTRALIANS EXHAUSTED
> FROM VISIT   ARRIVING KARACHI QUANTAS FLIGHT
> 307 FIVE PM FRIDAY JANUARY SEVEN   HEAPS OF LOVE
> BOO

In her own delightful way Betty shared the excitement of Louie's message:

"Waving my father's cablegram in the air, I called through the house, 'Hey, everyone, a cablegram from Boo. He's coming Friday.'

"At once doors were flung open. 'Did you say Friday, Mom?' Dave asked in unbelief.

" 'That's great!' Shirley laughed, 'but I thought he wasn't coming until March!'

"Jerry came in grinning, 'That guy's a regular genie. You never know when he'll show up. But can we be ready for him that soon?'

"Jerry was addressing me, but our cook Yaqoob stepped forward, his usually pleasant face twisted into a scowl.

"'No!' he complained. 'I not being ready that soon. I needing time, Mem Sahib. Windows not washed; guest quarters not ready; baking not done; food not bought. I not even knowing what Mem Sahib's father liking to eat.'

"'Don't worry, Yaqoob, my father will never notice dirty windows—he'll be much too interested in exploring the bazaars and meeting everyone. I'll make a list of his favorite foods and hang it on the kitchen bulletin board.'

"Yaqoob gave me an unfathomable look and shook his head. 'Too much work,' he complained. 'Not enough time.'

"'Quit worrying, Yaqoob,' I repeated. 'I'll help you.'

"'How long your father staying?'

"'Maybe a month, maybe a year.'

"Yaqoob frowned. 'I thinking I not liking working for two sahibs. Too much bossing. Too much "Yaqoob do this. Yaqoob do that." I may quitting.'

Leaving for Australia and Pakistan with his daughter Betty and grandchildren Shirley and David.

Betty and Jerry.

" 'Give it a try, Yaqoob,' Jerry interrupted. 'I think you'll like Sahib Talbot.'

" 'Sahib Talbot, Sahib Talbot,' Yaqoob muttered as he returned to his work, and we wondered if he were practicing my father's name or just complaining.

"At the market there was a din of voices and the air was seasoned with Eastern spices. It also bore the telltale scent of unwashed bodies and dirty clothes. Gnats and flies buzzed around my head as I surveyed a scene that was a kaleidoscope of color.

"I paused at a colorful display of papaya, mangoes, bananas, and eggplant piled on shelves tiered one above the other to form a giant pyramid against the market wall. A barefooted vendor clutched a heavy, knotted rope that dangled from the ceiling. I gave him my order, 'Up there,' I said, pointing, 'some of those mangoes.'

"The vendor pulled the rope taut, took a few running steps and swung himself through the air onto the top shelf. From this vantage point he pitched mangoes to my coolie. I ordered other vegetables and fruits, as the vendor swung from shelf to shelf.

"At the meat section, I said, 'I'll have some beef undercut.' The butcher grabbed a giant portion of beef and held it as if he were about to play a cello solo. Bracing the lower half of the meat between his feet, he sawed off a roast, disappointing a swarm of horseflies by wrapping my purchase in a newspaper.

"Yaqoob stepped through the kitchen door as I drove in. 'Mem

Sahib, you not forgetting to make list to hand in kitchen telling me what your father liking to eat?'

" 'No, Yaqoob, I'll do it now.' Hastily I listed a few foods—fish, meatloaf, roast beef, vegetables, pie, cake, ice cream. I tacked the list to the kitchen bulletin board.

"Friday came, and long before 5:00 P.M. we were at the airport gate. When Boo's plane landed, it was easy to spot him as he came through the doorway of the jet and began to walk down the ramp—the balding head with its silver fringe of hair, the broad grin—trademark of the cheerful mood that always seemed to envelop him like a cloak, the waving hat and then the shouted greeting, with Australian accent hurled our way, 'I sigh' (I say) 'Helloooo.'

"Yaqoob met me nervously at the door. 'Dinner not ready yet. Maybe in half hour, Mem Sahib,' he whispered.

"Half an hour gave us just enough time to show my father around the compound and introduce him to our neighbors before a perspiring, agitated Yaqoob announced, 'Dinner ready, Mem Sahib.'

"I had not planned the dinner menu. I spent little time in Yaqoob's kitchen, having learned early that my presence there only confused him. Under close supervision, Yaqoob became rattled, overly anxious to please, and sometimes made mistakes with the simplest recipe. Left to himself he was a creative artist. Yaqoob was so competent in the kitchen, I never dreamed he would misunderstand and think the foods I had listed for him were to be served all at one meal.

"We sat at the table aghast as course followed course: fried fish, French fries, and vegetables, which we ate with zest, followed by a crusty meat loaf, surrounded with more potatoes and vegetables swimming in rich, brown gravy. By the time we had finished the first course we were stuffed. By the time we finished the second—miserable! We were just pushing back our chairs to leave the table when Yaqoob appeared again—this time carrying a platter of roast beef and Yorkshire pudding. We exchanged stunned glances, but afraid of offending our friend and perhaps losing our most important servant, we valiantly attacked the roast.

" 'I swear I'm dying,' Jerry groaned. 'I don't even have room for an Alka Seltzer.'

" 'Shhh, Yaqoob will hear you,' I whispered. 'I know what's happened—that list I gave him—he's prepared the whole list! This means he'll be back any minute with the first of several desserts.'

" 'Oh no!' everyone gasped. But I had barely spoken the words when Yaqoob entered the dining room and set before us a rich, thickly frosted chocolate cake—which was followed by ice cream that tasted like cosmetics since our creative cook had flavored it with tincture of roses.

" 'You're not eating, Mem Sahib,' Yaqoob observed, looking at my unfinished, melting ice cream. 'You not liking rose ice cream?'

" 'Yaqoob—you prepared too much food,' I said at last, choking into my table napkin. 'We simply can't eat all of this.'

" 'But Mem Sahib,' Yaqoob protested, 'you hanging list of foods your father wanted on kitchen bulletin board. I only following orders. Mem Sahib, I sorry but cooking for two sahibs too much work. I must quitting.' Yaqoob shuffled despondently back to the kitchen.

" 'He doesn't understand,' I said. 'I'd better go talk to him.'

" 'No, let me go!' My father flashed his broad smile, 'I'm the extra sahib he's worrying about. I want to get acquainted with him anyway. I'll be right up.'

"Boo left the table and went to the kitchen while we went upstairs. After forty-five minutes, Jerry said, 'You'd better go down and check on him, Betty. Maybe he forgot we came up here.'

"I found my father and Yaqoob sipping tea together in the kitchen. They sat facing each other, their chairs tilted back, their feet propped on a high, three-legged stool placed between them. The soles of my father's polished leather shoes rested casually against the soles of Yaqoob's open-toed sandals.

"When I entered the kitchen, Yaqoob sprang to his feet smiling. 'Your father wanting only *one* meat at dinner, Mem Sahib,' he said, obviously relieved. 'Not too much work after all.'

"I looked at Boo, who was pulling himself from his chair. 'I'm tired, Betts,' he said. 'I'm going to my room and unpack. See you in the morning, Yaqoob. We'll visit some more then.'

" 'Goodnight, Boo Sahib,' beamed Yaqoob.

" 'Boo Sahib!' I laughed, after my father left us. 'Is *that* what you're going to call him?'

" 'Yes, Mem Sahib. Boo Sahib thinking "Sahib Talbot" too much stiff. We deciding "Boo Sahib" better name.'

" 'Well—if that's what he wants,' I said, not realizing that as my father collected friends, that absurd name would stick and he would be "Boo Sahib" to Pakistanis, American personnel, missionaries, and even a couple of ambassadors.

"'Is everything all right now, Yaqoob?' I asked as I turned to leave the kitchen.

"'Yes, Mem Sahib. Everything fine.'

"'You'll try working for two sahibs for awhile then?'

"'Yes, Mem Sahib. I thinking Boo Sahib okay!' Then softly but emphatically he added, 'I liking dat kind of mans.'"

Louie could be seen almost anywhere in Karachi—teaching a Bible class at one of the churches, or riding on the back of Elmer Fricke's motorcycle to the Arabian Sea for some prawns. Elmer was a Biola graduate, and Louie often preached to his congregation for him on Sundays. By tipping the guard, the two men found their way into the Tower of Silence, a sacred shrine of the Parsees. These people are Zoroastrians and worship the four elements, fire, air, water, and earth.

These Parsees cannot bury their dead, because it would desecrate the earth; neither can they cremate, because it would defile the fire; they cannot bury at sea, for it would contaminate the water; and they cannot pollute the air. The bodies are put in an open tower, where vultures consume all the flesh in ten minutes.

Louie made friends with almost everyone he met, and he enjoyed visiting the different churches in Karachi. One day Betty found him sitting in a pew of a church; he was copying down this hymn, which he recognized as one of his mother's favorites. Betty had it hand printed and framed for him. Here is one of the verses:

> I thank Thee, too, that all our joy
>   Is touched with pain,
> That shadows fall on brightest hours,
>   That thorns remain;
> So that earth's bliss may be our guide,
>   And not our chain.

ADELAIDE PROCTER

The Muslim people challenged Louie's heart, and missionaries invited him to rough it on a trip to Afghanistan; but he was scheduled to join Oran Smith and Dr. Feinberg in conducting a tour of Palestine and other countries. He joined Oran at Cairo in April.

Walking again the land the Lord had trod, Louie felt refreshed.

As pastor of Hinson
Memorial Baptist
Church.

On returning to Los Angeles, he was eager to see how the new campus was developing. Biola College had been accredited on February
24, 1961, by the Western College Association, and Dr. Sutherland
showed him buildings completed and others under construction.
As they watched the students, Louie's heart was thrilled.

"I say, Sam, I never dreamed it would be anything like this." He
was vitally interested in every aspect, but was still glad the burden
of the academics and construction was on the shoulders of Dr. Sutherland and Ray Myers.

When the Hinson Memorial Baptist Church of Portland, Oregon,
was looking for a new minister, Dr. William Kerr recommended they
ask Louie to serve for six months as interim pastor. He knew the
church well, and began his service there on November 26, 1961.

"The church was at a low ebb," according to Leona Nettler, "and
we lit our little lights from his big one. When he walked into the
church, the lights really went on. There was a lifting of spirits, a
raising of our sights."

"His humor had a way of reducing tensions at all times," commented the assistant pastor, Warren Steenson. "When Dr. Talbot
came, the potential schism that was in the church healed, and the
church forgot its troubles.

"World missions were brought to our door, evening crowds increased dramatically, and contributions grew. The old fire of the
pulpit genius forcefully came through. His sonorous voice made his

sermons sound as if they were coming from the pipe organ. When he was preaching, his was an unforgettable, forceful voice for God.

"His preparation for preaching was anxious moments of pacing the floor until it was time to deliver the sermon. To bring him from his study to the pulpit was like bringing a caged lion to the pulpit and then releasing him." Visitors came to the church by the scores, and many walked down the aisles to the altar to accept Christ.

No matter what the situation, Louie always had an answer. When asked to autograph a book for a prominent member of his new congregation, he wrote "To my good friends," but when it was called to his attention that he had written the wrong names, he promptly scratched it all out and wrote "To my *real* friends" and put in the proper names. The book was treasured the more for it.

Arrangements were made for Louie to live with Henry Copenhagen, a widower in his late eighties, who had a spacious home that he kept in meticulous order, that is, until Louie moved in with him.

Breaking ground for Talbot Theological Seminary. Left to right: Louie, Mrs. Ray Myers, Ray Myers, Dr. Charles Feinberg, and Dr. Sutherland.

The two men ate many meals out, but Louie's gourmet instincts tempted him to do some cooking himself. Cleaning up the kitchen, however, was another matter. Henry's daughters came in every week and put the whole house back in shape.

As chancellor of Biola, Louie came back to the campus for important events, such as giving the address at the ground breaking for Myers Hall, the key structure of Talbot Theological Seminary. Ray Myers turned the first shovelful of dirt for this fine building he was constructing in memory of his daughter Nancy, and in which he included an apartment for the chancellor.

The people at Hinson Church were enjoying Louie's ministry so much that efforts to secure a permanent pastor slowed down. He was in popular demand as a speaker; and although some of the officials of the church tried to discourage his accepting outside speaking engagements, he was on the go night and day. He did not give a thought to his health, and Mr. Steenson observed that Louie's health was deteriorating.

Then one Sunday morning in the prayer room just five minutes before the service, Louie said to Mr. Steenson, "I don't feel well. Can you take the service?" Louie went home to Henry's and rested.

Although a slight slurring developed in Louie's speech, he continued his ministry until one Saturday night in June. He phoned Mr. Steenson that he was not well, would not be able to preach the next day, and felt that his ministry was over. He wanted to drive home to California.

Bob Nettler arranged for the youth director to drive Louie to his daughter's home near Los Angeles. Audrey was a registered nurse, and with her care he began feeling better.

But the first of September he woke up in the middle of the night with intense pain and was rushed to the hospital and into surgery. He was there almost three weeks, and later complications developed, causing him to be quite ill.

On October 10 he wrote Bob Nettler, "I am making progress although I still spend the major part of my time in bed. In fact, I am dictating this lying on my back. But yesterday the doctors found that some of the setbacks have been due to an infection, and they are working on that with antibiotics now, so I expect to be on my feet pretty soon. However, I have been warned that I cannot expect to take any preaching appointments until sometime next year."

Louie recuperated at the home of his daughter Audrey, shown here
with her husband, the Reverend Charles Svendsen, and their children
(seated: Elisabeth; standing: Charles, Mary, and John).

For his seventy-third birthday that month he received about three
thousand cards.

But Louie had remarkable powers of recovery, and in February he
was back up at Hinson. He preached a couple of Sundays and in
March helped install their new pastor, Dr. Herbert Anderson. The
church gave Louie a warm and loving farewell.

Louie then took off for Australia, to visit his family there, to see
his old haunts, and to stroll along its sandy beaches and feel his
former strength return. He needed something to help him start life
anew when he returned; and his friends realized he needed a whole
team to keep him in order—a chauffeur and valet, a cook and housekeeper, a nurse and constant companion, a counselor and friend, and
someone to give him tender loving care. To sum it all up in two
words, a wife. Many were suggested to him, but when a missionary
had to come home from India because of an eye condition, Louie felt
that the Lord had chosen for him.

42

A WEDDING IN LIFE'S EVENING

WHEN I FIRST MET Louie, we were both standing in baptismal waters. I was one of many baptized that night by the new pastor of the Church of the Open Door. We had been interviewed by a church committee, and it was a routine occasion for him that he never remembered as distinct from any other.

Thirty years later we were married. One evening when we were discussing that baptism with some friends, he winked at me as he turned to the group with a wry grin, "If I had known Carol then as I know her now, I would have held her under!"

It was in 1931, when Dr. Philpott was pastor, that I first started attending the Church of the Open Door. Mel Trotter came to hold evangelistic meetings.

"How about helping out in the choir this week, Carol, while Mel Trotter is preaching?" asked Frances Neilsen. "The regular choir is being increased for the meetings."

I was a student at Woodbury College, and I had a heavy study load; but I sang in the choir—I thought I was doing my bit for the church.

Then one Sunday night as people were coming down the aisles to the altar, and we were singing, "Just as I am without one plea, but that Thy blood was shed for me," I became conscious that God, the Creator of the universe, was speaking to my heart. Suddenly I seemed alone with Him, unaware of the three thousand people around me. I felt Him ask me to accept the Lord Jesus Christ as Saviour and to give Him my life for His service.

I shrank back. "No, not that. I've studied and planned a career in the business world. I can't give that up." As I struggled against God's call, I broke out in a cold sweat.

Then in my mind I saw Christ on that cross for me and caught just

250

a small glimpse of the eternal love that put Him there. It overwhelmed me, the height and depth and wonder of it all, and I
realized that there was nothing greater in all the world than the
love of God. My dream of business success changed into fading tin-
sel as I felt His love flow through me and overflow into tears of joy.
In that moment I was born again, a new creature in Christ Jesus.

It was the following year that Louie became pastor of the church.

While I was reading the book *Mother India*, the Lord laid a burden on my heart for the little girls and women of that land. To prepare for missionary service there, I entered Biola as a student and
worked my way through as secretary to Dr. Sutherland.

When teaching the book of Hebrews, he included among his as-
signments the writing of sermons; but he never gave any of the
papers a grade better than B +. He felt that none of the students
put in the right mixture of exposition and illustrations. One day Dr.
Sutherland told the students to write a sermon on "rest" as given in
Hebrews.

I had worked for a time as secretary to Miss Mildred Cook on
The King's Business magazine, and she often had me take down in
shorthand messages of the pastor and other noteworthy speakers.
I had in my file of transcribed sermons a short devotional message
Louie had given extemporaneously at the close of a musical program
by the Haven of Rest quartet.

I studied and wrote my own sermon for the assignment, but as a
joke I held my paper back and turned in Louie's short message on
the subject. It received a B +.

Going into Dr. Sutherland's office, I confessed. "Here's my own
paper I wrote for that assignment on 'rest,' but the one I turned in
was a sermon of Dr. Talbot's, and you gave it a B +." He nearly fell
out of his chair laughing.

Considering it too humorous to let pass, he sent Louie the material, a note of explanation, and the remark, "Why don't you attend
my class and learn how to write a good sermon?"

Walking through the church offices waving that manuscript in a
good-natured way, Louie called out to his staff, "*My* sermon, *my*
masterpiece, only a B +." Then he telephoned Dr. Sutherland, "I
say, Sam, where did you go to school? You don't know a good sermon when you see one."

The two men joked back and forth about it for days. When the church put on a birthday party for Louie, Jim Vaus took the manuscript and acted out the whole scene for the church members, much to the merriment of everyone.

Because I was planning to go as a missionary to India, I was among the seniors chosen by the school to speak on Louie's radio program.

That was the first time he heard my testimony, and thirty years later Louie told me how the earnestness of it had stirred him to deeper commitment in his own devotion to the Lord.

After finishing at Biola, I left for India; but I sailed right into a war. While our ship, the *President Grant*, was unloading freight in Manila, Pearl Harbor was bombed, war was declared, and I was soon captured by the Japanese as a prisoner of war.

Shortly after they put me in Los Banos Internment Camp, impetigo spread all over me. Isolated from the others for fear it would spread through the two thousand people in our camp, I had to hold out my coconut shell for someone to pour water into it when I was thirsty. I was the camp leper.

As I thought of the children of India with all their skin diseases and of the thousands of lepers, I understood what it was like to be repugnant to others, to have people shrink away from you, to have people not touch or come near you for fear of contamination, to walk alone. I realized my training was not completed when I graduated from Biola. God was putting me through His university.

When I had learned what He wanted me to know, the Lord sent help. An American nurse in the camp fomented the sores and secured some medicine; and missionaries Cae and Peter Paget hauled buckets of water to wash my clothes and my two filthy sheets. I started to get well.

As the years passed and we lived on meager portions of rice and what edible weeds we could gather, some of the elderly died of starvation, and my hands became numb from beriberi. The last entry in my prison diary was January 24, 1945, "Beriberi. Right hand and arm so numb can hardly write this."

I went to the bamboo barracks we used as a chapel and held out my numb hands to the Lord, struggling with Philippians 4:19, "My God shall supply all your need according to his riches in glory by Christ Jesus." I needed food.

Gradually I realized the verse did not say, "You will never be hungry." And then the multitudes of India seemed to pass before me; they were reaching out starving, numb hands for food. I shuddered and wept for them, and knew God had supplied my deepest need—a heart prepared to understand and serve India. I had graduated from another course in His university.

Then at dawn on February 23, 1945, we heard the roar of planes overhead; clouds of billowing parachutes floated down as the paratroopers dropped; and tanks crashed through the fences. War was all around us. The bamboo barracks caught fire, and we piled into tanks and fled.

It was one of the most spectacular rescues of the war: 2,146 of us were snatched from behind Japanese lines. No soldiers were ever braver, no Americans were ever prouder of their country, no one loved it more than we did that day. Our military forces brought us to the United States on a troop transport.

After three and a half years as a prisoner of war, I arrived home in a weakened, malnourished condition. Among other things, I had worms from eating weeds, and the birds seemed to spread this bit of news.

While walking down the sidewalk one day in front of Biola, I saw Dr. Sutherland and Louie sauntering along together. When they spotted me, I noticed them nudge one another, and then Louie asked, "I say, Carol, did you get rid of all the worms?"

Looking at the two men and the mischievous twinkle in their eyes, I answered, "All but two."

Louie was still laughing when he reached his office; and his secretary, Lela Armstrong, said everybody had to hear all about my worms.

While regaining my health, I took more courses at Biola to get a degree, and for a time taught missions classes there. Graduation was to be in June. While preparing the program, Louie said to his secretary, "I'd like to liven things up a bit. Commencement exercises are too cut and dried."

They discussed it for a time, and then Louie came up with an idea, "Let's have Carol Terry give some of her war experiences. And don't tell her ahead of time. If she's called on without warning, the shock might make the testimony more lively and spontaneous."

Feeling that it was not fair to ask me to address four thousand people without preparation, Lela told me about the conversation.

"In that case," I replied, "He will be the one to get the shock."

The chancellor brings smiles wherever he goes.

When Louie changed my tassel, he was the one who received the shock.

In those days, the president changed the tassels of the graduates receiving degrees, so I gave my mortarboard to Louie's radio technicians, Earl Hunter and Bob Smith. They placed two wires in the tassel; they then attached the two wires to a small condenser, to which they gave an electric charge.

However, the day before graduation, Louie decided to upset routine a little more by having Ray Myers, the chairman of the board, change the tassels.

It was then that I told Dr. Sutherland the whole story, and he phoned Louie, "Dr. Talbot, those students have been looking forward all these years to your changing their tassels. It would be a shame to disappoint them on graduation day."

"Well, all right, Sam, if it means that much to them, I'll do it."

But since Louie was known for changing his mind on the spur of the moment, under my graduation robe I carried a pair of pliers as well as the condenser. If Mr. Myers changed the tassels, I planned to cut the wire and take the shock myself.

During the program, I was called upon to tell my war story as a surprise testimony. I did not disappoint anyone, but when I later marched across that platform and Louie's hand changed my tassel, he was the one who received the shock.

Lela explained it all to him later, and he accepted it with his great sense of humor. Now, however, the students change their own tassels!

In November of 1946 I sailed again for India and the Ramabai Mukti Mission, where thousands of children and women have found refuge and hope, medical care and education, and above all, our Lord.

During the sixteen years I served there, it was my privilege to be superintendent during the centenary year of Pandita Ramabai's birth, when revival swept through our midst under the ministry of

Dr. Akbar Abdul Haqq, who had interpreted for Billy Graham in New Delhi. Out of the two thousand attending our meetings, seven hundred accepted Christ. As we followed up with meetings under Augustine Salins, God worked deeply in the hearts of the believers. Backsliders and quarrelers were restored to fellowship with each other and with the Lord, and there was a renewed zeal for evangelism. For me, it meant a closer and deeper walk with God than I had ever known before.

But all during the years there, I had trouble with my eyes. Trucks traveling down a dirt road through our compound enveloped us in swirling dust, and my eyes were sensitive to its germs, which infected and filled my eyes with pus. The Indian doctors treated me for trachoma. Minor surgery on my eyelids was performed in India, England, and America—nine times in all.

When my eyes were so filled with pus that I could not work, the executive secretary of the mission suggested that I return to America and be a representative of the Ramabai Mukti Mission. That would free my eyes from the infectious dust and allow me to continue my ministry for the Lord within the mission fellowship.

I asked for one more opportunity to get help, and flew to Kulu Valley in the Himalaya Mountains. There an American surgeon was operating on the eyes of the Tibetans who had fled when the Chinese Communists invaded their country. There was no hospital. They were in tents, and I stayed in a mud hut, but the hands of Dr. Victor Rambo were among the most skilled in the world.

It was June 6 to 13, 1962, that I was in Kulu having surgery with the Tibetans, and it was that very same week Louie found himself unable to preach at the Hinson Memorial Baptist Church, in Portland. His health was deteriorating, and his memory was affected, perhaps because of a slight stroke. He was driven to his daughter's in La Canada, and surgery followed: I returned to the mission in India for continued service. In God's time and provision, we were to care for each other.

Dr. Rambo warned me to stay out of India's plains during the dusty six months. When the hot, dry season of 1963 approached, it was arranged for me to bring one of our orphan girls to America for adoption by a minister and his family in Boston.

Going on to Los Angeles, I went to the well-known eye surgeon Dr. Wendell Irvine. After completing his examination, he said to

At eighty years of age, Louie still causes hearts to smile and to learn as we chat in front of Talbot Theological Seminary with students Peggy Sanders Campbell of Biola College and Bob Thune of the Seminary.

Previous page: Golden wig and plumed headdress, New Guinea
Photo by L. H. Barnard in *Plumes and Arrows* by Colin Simpson

me, "I am not asking you to give up your work, but to give it up in India. So long as you are in that area, you will have this problem with your eyes." He then wrote the mission board that I should not return to India.

Although I was grateful that my sight had been spared, that in America my eyes would be free of that chronic infection and pus, and that there would be no more surgery, I felt that as far as my emotions were concerned this was one of the most difficult times I had known. A statement of Louie's I had heard years ago in one of his sermons came to my mind, "Never question God's providences."

I had to pray, "Lord, help me to trust You in this situation as I trusted You in the prisoner-of-war camp twenty years ago."

I could not bring myself to resign from the Ramabai Mukti Mission. After some months of taking meetings on the East Coast for the mission, I settled down in Los Angeles to fulfill its request that I prepare my children's stories for publication in book form. I spent almost a year on that project.

In the meantime, Louie's health had improved. He was taking limited speaking engagements and living in his old suite of rooms in downtown Biola. His secretary, Betty Bruechert, related this incident:

"I had an electric percolator in which we often made coffee in the office. When leaving on vacation, I said, 'Dr. Talbot, you can use this while I'm gone, if you like.'

" 'Well, that's fine.'

"But when I returned and started making coffee, I noticed that when I put water in the percolator, the water became tinged with blue. I scrubbed it and boiled water in it, but nothing seemed to do any good. After a while I asked him, 'Dr. Talbot, did you use the percolator while I was gone?'

" 'Oh yes, Betty. I used it for lots of things—boiling water, and doing my laundry.'

" 'You what?'

" 'I boiled my socks in it and they came out fine.'

" 'Were they blue socks?'

" 'All my socks are blue.'

"When telling my friends about this, I assured them I never used that percolator again!"

During that period of time, Dr. and Mrs. Kenneth Jacques drove

There was a new suite of rooms for Louie at Talbot Theological
Seminary.

Louie on Wednesday nights to Dr. Jack MacArthur's church in Bur-
bank, where Louie gave a series of lectures on his big chart, *God's
Plan of the Ages.* "He was a biblical encyclopedia," commented Mrs.
Jacques, "and while we were riding in the car, we often asked him
questions regarding the Bible. Each time he answered, his fingertips tapped the windshield. When we had our car washed, we
wouldn't let them wash the windshield at that place, because each
fingerprint represented the answer to a Bible question."

Observing Louie in action, Dr. Jacques commented, "Though he
was sometimes forgetful in other things, when he was teaching the
Word of God, his mind was sharp and clear. And though there
might be three thousand people wanting to greet him, when Louie
was talking to someone, that person had all his attention."

Then one day Louie saw me walking in front of Biola, and he
thought I looked worn and thin. "Are you having enough to eat?"
he asked me.

I nodded in the affirmative.

"Open your purse and show me exactly how much money you have."

A bit embarrassed, I opened my purse. He took me to lunch!

Louie had walked alone now for almost four years, and he started taking me to dinner. One evening he added something to it, "I'm going to the Griffith Observatory to watch a lecture on the stars. Would you care to come along?" We began watching the same lecture night after night, as the stars tranferred themselves from the skies to our eyes.

We were to be married on the Biola campus in the home of the president, but when Louie changed the date several times, Mrs. Sutherland smiled, "Well, I'll keep the front room dusted."

Louie could be a very private man; and as he made Taud wear her engagement ring on a chain around her neck, so he would not let me wear mine. On the day before the wedding, his daughter Betty arrived from Denver. He was going out with his two daughters while I was busy with wedding preparations. As they were leaving my room, I asked him to come back a minute. "Since we are being married tomorrow, may I wear my engagement ring today?"

"Yeah, sure," he answered in his bighearted way and started off with Audrey and Betty.

"Will you come back a minute?"

Looking surprised, he returned.

"Will you put it on for me?"

"My land! Can't you put it on yourself?"

"No."

He placed it on the appropriate finger, embraced me, and although he was seventy-four years old, went happily off with his daughters like a schoolboy excited about a first date.

For a few moments I stopped all my bridal activities and gazed at that diamond ring on my left hand. Possibly the greatest happiness that can come to a woman was mine at that moment. The most wonderful man I had ever known in my life had just placed his ring on my finger. It was a sacred moment.

Because the Lord had become supreme to me, only one whose reverence for Him was greater than mine could have become my heart and life. Louie was that one. Although he had a tremendous capacity for enjoying life, the core of the man was his deep reverence

A wedding in life's evening.

for the Lord and his unshakable faith. Of his many qualities,
Louie's reverence and faith were what I admired most. I also loved
his spirit of tenderness. These lines by Martha Snell Nicholson
flowed through my mind:

> We are to be married [tomorrow].
> He is my ecstasy and radiance,
> My dreams,
> My laughter and my song.
>
> .   .   .   .
>
> He is the shade of poplars
> Growing beside still waters.
> He is peace in the heart of deep woods.
>
> He is integrity and truth
> And unshaken uprightness;
> He is delicacy of thought and perception,
>
> .   .   .   .
>
> He is the moon and stars,
> The great round sun at break of day,
> The free wide spaces of the plain and sea.
>
> .   .   .   .
>
> He is a man, strong.
> He is a lover, compelling, ardent,
> He is as tender as my mother
> He is the strength of my limbs,
> The beat of my heart,
> The wings of my spirit.
>
> .   .   .   .
>
> We are to be married [tomorrow.]
>
> .   .   .   .
>
> If all this ecstasy is ours on earth,
> What will it mean to be the Bride of Christ!

Before resuming my honeymoon packing, I knelt in worship before
the Lord who had brought me through many storms and now encircled me with His rainbow of blessing.

On the wedding day, February 5, 1964, Louie's daughter Betty
played hymns and the guests stood for the wedding. Dressed in an

ensemble of candlelight-pink brocade, I entered the room on the arm of my brother George, who whispered, "Slow down." In my hands was a small white Bible with ribbon streamers. Audrey was my attendant, and her husband, Charles, stood with Louie. After Dr. Sutherland performed the ceremony, Dr. Jack MacArthur led in prayer.

But Mrs. Sutherland had done more than "keep the front room dusted." There were floral arrangements, and the bridal table was enhanced by little lights illuminating silver bells surrounding the wedding cake and refreshments.

As we left for a short honeymoon, I knew life with Louie would be exciting and thought I loved him with all my heart, but that love was to reach a depth I never dreamed was humanly possible. He was to become more than life to me.

43

"FOR THIS I WAS BORN"

AFTER A BRIEF HONEYMOON, we moved into an apartment in Leisure World at Seal Beach. Our first guests were my brother Jack and his wife Crysta. Jack had managed to stay clear of most ministers and took a rather dim view of having one in the family. I wanted so much for the two men to be friends that I gave Louie detailed instructions on what to do and say.

"Take it easy with my brother Jack, won't you? No religious discussions, please, for this first visit, and by all means pay for the expenses of the day."

"Oh sure!" Louie was most agreeable.

Since Jack enjoyed the sea, we all went for an excursion in a motor launch, and Louie dutifully picked up the tab. Everyone liked fish, so we went to a seafood restaurant for our dinner, and the whole day sailed happily along.

But when the waitress put our dinner check on the table, Louie and Jack were engaged in a conversation and neither of them noticed it. After a bit, I nudged Louie, but he was having such a good time talking with Jack that I hesitated to interrupt.

A few minutes later, I gave him a little kick under the table.

Looking at me, Louie asked, "What are you kicking me for?" Then Jack asked him a question, and the matter of the kick was dropped.

Finally the conversation tapered off, and there sat the check on the table. Jack reached over rather slowly and picked it up.

I snatched it from his hand and gave it to Louie. "You're our guests today, Jack, just as though you were in our home."

But Louie spoke up, "If Jack wants to pay this, why don't you let him?"

I just gasped, and then he said to my brother, "Jack, do you want to pay this or don't you?"

At home in Leisure World.

Jack nodded, "I'll pay it."

Leaning toward Louie, I whispered, "What's come over you?"

In a low voice that I was afraid my brother would hear, he answered, "We can't get to feeding all your relatives like this."

Stunned, I blinked back the tears I felt coming.

Then Crysta spoke up, "Carol, I wonder if they're pulling something on you."

Quickly I looked at both men, and their eyes were dancing with mischief. Then they burst out laughing.

What had happened was that when Crysta and I had gone to the powder room to freshen up after the boat ride, Louie had shared with Jack every single thing I had told him. Then he gave my brother a twenty dollar bill. "I'm going to ignore the check, Jack, no matter what Carol says. After a while you reluctantly start to pay it with this money, and we'll see what we can do to get Carol upset."

The rest of the time together was all fun. Louie and Jack became great friends, and my brother chuckled all the way to his home near Sacramento. Jack grew to love the Lord and to love Louie; and I learned what Taud had known. Just let Louie be himself.

Not feeling up to handling heavy traffic on the freeways, he asked me to take over the driving of our car. One day while we were going along the Hollywood Freeway, a policeman signaled us over to the side of the road and gave me a ticket for tailgating a truck. With an impish look in his eyes, Louie leaned over and said, "That's right, officer. Give her a ticket. She tailgated *me* until I married her!"

When word of our marriage spread around, Louie received some amusing letters from friends who enjoyed ribbing him. His favorite came from Dr. George Palmer, who knew both of us very well:

"How in the world did you ever get Carol to say 'yes'? It seems to me that she has had enough trouble through her life without taking you on! Poor girl, my sympathies are certainly with her. I know that she has had serious eye trouble, but I didn't think it was that bad!"

Life with Louie was quite different from the twenty years I had spent overseas, first in the concentration camp and then at the orphanage. I was accustomed to doing everything according to a strict schedule, but Louie was not.

As soon as dinner was over one evening, I jumped up to wash the

The chancellor marries students Heather Jacques from Biola and
Stephen Brown from Talbot Theological Seminary.

dishes. "Leave them for now and come watch the news with me," Louie suggested.

"I can't leave the dishes dirty. Let me wash them first."

"The dishes will wait."

Putting them in the sink, I watched television all evening with him, though I squirmed a bit uncomfortably at the thought of those dishes.

As soon as he turned the television off, I headed for the sink.

"Let's have prayer and go to bed. I'm tired."

"But the dishes. . . ."

"They'll be there in the morning."

After running some water over them, I went to bed but tossed restlessly thinking of all the insects those dishes would attract in India.

The next morning when I walked into the kitchen there was not a dirty dish in sight. I looked incredulously at Louie. Because at Biola, he had been accustomed to getting up about four o'clock in the morning and taking the elevator man out for a cup of coffee, now when he woke up at four, he made coffee, washed and dried all the dinner dishes, and put them away. I learned that our fellowship together was far more important than washing dishes on schedule.

I really did not know Louie very well and was still a bit in awe of him. Putting the trash in a paper shopping bag, I started out for the communal trash bin. He walked up and took it out of my arms.

"No!" I said. "You're not going to carry the trash!"

"Why not?"

I walked beside him and thought, *The chancellor of Biola carrying trash?* And I realized that day what a truly humble man I had married.

I was startled one morning to find my toothbrush on the floor of the bathtub. Picking it up, I asked Louie, "How did my toothbrush land in the bathtub?"

"I was scrubbing my corns with it."

"Have you used it for anything else?"

"Yeah, scrubbing my fingernails and toenails, and brushing my hair."

"If you must use a toothbrush for all that, why don't you use your own?"

"I can never find it."

I bought him a whole glassful, and hid mine.

Although we had our times of Bible reading and prayer together, I was accustomed to having rather long periods of kneeling in quiet communion with my Lord, and I felt the need to continue that time alone with Him. But in an apartment, there is no place to be alone. I tried going into the den and closing the door, but he thought I was upset about something. When I stayed in the bathroom, he thought I was sick.

I presented the problem to the Lord, and He worked it out for me.

Louie's snoring often kept me awake. One night when it made me restless, the Lord seemed to say, "This is your opportunity to be alone with Me."

I slipped out of bed, went into the den, and had as long a time in private fellowship with my Lord as my heart needed.

But one night Louie woke up and wandered around. When he saw me kneeling by the davenport in the den, he quietly knelt beside me and had his time of communion with the Lord. It was a sacred moment. When those times happened, they became some of our most treasured moments together. They were unscheduled and unhurried; each of us was alone with the Lord and yet we were together at His feet.

Louie was pleased when his granddaughter Shirley entered Biola

Luncheon at Biola. Dr. Sutherland, Louie, Mrs. Sutherland, and me.

At meetings and ban-
quets across the nation,
he charmed everyone,
including me.

as a student, and he was glad that he had made a donation toward
the building of the women's dormitory in which she lived.

Because the school was going to surprise Louie with a program on
his seventy-fifth birthday, I asked Shirley to stay all night with us,
and the next morning we drove her to the campus. We stopped at
the home of Dr. Sutherland, who remarked, "I have to speak at
chapel this morning. Come on over with me, Dr. Talbot, and lead
in prayer."

When the two men walked into the auditorium, all the students
stood and sang "Happy Birthday, Dr. Talbot," and the school put
on a "This Is Your Life" program. There was birthday cake for all
the students, a Biola luncheon for Louie, and a radio program fea-
turing greetings from some of his lifelong friends. No one could
have had a happier seventy-fifth birthday.

Louie and I spoke at Biola's summer conferences at the campus,
at Mount Hermon, and at The Firs in Washington. We shared in
the humor and messages, and it was a harmonious combination. We

Dr. Sutherland, Dr. Feinberg, and Louie at commencement exercises on the campus.

were called to speak at meetings all along the Pacific Coast and back East as far as New York.

But during the night of August 27, 1965, I was awakened by a sound in the bathroom. Springing out of bed, I ran and found Louie lying on the floor. An ambulance took him to the hospital, where they found that a stroke had affected one leg.

Billy Graham was holding his crusade in Denver at that time, and he sent Louie this telegram:

> REGRET TO HEAR THAT YOU ARE SICK AM PRAYING FOR YOUR SPEEDY RECOVERY YOU HAVE BEEN ONE OF GOD'S GREAT SERVANTS IN OUR GENERATION WE NEED YOU GOD BLESS YOU
>
> BILLY GRAHAM

Louie had remarkable powers of recovery, and he was soon swimming in the communal pool near our home and basking in the hot therapy pool. We canceled all speaking engagements for the rest of the year and lived a leisurely life. He enjoyed sitting on our verandah and watching the golfers tee off on the short golf course that started in front of our apartment. He was soon on that course himself, and when I saw him take off after his golf ball, I knew that his legs were in good shape again.

Those were years of enjoying activities on the campus, and we often stayed there in the suite of rooms Ray Myers had provided for Louie in the main building of Talbot Theological Seminary.

He enjoyed watching the students as they went to classes, rooting at their basketball games in the gymnasium, attending their concerts in the Crowell music building, with its Lansing Recital Hall and magnificent pipe organ. He delighted in fellowshipping with graduates at alumni reunions and in browsing among the books at the Rose Memorial Library, which he had urged Danny Rose to give to Biola.

The students love their chancellor.

The students loved their chancellor, and when he was introduced at convocations, they give him a standing ovation.

We had a speaking engagement at the First Brethren Church of Long Beach. The pastor, Dr. David Hocking, is six feet five inches tall and weighs over two hundred and fifty pounds. He often smiles over Louie's reaction to him. "I met Dr. Talbot for the first time when our pastors met for prayer just before going out to the platform. My height caught his attention. He took a long, slow look at me, from my feet to the top of my head, and remarked, 'When God was making people and He came to you, things must have gotten out of hand!' "

When I had to address an important meeting, I asked Louie to give me some thoughts for the message, and he replied, "Speak on 'I am the light of the world.' The Lord Jesus Christ is light as to who God is; He is light as to who you are; and He is light as to eternal destiny. As light is one with the sun, so Christ is one with the Father. He is the effulgence, the outshining of God's glory. The sunbeam shines even into alleys and on garbage heaps. But the debris does not defile that shaft of brightness. Light changes the garbage, lifts its moisture into the sky, and turns it into a beautiful rainbow in

Dr. Glenn O' Neal
of Talbot Theological
Seminary chats with
Louie and
Dr. Sutherland.

the heavens. And the Lord Jesus Christ does this for us when we let His light shine on the garbage in our lives, changing it into a rainbow of God's promises, His faithfulness, His mercy, and His glory."

As I was wondering whether to include those words in this book, a rainy sky drew my eyes to the window, and I was startled to see a magnificent rainbow arching the sky. I had my answer, and could only stop and worship God in awe and wonder.

We were a bit late one day for a meeting, and as we were driving down the freeway, my speedometer climbed to seventy miles an hour. After a few moments, Louie remarked, "I believe we each have a guardian angel, but when you drive at this speed, I think our guardian angels get out of the car."

Louie was eighty years old the month in 1969 when Billy Graham held his crusade in Anaheim, and he attended almost every meeting.

On Louie's eightieth birthday, Biola had special radio broadcasts, a big luncheon, and a student assembly filled with humor and tributes. The school presented him with a golf bag and handcart. One student came up and gave him a pair of legs from a cardboard skeleton to use when his own gave out on the golf course; another brought a beribboned rake for him to use as a putter; and a small shovel was given to him so that he could get out of sand traps.

Among the letters read was this one from Billy Graham; it was accompanied by an autographed copy of Mr. Graham's biography.

October 8, 1969

Dear Dr. Talbot:

I am writing to thank you for the warm words of encouragement in your letter of September 27.

There are few clergymen over the years that I have admired and respected more than you. You have no idea what a word like yours means to an evangelist like me.

You are now approaching your eightieth birthday, and you have been a faithful warrior in the Kingdom of God. Your loyalty to the Word and enthusiasm for the Gospel has always been an inspiration to me.

What a glorious time we are going to have in Heaven together, exchanging experiences!

Mrs. Mooney told me that you had been in the audience several times. I wish I'd had an opportunity to see you.

With warmest greetings and congratulations, I am

Cordially yours,
[Signed] Billy

Although Louie still preached occasionally at eighty years of age, he relaxed and enjoyed things for which there had been little time in his life. He was a great sports fan, and we attended a number of tournaments; there he saw all the tennis greats play, and he met and conversed with some of them and with the fans. While we watched the final Olympic trials in Long Beach, Louie seemed to be swimming and diving right along with the contestants.

But he was struck down with viral pneumonia and became very ill. One night at the hospital everyone, including Louie, thought he only had a few more hours. When he noticed tears rolling down my cheeks, he said, "What's the matter with you? *For this I was born. For this I've lived all my life—to see my Saviour face to face.* It will be all glory. I can hardly wait."

When he awakened the next morning, Louie thought he had died and gone to heaven. Looking around at the bleak hospital room, he said, "If *this* is heaven, I certainly misled a lot of people while I was down on earth!"

Louie recovered sufficiently to come home, but his strength was limited. When we were at the Biola campus, he prayed in the Rose of Sharon Prayer Chapel for Dr. Richard Chase, who became president when Dr. Sutherland retired. Louie had sent him the same

Dr. Richard Chase, new president.

charge he gave Dr. Sutherland at his installation: that when it came time for him to turn the torch over to his successor, it would be burning even more brightly then when he had received it.

And there at the little chapel, he prayed for the students in the seminary and college and for those to come in future years, one of whom, Miss Bevin Hedahl, typed the manuscript for this book. She fitted the typing and her studies into a schedule that included attending classes at Biola in the daytime and working eight hours a night at a hospital. It was for young people of this caliber that Louie worked to save Biola from extinction in the depression years.

He enjoyed short visits to Disneyland, where he delighted in the jungle ride and other attractions. But when he came out of the Tiki Room, he was very quiet. One night I woke up at two o'clock and found him sitting thoughtfully in the living room. "What's the matter? Can't you sleep?"

"I'm thinking about the Tiki Room. As I watched those colorful birds and orchids all singing and moving together in rhythm, it made me think of those verses in Scripture, 'Let every thing that hath breath praise the LORD,' and 'the mountains and the hills shall break forth before you into singing, and all the trees of the field shall clap their hands'" (Psalm 150:6; Isa 55:12).

But at a birthday luncheon for his sister Gladys, with Mr. and Mrs. Gordon Hooker and Eleanor Nyman Witt as guests, Louie crumpled before our eyes. A rescue squad took him to the hospital, and a long period of convalescence followed. During that time, Dr. John Lungren and Dr. Arthur Buell cared for his medical needs.

Louie had often said, "Man is immortal until God's time to take him." That time came for him on January 22, 1976, when his valiant body weakened at the age of eighty-six.

The family had left the hospital, and Dr. Sutherland was standing by as I bowed my head at Louie's bedside. Feeling that the holiest moment of his life was approaching, I prayed, "Dear Lord, I believe Thine angels are in this room now ready to take Louie into Thy presence." And as I opened my eyes and looked at him, he quietly took his last breath. It was just before dawn.

Al Sanders later commented that the "hospital room became the staging ground for a trip that would transcend all of his thousands of miles of Christian travels around the world," as Louie left to enter

With all the flourish and dash of youth, Louie at eighty years of age
escorts me to the Biola students' spring banquet.

the presence of the King of kings. The moment for which he was born had come, and no one can comprehend what joy was his when he met his Saviour face to face.

By invitation of the pastor, Dr. Malcolm Cronk, Louie's service of triumph was held Sunday afternoon at the Church of the Open Door, where he had served for so many years; but his real memorial will always be the people God touched through his ministry and every student who graduates from Biola College and Talbot Theological Seminary. To them he hands the torch held high by our forefathers in the faith.

As we gathered at the graveside on Monday, a bare branch of a tree that was arched against the blue sky pointed directly at Louie's casket. Just as the service started, a dove flew down and lit on that branch; it watched those sacred moments, and then quietly flew away.

THE KING'S BUSINESS

June 1946.

Dear Graduates:

It is with mixed feelings of joy and sorrow that I address a final letter to you. Although we regret to see you leave the halls of Biola, we know that we cannot keep you always. While we have enjoyed exceedingly your stay with us, we realize that God is calling you to distant fields of service for which He has been preparing you. So we bid you Godspeed and we assure you that our prayers will ever follow you.

It may be that in this life we all may never be together again. Oh, there will be class reunions which we anticipate with pleasure, but without doubt on some of those occasions there will be vacant places. However we look forward to that day on which we shall enjoy in the presence of our Lord a glad and grand reunion, when we shall never part again. I trust that at that time everyone of us, through faithful service may have many sheaves to lay at the feet of our Lord Jesus Christ.

My heartfelt prayer for you is that the light of His presence may attend you all the days of your life, and that you may be of the greatest possible use to Him in the evangelization of the world in this generation.

Ever yours in His wonderful service,

Louis T. Talbot

Appendix

Theological Convictions of Louis T. Talbot

I

The Bible, consisting of all the books of the Old and New Testaments, is the Word of God, a supernaturally-given revelation from God Himself, concerning Himself, His being, nature, character, will, and purposes; and concerning man, his nature, need, duty, and destiny. The Scriptures of the Old and New Testaments are without error or misstatement in their moral and spiritual teachings and record of historical facts. They are without error or defect of any kind.

II

There is one God, eternally existing and manifesting Himself to us in three Persons—Father, Son, and Holy Spirit.

III

Our Lord Jesus was supernaturally conceived by the power of the Holy Spirit and born of a virgin—Mary, a lineal descendant of David. He lived and taught and wrought mighty works and wonders and signs exactly as is recorded in the four gospels . He was put to death by crucifixion under Pontius Pilate. God raised from the dead the body that had been nailed to the cross. The Lord Jesus after His crucifixion showed Himself alive to His disciples, appearing unto them by the space of forty days. After this the Lord Jesus ascended into heaven, and the Father caused Him to sit at His right hand in the heavenly places far above all rule and authority and power and dominion and every name that is named, not only in this world, but also in that which is to come, and put all things in subjection under His feet and gave Him to be Head over all things to the Church.

IV

The Lord Jesus Christ, before His incarnation, existed in the form of God, and of His own choice laid aside His divine glory and took upon Himself the form of a servant and was made in the likeness of men. In His preexistent state, He was with God and was God. He is a divine Person possessed of all the attributes of Deity and should be worshiped as God by angels and men. "In him dwelleth all the fulness of the Godhead bodily." All the words that He spoke during His earthly life were the words of God. There is absolutely no error of any kind in them, and by the words of Jesus Christ the words of all other teachers must be tested.

V

The Lord Jesus Christ became in every respect a real man, possessed of all the essential characteristics of human nature.

VI

By His death upon the cross, the Lord Jesus Christ made a perfect atonement for sin; by His atonement the wrath of God against sinners is appeased and a ground furnished upon which God can deal in mercy with sinners. He redeemed us from the curse of the law by becoming a curse in our place. He who Himself was absolutely without sin was made to be sin on our behalf that we might become the righteousness of God in Him. The Lord Jesus is coming again to this earth, personally, bodily, and visibly. The return of our Lord is the blessed hope of the believer, and in it God's purposes of grace toward mankind will find their consummation. "The return of our Lord" is to be premillennial and the millennium is to be the last of the dispensations.

VII

The Holy Spirit is a person and is possessed of all the distinctively divine attributes. He is God.

VIII

Man was created in the image of God, after His likeness, but the whole human race fell in the Fall of the first Adam. All men, until they accept the Lord Jesus Christ as their personal Saviour, are lost, darkened in their understanding, alienated from the life of God through the ignorance that is in them, hardened in heart, morally and spiritually dead through their trespasses and sins. They cannot see nor enter the kingdom of God until they are born again of the Holy Spirit.

IX

Men are justified on the simple and single ground of the shed blood of Christ and upon the simple and single condition of faith in Him who shed the blood, and are born again by the quickening, renewing, cleansing work of the Holy Spirit through the instrumentality of the Word of God. The Holy Spirit indwells all believers, having baptized them into the body of Christ at the time of regeneration, and although there may be many fillings, there is only one baptism of the Holy Spirit.

X

All those who receive Jesus Christ as their Saviour and their Lord, and who confess Him as such before their fellow men, become children of God and receive eternal life. They become heirs of God and joint heirs with Jesus Christ. At death their spirits depart to be with Christ in conscious blessedness, and at the second coming of Christ their bodies shall be raised and transformed into the likeness of the body of His glory.

XI

All those who persistently reject Jesus Christ in the present life shall be raised from the dead and throughout eternity exist in a state of anguish and separation from God.

XII

The Church consists of all those who, in this present dispensation, truly believe on Jesus Christ. It is Christ's Body and Bride, which Christ loves and for which He has given Himself.

XIII

There is a personal devil, a being of great cunning and power, "the prince of the power of the air," "the prince of this world," "the god of this age." He can exert vast power only so far as God suffers him to do so. He shall ultimately be cast into the lake of fire and brimstone and shall be tormented day and night forever.

INVITATION

Because Louie always included in his messages an opportunity for people to accept the Lord Jesus Christ as personal Saviour, he would want that opportunity offered here.

Believing that Christ died for sinners and for me, I do now accept Him as my Saviour and Lord, and so confess Him before men.

Signed _____ Date _____

Books by Louis T. Talbot

Addresses on Romans
Bible Questions Explained
Christ in the Tabernacle
Ephesians, an Exposition
An Exposition on the Book of Revelation
God's Plan of the Ages
More Objects that Talk and Teach
Objects that Talk and Teach
The Prophecies of Daniel
Still More Objects that Talk and Teach
Why Four Gospels?

Genesis (in bound pamphlets)
Hebrews (in bound pamphlets)

hundreds of booklets

Films Produced by Louis T. Talbot

Africa Awakes
Bolivia
Christ in the Tabernacle
Colombia
Egypt's Broken Fragments
Four Thousand Miles up the Amazon
Himalayas
Human Pincushions and Fire Walkers
India's Sorrows
I Saw Bethlehem on Christmas Day
I Saw Borneo
I Saw Petra
I Saw the World's Need
Japan
Jungle Indians of Peru
Land of Promise (Holy Land)
Land of the Pharaohs
The Land Time Forgot (New Guinea)
Pygmies of the Belgian Congo
Red Terror over Malaya
Siam
Venezuela

SOURCES

I have not wanted to weary the reader by identifying in the text every quotation. Listed below are the main sources. Quotations from printed material have been listed in the notes.

1. People who loved Louie and shared their memories by tape, letter, and interview.
2. The books, booklets, and magazine articles he wrote.
3. His sermons, letters, and files.
4. His radio broadcasts, sometimes edited for brevity.
5. His films.
6. Board minutes of Biola and the Church of the Open Door.
7. Records of schools Louie attended.
8. The files of Dr. Ray Myers.
9. Church bulletins.
10. *The King's Business* magazine.
11. *Faith for the Family,* by Mildred M. Cook.
12. Experiences and conversations during our years of married life together.

ACKNOWLEDGEMENTS

My warm appreciation is expressed to members of the family and friends who shared memories and pictures, and to the schools and churches that searched their archives. The whole book is a network of people who loved Louie.

I especially want to thank those who read the manuscript and others who helped along the way when I encountered rough terrain:

Dr. J. R. Allder	*Dr. James Henry*
Dr. Foster Bens	*Dr. George Peek*
Mrs. Betty Bruechert	*Mr. Norman Rohrer*
Mrs. Ruth Byrne	*Dr. S. H. Sutherland*
Dr. Richard Chase	*Mrs. Cornelia Westlund*
Miss Mildred Cook	

FROM CREATION TO RE-CREATION

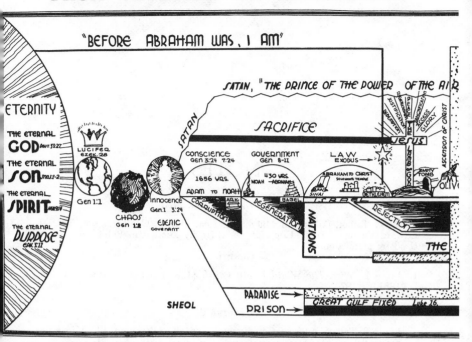

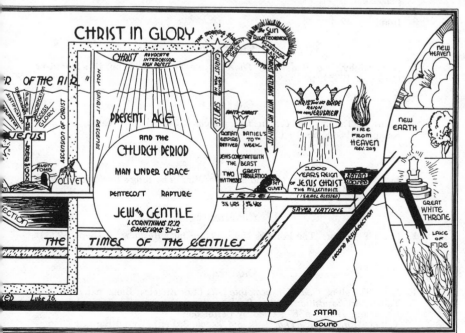

Louis T. Talbot, *God's Plan of the Ages* (Grand Rapids: Eerdmans,, 1972).
Used by permission.

NOTES

Shoes to Match the Road

Louis T. Talbot, "Shoes to Match the Road," from *God's Minute, Vol. II,* Edward Viening (Ed.). Copyright © 1970, by Zondervan Publishing House. Used by permission.

Chapter 2

1. Loyal L. Wirt, *The World Is My Parish* (Los Angeles: Warren F. Lewis, 1951), p. 97.

Chapter 3

1. Louis T. Talbot, *Addresses on Romans,* 2nd ed. (Wheaton, Ill.: Van Kampen, n.d.), p. 77.
2. Ibid., p. 73.
3. Ibid., pp. 42-49.

Chapter 5

1. R. P. Shuler, *Bob Shuler Met These on the Trail* (Wheaton, Ill.: Sword of the Lord, 1955), p. 162.

Chapter 6

1. Louis T. Talbot, *The Prophecies of Daniel,* 3rd ed. (Wheaton, Ill.: Van Kampen, 1954), pp. 10-11.

Chapter 10

1. James O. Henry, "Black Oil and Souls to Win," *The King's Business* 49 (Feb. 1958): 11-41.

Chapter 12

1. Louis T. Talbot, "The Fortress Held," *The King's Business* 24 (Sept. 1933): 292-294, 299.

Chapter 13

1. Louis T. Talbot, *God's Unspeakable Gift* (Los Angeles: Biola, n.d.), pp. 8-9.
2. Talbot, *An Exposition on the Book of Revelation,* rev. ed. (Grand Rapids: Eerdmans, 1973), p. 87. Used by permission.
3. Talbot, *More Objects That Talk and Teach,* 3rd ed. (Grand Rapids: Zondervan, n.d.), pp. 73-74. Used by permission.

CHAPTER 14

1. Louis T. Talbot, Church of the Open Door Bulletin, Oct. 14, 1934.

CHAPTER 16

1. H. S. Risley, "Breaking the Log Jam," *The King's Business* 29 (Sept. 1938): 291-292.
2. Mildred M. Cook, "Flame of Sacrifice," *The King's Business* 29 (Oct. 1938). 327-329.

CHAPTER 18

1. Louis T. Talbot, *An Exposition on the Book of Revelation*, rev. ed. (Grand Rapids: Eerdmans, 1973), p. 42. Used by permission.

CHAPTER 20

1. "Building It Anew Debt Free," *The King's Business* 34 (Nov. 1943): 402, 439; 35 (Jan. 1944): 13; 35 (Feb. 1944): 42; 35 (March 1944): 83.
2. "Praise Be Unto Our Great God," *The King's Business* 36 (April 1945): 124.

CHAPTER 24

1. Louis T. Talbot, "I Saw China's Need," *The King's Business* 38 (Nov. 1947): 10-11, 14.

CHAPTER 27

1. Betty Bruechert, "The Bible by Radio," *The King's Business* 59 (Jan. 1968): 27-29.

CHAPTER 28

1. Louis T. Talbot, "I Talked to General MacArthur," *The King's Business* 40 (Nov. 1949): 5 (combined with oral report).

CHAPTER 29

1. Louis T. Talbot, "I Saw the Wild Men of Borneo," *The King's Business* 40 (Dec. 1949): 9-10, 15, 17, 34; letter to his family from Borneo, Oct. 1949.

CHAPTER 30

1. Louis T. Talbot, "I Saw India's Sorrow," *The King's Business* 41 (Jan. 1950): 6-9.

CHAPTER 32

1. Louis T. Talbot, "I Saw the Place Where the Lord Was Laid," *The King's Business* 41 (May 1950): 8-9.

CHAPTER 33

1. Louis T. Talbot, *I Saw Petra, The Rose-Red City of the Dead* (Glendale, Cal.: Church Press, 1951), pp. 8, 25, 30.

CHAPTER 34

1. Louis T. Talbot and J. Russell Davis, "Four Thousand Miles Up the Amazon," *The King's Business* 42 (April 1951): 9, 36; "Adventuring for Christ in the Andes," *The King's Business* 42 (May 1951): 7-9; "Adventuring for Christ Along the Orinoco and the Amazon," *The King's Business* 42 (June 1951): 7-12; "Adventuring for Christ in Peru," *The King's Business* 42 (July 1951): 12-14, 23, 26; "Adventuring for Christ in Latin America," *The King's Business* 42 (August 1951): 8-10.

CHAPTER 36

1. Louis T. Talbot, letters to Dr. S. H. Sutherland from Goroka, New Guinea, Nov. 28, Dec. 5, 1953; radio addresses June 7, 9, 11, 14, 1954.

CHAPTER 37

1. Louis T. Talbot, letters to Dr. S. H. Sutherland from Singapore, Dec. 25, 1953; Indochina Tribesland, Jan. 2, 1954; Banmethuot, Vietnam, Jan. 10, 1954; radio addresses June 16, 18, 1954.

CHAPTER 38

1. Louis T. Talbot, letters to Biola from Africa, Feb. 1, April, 1954; four radio addresses, n.d.